14.⁹⁸

THE COWBOY IN ART

THE COW

by Ed Ainsworth

BOY IN ART

The World Publishing Company • New York and Cleveland

*For generous assistance in the creation of this book
the publishers extend their grateful appreciation to*
Trailside Galleries of Jackson Hole, Wyoming
Desert Southwest Art Gallery of Palm Desert, California
Saddleback Art Galleries of Santa Ana, California, and Phoenix, Arizona.

Published by The World Publishing Company
2231 West 110th Street, Cleveland, Ohio 44102

Published simultaneously in Canada by Nelson, Foster & Scott Ltd.

FIRST PRINTING   DECEMBER, 1968
SECOND PRINTING   JANUARY, 1969

1624317

Quality 12-17-71

John Wayne. (Universal Studios.)

FOREWORD

The cowboy is now a part of American history. For a hundred and fifty years his adventures and escapades have formed the legend that has become the folklore of America. The frontiersmen and patriots in Texas, where the genuine American cowboy came into existence, were simple, direct men. They believed in things like liberty and minding their own business. When the first cowboys were herding longhorns up the Chisholm Trail from Texas to Kansas they were a pretty tough lot, but they had to be. It was a rough era in our history. There was no room for nuance or time for luxury.

Out of the lives of these cowboys have come all sorts of stories and legends, some true and some fiction.

But the most authentic and dependable evidence of what the cowboys really were has come from the artists who pictured them in their true environment, risking their lives in stampedes, freezing or sweating, under the stars, by lonely campfires, rowdying in saloons, fighting, branding and whooping it up around the chuck wagons. These paintings have come to be a part of the American tradition.

I am glad to see that in *The Cowboy in Art* the spirit of a great era comes alive once again in text and illustration. The cowboys were a terse lot who didn't say much for themselves. This book, fortunately, says it for them in the paintings by these fine artists.

My hope—may you enjoy them as I have.

JOHN WAYNE

CONTENTS

LIST OF ILLUSTRATIONS

Chapter heading drawings by Don Perceval

THE COWBOY IN ART

GENESIS ON HORSEBACK

When the Almighty put hoofs on the wind and a bridle on the lightning, He called it a horse. Then He summoned a fitting companion to ride His whinnying creation down the long arroyo of Time, and commanded: "Horseman, get on!"

It was the right combination. Man on horseback has been pounding sparks ever since. A horse gave a man height, and four legs. If early man lacked a horse, he invented one. He combined himself with the horse idea and called the unified animal a centaur, half horse, half man. He gave the horse wings and called him Pegasus, the flying king of the skies. He hitched horses to the Chariot of the Sun and watched them speed forever West.

He used the horse for war. The neigh and the battle cry resounded in chorus.

But the Almighty also had invented cattle. This set things in motion: All Nature moves towards climaxes. The horse, the horseman and the cattle moved towards theirs. It took a long time and many discoveries and a man called Columbus and a new land called America. But, eventually, it happened. Time, place and circumstances coincided.

Amid the tall grass and beside the big rivers and on the vast plains, with all the bulls and cows running wild, and buffaloes thrown in, the Almighty needed a special kind of horseman, and He needed him fast.

So He cupped His hands and hollered for help.

This new feller came riding up with leather pants and a lasso in his hand and a big hat and cheeks like bullhide and a yen in his soul to herd those cow critters. He didn't say much, he just started roping and branding. Even the Almighty was a little surprised. He couldn't quite figure what to call this strange helper. But He finally came up with it.

From the top seat in the Big Grandstand, He leaned down and in the Voice of Ages that shook the arena, thundered:

"Ride 'em, Cowboy!"

1
LONG TRAIL

Tenth-century Spain

Cowboys can claim a lot of fancy kinfolks. Old Charlie Goodnight is connected by stirrup and spur to King Arthur of the Round Table and the Texas Panhandle is next door to Camelot. Annie Oakley is a kissing cousin of Ben Hur, and Casey Tibbs traces some tricks to the bull riders on Crete.

Few people recognize the family connections, but the same brand is on a Montana fence rider and Sir Launcelot, and Tex Ritter singing "Ghost Riders in the Sky" is sharing his high notes with some troubador spearing a knight in song for Richard the Lionhearted. The cowboy urge was in the herdsmen of Mesopotamia and the kings of Spain, but they lived too soon. The real cowboy had to wait out on the horizon for many a century before he got his cue to come loping up into the light of the campfire.

Everything had to be just right for his entrance. From the day when Noah saved the cattle and horses along with all the other pairs of animals, the raw ingredients had been available, although for a long spell nobody put them together. Hieroglyphics on the mud bricks of Babylon and in the pyramids of Egypt show no steers on a Chisholm Trail. The sculptors of Greece never fashioned a Buffalo Bill. The lasso failed to inspire a Beethoven symphony. Leonardo da Vinci and Michaelangelo produced no paintings of Tom Mix or Bill Hart in a rodeo.

A philosopher has said, "Man's noblest position is on horseback." Yet Aristotle never mentioned a wild bronc rider.

These omissions, regrettable as they are, were inevitable. The emergence of the true cowboy was waiting for the formation of the United States and the arrival of the nineteenth century. At the proper time, the trail boss guided his herd over the rise onto the Staked Plains of history. Nobody seemed to ask why it took so long or why it happened just when it did.

Even the cowboy did not realize he had come into the spotlight. No lights blinded his eyes. No applause rang in his ears. He was just doing a job. The sun burned his neck, the cold bit into his bones, the mud stuck on his boots, the ornery steers fought at the end of his rope, and if he got drunk it was not to find happiness but to blot out the weariness and the stink of sweat and the thought of the goddam lonely stars. He would have been the last guy on earth to think of himself as a hero or as the subject of popular interest.

This was natural, because he was the product of a slow evolution. He did not gallop onto the open range and cry out that he was a cowboy. His unawareness of the romantic aura that was to surround him was due to his acceptance of his work as a commonplace, a routine of interminable hours devoted to doing the necessary jobs around cattle to bring them to the beef stage. Even his proficiency was part of this attitude. He had to be able to ride to get a job; he had to ride well to hold it. He had to handle a rope properly to keep from getting dragged off his horse, and killed. The fence building and the branding and the castration were monotonous bits of the pattern. Everything he did had a precise purpose. If he wasted any motion he got fired. The cowboy, as a result, became the epitome of practicality.

If time was an element in the evolution of the cowboy toward his destiny (unwilling though he might be to admit that he had one), so too were the elements of geography, surroundings and animal environment. America, it is true, was the place of his appearance on earth. This happened late because of a basic lack at first of certain essential elements for cowboy life.

A cowboy must have two things in order to function: horses and cattle. America, at the time of the discovery, had no horses. It had no cattle.

Herds of bison roamed its vast plains, but the aborigines who sought to kill them for food were forced to do so on foot at great peril to themselves. So, while the buffalo were in a sense the native livestock, the other essential element for a "buffalo boy"—a riding horse—was unknown. The Sioux and the Comanches and the Pawnees had to wait for history to bring them a steed.

History, though, seemed little concerned with hastening the era of the prospective Indian "buffalo boys."

In her cavernous womb, other multiple embryos were taking shape for their successive births to hasten the day when the cowboy himself could be delivered. These embryos were of diverse natures. They included a particular kind of horse, with an incurving face and large eyes and hoofs like steel, developing thousands of years ago amid the endless sands under the burning sun of Arabia beside the Red Sea . . . the envy and greed of Egyptian monarchs that caused these horses to be captured and taken to the deserts of North Africa beside the Mediterranean . . . the need of Hannibal, the Carthaginian general, for a new kind of war steed to use in his invasion of Italy, so that he developed the powerful strain called the barbs, by using Arabian stallions on African mares . . . the invasion of Spain by the Moors, who stayed there for seven hundred years, glorying in conquest and the magnificence of their incomparable cavalry horses . . . the ultimate expulsion of the Moors by the Spaniards with the capture of the last stronghold, Granada, and the immediate, resultant commissioning in 1492 of Christopher Columbus by the king and queen, released now from war pressures to think of colonial expansion, to go on a westward voyage . . . the Discovery, and the

One of the first horse pictures in the world, from the caves of Altamira near Santillana, Spain, reputedly done 25,000 years ago

taking of the first horses to the New World.

Prior to these developments in the realm of exploration came the seemingly unimportant adoption by the Spaniards of the Middle Ages of a game of skill and daring played on horseback. At the time, it seemed to be merely an exercise, but in its lasting effects it came finally to be a vital factor in determining the nature of the saddle used by vaqueros and cowboys on a continent that had not yet been found. The game was *cañas*, known by the Arabs as *El Jerid*. It was brought to Spain in the eighth century by the conquering Moors, and, later on, was taken over by the revitalized Spaniards who found it a congenial way to train for reconquering their country. It was played by galloping riders who threw canes, like lances, against each other somewhat in the fashion of spear-fighting, but it was different from the jousting of knights who sought to unseat each other by actual contact and collision. The object, instead, was to catch the canes, or to elude them by lightning-like maneuvers

in which it was necessary for horse and rider to act as a unit—as one wily, agile animal. Necessarily, this developed a race of superb horsemen, capable of the most subtle handling of their mounts.

In the game, the *hombres* definitely were separated from the *muchachos*.

It was a matter of saddles and stirrups. The old-timers in Europe rode in a weird sort of shallow bucket with a low cantle known as a bur, with their feet straining to reach the stirrups which hung almost to the ground on long stirrup leathers. Once he was in this kind of saddle, a man was butt-bound to his horse, unable to lift himself by the stirrups. This awkward method of saddling was known as "cavallevio a la estradiota."

In the game of *cañas*, though, the dashing Spaniards who wanted to show their manhood borrowed a chapter from the Moors. They rode, as it was known, *a la gineta*, in a Moorish saddle with a high cantle, relatively short stirrups, one rein and a "high hand," turning their horses by simple pressure on the neck rather than by using the bit in the mouth. At full tilt, then, in the game of *cañas*, these Spaniards rose in the stirrups, braced against the upward-rising cantle in the back, held the saddle horn with one hand and, thus reinforced, hurtled the canes at each other with incomparably greater agility, firmness and accuracy than they could have done while hamstrung in a bur.

These daring riders were the grandfathers of the Spanish and Mexican vaqueros, and their saddles were the sires of the stock saddles of the American continent, tailored to the temperaments and needs of horsemen as yet unborn.

Even so, another element was needed to add to all these before the cowboy could canter forth in his full stature. As the ships of the early explorers of the New World went forth from Spain, Portugal, England and many nations of Europe, it apparently was

Horse of the trapper and trader, by Fred Fellows.
(Van Kirke Nelson, M.D., Kalispell, Montana.)

by accident that the erratic vessels landed where they did and that the respective colonizers set up the flags of their kings. However, for the future cowboy, a happy circumstance guided the apportionment of the climes to which the different nations laid their claims.

Spain and Portugal—themselves semitropical—got the compatible southern latitudes, where nature was lush, the blood ran hot, fecundity was a way of life, rich verdure awaited the cattle herds in enormous expanses of plains, valleys and mountainsides, and man on horseback was an essential to manage those herds, which were larger than had ever been imagined before on earth.

England, on the other hand, as a small nation used to quiet pastoral ways and the herding of a few cattle on foot—mostly by farmer-type rustics with no desire to go bouncing around on a plow horse—colonized in America the bleak northern regions where a cow sloshing in the snow of a backyard pen was the accepted version of "cattle raising."

Yet, strangely enough, the pressures of frontier life affected both the Spanish in their sunshine and the transplanted English in their sleet storms in such a way that they slowly began to converge—actually unknow-

ingly—toward the American Southwest, where both were to participate in a combined drama of men, cattle and horses.

The Spaniards moved toward this rendezvous of the future by way of the vaquero and the *charro*. The Anglo-Saxons headed the same way in the guise of explorers and plainsmen. One group was moving up across Mexico toward Texas and the Californias, and the other was pressing through the forests and across the grasslands of Kentucky, Missouri and the Louisiana Purchase. Neither gave any real thought to the other. The vaqueros and the *charros* were too busy herding and branding, and the American plainsmen were too much on the alert for tomahawks and scalping parties to be aware of the trends of history.

Both the Spaniards and the Americans were hardy, enduring, brave, adventurous and fiercely proud. All these ingredients were needed in the forthcoming cowboy. The quality of superb horsemanship was shared by both. The Mexicans, in a transplanted system brought from Spain, divided themselves quite naturally by heredity and tradition

Early-style cowboy boots, by Maynard Dixon.
(Edith Hamlin, San Francisco, California.)

"Throwing the Rope," by Maynard Dixon. (Edith Hamlin, San Francisco, California.)

The transplanted English in the American colonies practiced some social distinctions too, but in the amalgamations of the colonists a new race, the frontier American, emerged. He was a composite of the country gentleman of Virginia and the other colonies who rode to hounds and risked his neck in steeplechasing, and the sturdy English yeoman and tradesman who walked more than he rode. The blending of the two, under the influence of republican institutions developing far from the mother country, produced these American frontiersmen who were equally at home afoot or in the saddle.

These Mexicans and these Americanos del Norte of almost-balanced capacities were the hellbent horsemen riding from their respective directions to collide, as a prelude to the eventual, swift evolution of the cowboy. In the veins of one flowed the red cells which had animated the knights riding across the Vega (plain) below the Alhambra against the Moors in the siege of Granada. The hardy hearts of the other pumped the blood descended from Paul Revere. When they met, they were bound to create the fiercest compe-

between the rich landowning hidalgos, or gentlemen of noble birth, and the serving class. The working riders who cared for the herds on the big haciendas and spreading ranchos of the hidalgos became vaqueros, horsemen so skilled by necessity in their duties around cattle that their fame began to spread throughout the world. The hidalgos themselves, carrying in their veins the hot blood of Spain, were not required by necessity to become daring riders although they chose to do so for sport. They organized dangerous games on horseback calling for the greatest possible skill, and designated themselves *charros*.

"Pack train," by Harold Hopkinson

tition among horsemen ever seen on earth—not in any jousting tournament of rustling silks, floating banners and fair ladies, but under the burning sun and in the howling wintry northers of the plains and amid the dung of wild cattle and the sweat of running horses. Each was certain he was the best rider on earth. Each was ready to prove it, with *reata* and lasso and saddle and spur.

For the Mexicans, the wild bulls of the thorn jungles and mesquite thickets of Sinaloa and Chihuahua and Sonora provided an unending test of skill and daring. For the Americanos, the millions of buffalo on the grasslands offered an equal challenge for dangerous hunting on horseback. From these respective training grounds, the antagonists moved toward Texas, the ultimate arena, for their final testing.

On their way, they began to assume heroic proportions even though they were unaware of it in their absorption in daily tasks. They suddenly became a subject of intense interest to a certain kind of perceptive man, who down the ages, has chronicled the bizarre and the feats of the mighty. Horse artists, as far back as twenty-five thousand years ago, painted images of the graceful equines they admired so much, along with bison, in the sacred cave of Altamira penetrating a grassy hilltop near Santillana, Spain, and elsewhere in European caverns. Blind Homer glorified Ulysses in verse. An ancient Greek sculptor, Myron, carved "The Discus Thrower" in marble. Troubadours sang the deeds of clanking crusaders. Van Dyck, with enduring skill, depicted kings on prancing steeds.

Now, in their appointed turn, came the painters of the horsemen of America.

Suddenly, the bison hunter and the mounted cattle herder were recognized as subjects for art. The chase of a buffalo was transformed into poetry in motion on canvas. The whirling loop of the lasso settling on the neck of a running steer was caught in a frozen moment of time. The workaday rider was metamorphosed into a living memento for posterity. These painters, these creators, these chroniclers in pigments added some magic ingredient of their own to the whirling dust, the frenzied eyes, the clattering hoofs, the straining muscles of the men and beasts, the twisting bodies, the branding fires and the threatening horns. They saw deeper than the dingy clothes, they peered beneath the big hats, they gave new meaning to the frayed boots.

They transformed transient events into lasting form.

All this resulted in a paradox. The unimaginative Western horseman considered himself totally uninteresting. Yet he became, in the public imagination, the Knight on the White Horse, Sir Galahad with a Bull Durham cigarette, Paul Revere in a Stetson. He was totally utilitarian, and so, like all genuinely utilitarian objects, he represented perfection in his own sphere. He became a symbol. To shopgirls and office clerks and schoolboys amid crowds, tall buildings and a deadly boredom, this horseman was Adventure astride a wild horse. He forever galloped across the prairie of romance and twirled his lariat toward the neck of an elusive dream. It mattered not at all in this concept that the Western horseman's horizon was limited to the momentary task in hand. To his admirers he seemed to be looking out forever with shining eyes toward the distant and misty mountains of a beckoning Valhalla.

From everywhere came the artists glorifying the horsemen—some from Europe, some from New England, some from the new parts of America. They shared the common quality of perception. They went forth in wagon trains, by dugout canoe, on horseback and afoot to the scene of the buffalo hunts and the cattle roundups in the 1830s and 1840s, even before the birth of the true Cowboy.

"Buffalo hunt." Artist unknown. (Santa Barbara Museum of Art.)

They were drawn irresistibly to the buffalo lands and the roaming grounds of the wild cattle. They endured cold and heat and exhaustion and danger. They slept on the ground, treasured their paints and pencils like gold, and drew pictures of Americans, Indians, horses, buffalo, cattle and the mountains and limitless grasslands.

Long before the Texas cattle drives, these painters designed the setting for the cowboy, who, in his true proportions, was as yet unborn. George Catlin, Alfred Jacob Miller, Titian Ramsay Peale and all their confreres became the progenitors of America's Cowboy Art period.

They signified, indeed, that this was the moment when the "cowboy" must ride out onto history's stage—as a result of the competition between Mexicans and Americans in Texas. This competition came about because of an astounding series of happenings in the New World. Some of these events did not

happen entirely on land. Some took place on the sea.

These were in the days just after the discovery of the New World by Columbus. The Spanish were entrenched in Cuba, and from there launched exploration and freebooting expeditions westward. One of these, under the command of Juan de Grivalja in 1518 (only twelve years after the death of Columbus), sailed along the coast of Yucatan, or Tabasco, and by San Juan de Ulúa, site of the present Veracruz, and terrified the native Indians who observed the great ships with awe. This voyage paved the way for another and far more important expedition.

A fleet of eleven vessels sailed from Santiago de Cuba on February 10, 1519, under the command of a mighty captain named Hernando Cortés, bound for a place called "Mexico" and carrying sixteen horses and mares toward a strange destiny.

A TOP HAND FOR THE OLD WEST

When it came to painting the whole gamut of the Old West, from black-robed priests to cowpunchers and from conquistadores to Indian warriors, it took a South American to show us all the tricks.

His name was Joe Mora, and he came from Uruguay. He was the son of Domingo Mora, Uruguayan sculptor, and a brother of Luis Mora, the painter.

Joe Mora, born in Montevideo in 1876 and brought up in New York and Boston, became so enamored of the Western way of life that he devoted many years to depicting the stirring history of Mexico, California and the Indian country in paints. By the time he was twenty-one he was a newspaper artist on the *Boston Traveler* and the *Boston Herald*. Then in 1900 he began doing book illustrations. He traveled on horseback throughout Mexico and California and conceived and executed the Fr. Junipero Serra Sarcophagus at Carmel in honor of the founder of California; a Cervantes memorial in San Francisco; and thirteen dioramas for the Will Rogers Memorial Museum at Claremore, Oklahoma.

In his book *Trail Dust and Saddle Leather* (1946), Mora presented a monumental account of the horse in America, with dozens of illustrations showing the gear of the riders, the breaking of horses, the handling of cattle and the adventures of cowboy life.

Toward the end of the book he wrote: "If the old Cowboy was a hell-cattin,' shootin' hombre either in his cups or out of sheer animal exuberance he was an American creation."

And an American creation was Joe Mora, too!

Conquistador

2
THE DEVIL BEASTS

Fifteenth-century Spain

America's first "cowboy artists" were drawing pictures of their own native subjects in the lush jungles of the tropical coastland before they ever saw a horse.

Their transition to "horse art" was startling.

The Indians of Tabasco, along the Mexican coast in Yucatan and northward, were creating murals and other kinds of portrayals long before the discovery by Columbus of the island of San Salvador and the successive explorations which ended forever the isolation of the Caribbean tribes. Indian *lienzos*, or murals, showing battles and other great events, were painted in pigments on long pieces of woven cotton cloth. Many other decorations and paintings were done on stone and wood indoors and out. These types of artistic expressions were a sequel to the architectural masterpieces created by races who,

in the dim past, had lived in the same jungle environment and had left crumbling evidences of their knowledge and skill in the form of temples and pyramids.

So, on the Mexican coast between the 96th and 97th parallels of latitude, on the shore of what was to become known as the Gulf of Mexico at the precise spot later to be called San Juan de Ulúa, or Veracruz, the stage was being set for an event unparalleled both for history and art. Up and down the irregular sea front, in quiet bays and on jagged promontories battered incessantly by crashing waves and amid the tangled creepers and crimson flowers of the jungle itself where parrots screamed and snakes slithered, a message was flashing. By runner and drum talk and, seemingly, telepathy, the word was spread with greater speed than a running jaguar that the giant canoes with the white wings were back again, floating low in the sea, and that they were moving slowly northward as if seeking a special place to move in and seize some helpless prey.

This was not a new sight to the Indians, but it was no less frightening on that account. Within a period of recent moons the same kind of immense canoes with bearded men peering from them had moved along this same coast, spreading terror and wonderment, but eventually disappearing. This time the monstrous apparitions appeared to be more purposeful, more ominous.

From far south had come the news of a battle with the invaders. But it was not the news of the battle itself that was having so devastating an effect, it was something else entirely. An exhausted runner had arrived bearing a hastily scrawled picture on a piece of cotton cloth. It represented a creature never before seen by any Indian even in his dreams.

It had a long body with four legs and a tail like straws, and, unbelievably, the torso of a man rising from its shoulders. The tidings were that hordes of these devil-beasts had suddenly appeared as if from nowhere during the battle, and that "the men with the four legs" which could run with the speed of a hurricane had speared innumerable Indians who were unable to flee fast enough to escape. The devil-beasts supposedly had gone back, after the battle, to their lair in the bowels of the giant canoes and now were approaching to add new victims to their list of death.

Soon, the Indians' premonition of evil was borne out. The winged canoes began moving closer toward shore. This took place in a long, curving bay dotted with three islands. On one of the islands the Indians' greatest magic was concocted. It was known as the Island of Sacrifice, because here, by the light of leaping flames and amid the awful cries of blood lust, the appointed victims were put to death to appease those gods who

demanded it. Now, except for the chattering of parrots, as the canoes came nearer and nearer, there was a deathly silence on the Island of Sacrifice and even along the shore of the mainland.

From the tops of trees and from behind the immense sand dunes and from coverts in the jungle, the Indians peered forth in awed expectation. They clutched their bows and arrows and their whetted spears, and waited. Out in the bay, the silent, gliding monsters came past the Island of Sacrifice and toward the larger island directly offshore. As they approached, the Indians could see the dreaded bearded faces once more. Eyes peered from behind those fierce hairs and struck new terror in the hearts of the on-lookers. Finally, from the canoes came cries in a strange tongue, and huge objects shaped like double hooks plunged down and into the sea. The canoes stopped. Their wings folded.

Even though it could not be observed from the canoes, great activity was going on among the Indians. The intelligence corps of two great native nations were already starting

their duties. One group belonged to the inland Tlaxcala tribe and their allies. Their cacique, the supreme chief, had ordered immediate preparations for defense, and part of this included the close observation of this strange enemy and the reporting of every detail. A vital part of this spying was being carried on by native artists who were drawing pictures on pieces of cotton cloth for distribution to faraway allies to keep them informed concerning the imminent peril.

The other nation, enemies of the Tlaxcalas, was that of the Aztecs, who had swept into Mexico only about two centuries before and had created a tremendous empire with its capital in a vast inland valley, an old lake bed at more than 7,000 feet elevation, where waterways, fortifications and moats made it almost impregnable. The Aztecs were con-stantly at war with the Tlaxcalas, with victories and defeats alternating and boundary lines constantly shifting. The tremendous intelligence corps of the Aztecs, which functioned in a vast area of Mexico from the peak of Popocatepetl to the shores of the great waters, was sending its runners to the capital with news of the threatening canoes and the bearded men, and rumors of other creatures even more horrifying. The men straining every muscle in their relay race of two hundred miles from the sea to the capital and to the palace of their emperor, Montezuma, knew that the tidings they bore would unleash a powerful war effort.

At first, they carried with them only oral messages of what had been observed as the canoes moved toward shore and stopped there, with the bearded men looking forth threateningly at the land. However, when the first exhausted runner reached the palace and gaspingly delivered his message, Montezuma's aides immediately informed the Emperor and a task force was sent toward the coast at once.

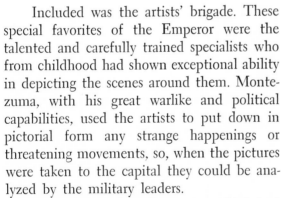

Included was the artists' brigade. These special favorites of the Emperor were the talented and carefully trained specialists who from childhood had shown exceptional ability in depicting the scenes around them. Montezuma, with his great warlike and political capabilities, used the artists to put down in pictorial form any strange happenings or threatening movements, so, when the pictures were taken to the capital they could be analyzed by the military leaders.

So swift was the relay system which brought the first news to the capital (the runners having started long before the canoes moved in close to the jungle shore) that the artists actually reached the scene before the bearded men attempted to come ashore.

Both the Aztecs and the Tlaxcalas, as if by some unspoken truce forced upon them by the common danger, observed the canoes without paying any attention to each other, deferring their own perpetual hostilities until the present danger had been met.

The event was stupefying when it occurred. At first, the military observers and the artists noted an unusual activity among

the bearded men on the back of the canoes. The men ran about, loud voices sounded, and strange shapes appeared. Full view was obscured by the bearded men as they crowded around the monstrous objects, but enough could be seen to cause consternation and dismay. The great beasts of which there had been so much talk seemed to be emerging from the interior of the canoes.

The beasts did indeed appear to the gaze of those on shore to be half monster and half man—the body of an animal and the torso and head of a man. To the Indians peering at a sight they could hardly credit, the day of doom now loomed as a certainty. No rites were known to appease such creatures, no incantation was powerful enough to halt their imminent landing and the ensuing destruction of all who might try to stand in their way.

Drawings done by Aztec artists of Montezuma's "intelligence corps" soon after arrival of Spaniards with first horses in America. Center picture shows Spaniards passing the volcano Popocatepetl (Aztec for "Smoking Mountain"). Originals of these drawings are preserved in museums throughout the world.

At this precise moment, the intelligence force and the artists of Montezuma arrived. With them they bore terrifying instructions for these coastal Indians, the vassals and necessarily the allies, although perhaps unwilling ones, of the Aztec Emperor. The orders were to greet the bearded ones as gods, and particularly their leader who, Montezuma had concluded from the first oral messages brought to him, must be the reincarnation of "the Fair God," Quetzalcoatl, the great deity of the Aztecs who had left his people in the dim past with the message that he would return in the future. Montezuma had concluded that the "future" had arrived.

A dreadful dilemma was created for the Indians.

Either they must go forth from their hiding places and greet the "gods" and their awful monsters, or by defying the orders of Montezuma, face certain death from the Emperor himself. They debated. Finally they

reached a decision. They would face the monsters rather than the wrath of Montezuma.

Immediately, two Indian dugouts were dragged down to the beach, and the bravest selected for the venture started for the largest of the invading canoes where bits of colored cloth were flying at the top of the long poles above it, signifying it was of special importance. To their astonishment, as they neared the giant canoe, they saw among the bearded men an Indian woman dressed in the native costume of Tabasco. She spoke to the Indians in their own tongue and told them not to be afraid, that the bearded ones were their friends and were bringing gifts.

"What is your name?" the head man of the Indians asked the woman.

"I am Doña Marina," she replied, "and I now speak the language of these strangers as well as our own, and can interpret for you anything you wish to say."

"Where is their tatuan?" asked the Indian leader.

"Their chief is this noble stranger here, and his name is Hernando Cortés," answered Doña Marina, bowing toward a young man of about thirty-five.

However, the Indians hardly saw Cortés: their eyes were fixed upon the monsters, now seen close at hand for the first time, and they could hardly spare a glance for the figures in human form even though they might be gods. The monsters were almost as tall as a man, with long, powerful legs ending in round feet that looked as hard as stone, and, most terrible of all, from the back of each one appeared to sprout the head and shoulders and arms of a man.

The Indians, copying Doña Marina, bowed as if to Cortés but in reality to the dreadful apparitions standing on their four feet beside him. Momentarily, they hesitated when Doña Marina invited them to board the canoe, but, remembering Montezuma and his threat of death, at last they climbed the ropes thrown down to them by the bearded men and stood amid the monsters.

Cortés said something to Doña Marina and some of his men, and at once the Indians were given cups of wine and were handed wondrous blue beads of a kind they had never seen before. The monsters, under the control of the man-beast on their backs by means of straps running to bits of metal in their mouths, were taken to another part of the canoe because of the uneasiness of the Indians, and Cortés, through Doña Marina, began asking many questions of the Indians, about their country and their leaders.

Finally, as the Indians prepared to leave after having told about the Emperor Montezuma amid his golden ornaments in his distant palace in a place called "Mexico," they summoned up their courage and, pointing, asked a question of their own.

"What," they queried in awe, "is the name of the monster with the four legs and the head of a man?"

For the first time Doña Marina hesitated. She knew no word for an answer in the language of Mexico. This was a creature never seen before in the world of the Aztecs and the other tribes of the country. Questioningly, she turned to Cortés.

"Tell them in my language," he commanded.

Doña Marina turned again to the Indians.

"My lord and master instructs me to say that henceforth you shall call the monsters, as he does, by the word *caballo*."

And, on the next day, in the sight of thousands of wondering Indians, the *caballos* were taken ashore. With their feet like rocks and the aura of horror about their man-heads, they stood where none of their kind had ever stood before, excepting only those pygmylike creatures of the same family in prehistoric times, the eohippus, now long extinct.

Horses had come to America.

3
WHIP AND SPUR

Voyage period of Columbus, 1493–1494

Those hoofprints in the sand of San Juan de Ulúa, beside the great dunes and the jungle reaching toward the sea, started a trail so far-spreading that during the next few centuries millions of running hooves sculptured the soil of a continent and carved indelible chronicles in a new land. Yet, as the gaunt and stiff-jointed horses stood there in the sunshine of that Good Friday of 1519 under the fascinated gaze of the surrounding Indians, they appeared almost incapable of becoming the Adams and Eves of an equine avalanche engulfing valleys, mountains, and deserts, and catapulting for thousands of miles into the illimitable West. They had been suspended so long in their slings in the crowded, pitching Spanish vessels that only the hardihood of their long ancestral line permitted them even to survive. They were worthy scions of the Arabians and barbs that

had been accustomed to travel the endless sands of Asia and North Africa with little water and only a handful of dates for food. Now, to the eyes of their Spanish masters, they seemed shrunken and bony, hardly capable of venturing into battle—if battle was required, as seemed almost certain despite the apparent initial friendliness of the Indians. Yet their recuperative powers were so great that within a day they were prancing and vigorous, animated by the nourishing grasses of their strange new home.

From the moment the horses set foot on land, they began to figure in adventure and intrigue. Both Cortés and Montezuma, wily military leaders and consummate politicians, pitted not only their wits against each other but also the horses as symbols both of offense and defense. Cortés depended upon the psychological effect of his cavalry to carry him

"Los Charros," by Edward Borein. (Harold G. Davidson, Santa Barbara, California.)

through any conflicts he might encounter in the conquest on which he was embarking— upon the fear inspired by the galloping, snorting devil-monsters to rout the enemy. At first, after hostilities with the Aztecs began, his judgment did in fact prove to be correct.

Montezuma, with his own great canniness, was ready to retaliate. This was due in large part to the Aztec artists. When, before he had seen a horse in the flesh, the pictures made by the intelligence corps were shown to Montezuma, he was told that the monsters appeared to be half animal and half man, that they could not be killed and that they devoured their prey. The Emperor refused to credit this. After studying the pictures, he issued orders that, in the event the strangers appeared not to be the returning Aztec gods and proved to be only mortals, the monsters with them were to be made the object of spe-

cial attack to determine whether they could be killed. The Emperor had concluded that the monsters were not, as so many of the Indians thought, centaurs, but were two creatures—some strange animal ridden by a man.

As war broke out with the Spaniards, horses were indeed killed with arrows and lances, and their heads were cut off and hung beside the heads of slaughtered Spaniards at the entrances to the Aztec capital to disprove the myth they were immortal. However, neither the ensuing wars nor the rigors of heat and blizzard in Mexico's varying climes were able to stem the wave of fecundity being generated there at San Juan de Ulúa in the springtime of the first year of the Conquest. The horses of Cortés, like those of Noah, joyously heeded the Biblical injunction to be fruitful and multiply. They bred in Mexico with such abandon that, as the Spaniards

"Setting Him Up," by Edward Borein. (Dr. H. J. Burtness.)

spread west, north and south from the landing spot on the east coast, the horses became so numerous that they broke the bonds of domesticity. Many escaped into the forests and thorn jungles and, living there in bands, became feral, as wild as the jaguars and deer among which they roamed.

It was from this wave of multiplication that, eventually, there emerged the term which was to identify a whole race of horses, signifying the freedom of the great spaces where they roamed. The Spanish and Mexican term *"mesteño"* for the wild horses was transformed in time into the Anglo-Saxon "mustang," emblem later on of an era and the cue for the entrance of the "cow boy."

The cowboy, though, was dependent for his materialization upon the development of his Latin predecessors, the vaqueros and the *charros.* The vaquero in Mexico promptly became as necessary as the muleteer. As soon as the conquest of the Aztecs was completed, the vast realm which they had ruled became

a part of the Spanish Empire, and all the transplanted customs and arts of the homeland began to be practiced. In 1521 only two years after Cortés landed at San Juan de Ulúa and established the city of Veracruz—which finally occupied three different sites—the first cattle were landed there to join the horses in creating the necessary ingredients for ranchos and haciendas. Gregorio de Villalobos brought these original cattle from Santo Domingo. Then Cortés himself created the setting for ranch life in Mexico. He established a magnificent hacienda a short distance south of Mexico City and named it, appropriately, "Cuernavaca," meaning "Cow's horn." From his hacienda in Cuba he imported cows and bulls, and helped start the tidal wave of livestock sweeping north and west through Mexico and beyond.

A Registry of Brands was started in Mexico in 1529, and a large number of brands was registered even during the first decade.

The muleteer had become indispensable in the extension of Spanish exploration in America by caring for the horses, mules and burros used by the troops. Now, too, the vaquero entered into the great enterprise of colonial expansion by herding on the big ranchos the cattle needed to accompany the soldiers and priests who were constantly pressing forward into the beckoning lands of the heathen.

Within an incredibly short time after Cortés' landing at Veracruz, it was possible to gather up enormous numbers of horses and cattle hundreds of miles away for new adventures in exploration. When Coronado started out in 1540, only twenty-one years after the Conquest, in search of the Seven Golden Cities of Cibola, he did not leave from Veracruz or Mexico City, great supply centers, as might have been expected. Instead, far to the north and west, in a tiny place called Compostela close to Tepic, he assembled his forces and collected five hundred cattle, extra horses,

"Fremont at Monterey," by W. H. D. Koerner, from "Folded Hills" by Stewart Edward White, in The Saturday Evening Post, *1934. (Ruth Koerner Oliver, Santa Barbara, California.)*

goats, sheep and hogs, already plentiful in that distant area to which they had been introduced so recently.

On Coronado's fruitless trip, during which the "Golden Cities" proved in the New Mexico region to be mere clusters of mud huts, he took horses and cattle into a region which had never known them. He saw in the land of New Mexico and the Rio Grande the buffalo, which were as novel to him as the horses and cattle were to the Indians. He could not at that moment of frustration along the banks of the inhospitable Rio Grande, when he and his men were disappointed at failing to find the treasures of which they had dreamed, realize that the Indians he glimpsed would one day transform themselves into ferocious mounted warriors when they, too, obtained horses such as those they now saw for the first time. He was, in effect, giving the Indians a preview of the creature destined to enable them to ride down the buffalo, harass generations of white invaders and immortalize themselves in the Battle of the Little Bighorn.

Hunger, danger and a total lack of golden booty were all that Coronado and his companions could think of on their weary return to Mexico. Yet his expedition was the first probing of a region where the Spanish horse was assuredly about to become, next to man himself, the leading figure in a momentous enactment such as had never been seen before on earth. Up from southern and central Mexico, the onward push of mounted men began with such unparalleled vigor that its progress become irresistible. Through valleys and over mountains it went, into Chihuahua and to distant Sonora.

Its movement was in the shape of a Spanish spur, like a V standing for "vaquero." One prong was aimed at Texas, the other at California. Along these diverging routes, with stops for battles, colonization, growing of crops and the birth of new generations of children, the conquistadors and their successors kept up their inevitable progression. They crossed the Rio Grande onto the vast plains of Texas and went by sea and also across

"Reata," by W. H. D. Koerner, from "Ranchero" by Stewart Edward White, in The Saturday Evening Post, 1932. (Ruth Koerner Oliver, Santa Barbara, California.)

"Don José Sepulveda, 1856," by French artist Henri Penelone. Don José Sepulveda was a member of the celebrated Spanish family in early California. (Charles W. Bowers Memorial Museum, Santa Ana, California.)

the Rio Colorado to the lush coastal grasslands of California.

Once in these new settlements, the horse and his rider found the environment ideal for their ultimate development. In Texas, a realm so vast it was hard for the settlers themselves to realize its bounds, the horses escaped from their owners and began to create an immense population of their own in the wilds, to an extent never seen in interior Mexico. Likewise, the cattle became "wild game" in the wooded lands along the Pecos and the Brazos and the Texas Colorado, unbranded mavericks subject only to the *reatas* of those daring riders who could catch them. In California, on the big ranchos and amid the hills, the unnumbered cattle ran in such hordes that they were slaughtered at will, and their hides became the monetary currency of the colony, at two dollars each.

During this time, the vaqueros were in the ascendancy, seemingly secure in their enviable position as the finest riders known in the world. However, their reign was being threatened. Out from the Atlantic coast of the newly formed United States of America was spreading another array of hardy horsemen, moving inexorably toward their own goals, which were in many cases as yet obscure and unseen. Just as the vaquero had traveled in two directions along the sides of a symbolic spur, so also did the Americanos del Norte have their own emblem of expansion. They rode onward as if guided by the symbol of a wide U in a Flying Half Circle branding iron. One segment of this made its imprint down toward the Red River and Texas, the other across the buffalo plains and the peaks of the Rockies to the Sierra Nevada and California.

The V and the U were headed for collision.

So the ancient Mexican vaquero, proud in his tradition, arrogant in his manliness, rode toward a showdown with the embryonic American "cow boy," lusty and lean, spoiling for a fight.

INCANTATION FOR A BRANDING IRON

Branding of animals is so ancient a practice that the art of forging the branding irons is surrounded with incantations. The forger was an artist in metal.

From venerable Toldeo, so celebrated for its unexcelled steel, has come down to us, through Mexico, the traditional chant of the forger as he plunged the red-hot iron into the water to temper it:

Blessed be the hour in which Christ was born—Saint Mary who bore Him—St. John who baptized Him—The iron is hot—the water hisses—

The tempering will be good—If God wills.

Tempo and length of the chants for the forging were rigid because they determined the exact time for the best results with the metal during its immersion.

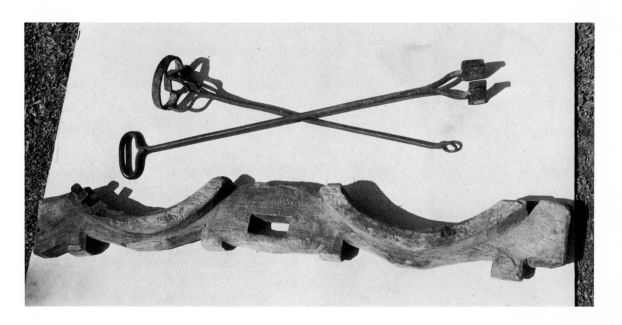

4

BIRTH OF THE COWBOY

Conquistador in the New World, 1500

Three wars and a big appetite for beef stew combined to put the American cowboy in the saddle of history.

Two of the wars brought into collision the Latin and Anglo-Saxon civilizations, which were contending for territory and domination. The third resulted in the big appetite within the United States. The military clash between the long-established Spanish-Mexican forces and the restless, probing Americano del Norte frontiersmen forever pushing westward had become inevitable by the time of the Texas Revolution. It was a physical confrontation of two opposing peoples, the former looking east and the latter west.

In these big corrals called Texas and California it was hard to tell who was wilder, the horses or the men. Maybe there is the text for a sermon on "Love of Liberty" in the fact that of all the fifty states of the union, only

Texas and California were independent republics before they became part of the United States. The men so prized individual freedom that they took part, in Texas in the Revolution, and, in California, in the Bear Flag Revolt against Mexican authority. Part of this was due to the immensity of Texas and California, where a fellow never had to mess around much with neighbors. The vastness got into a man's thinking. He looked out every day over the prairies or up to the Davis Mountains or the Sierras, and moved his elbows around to see that nobody was jostling him. The same sort of spirit was bred into the horses, too. They had their own ideas about liberty and were ready to fight for it just as the men were. If a man caught a wild horse it was a personal duel. Somebody had to give in or get killed, and nearly always it took a hell of a fight to see which way it was

going to be. If the man won, he had himself a good mustang for life. If the horse won, they buried the man out on the lone prairee.

It did not matter much in regard to the love of liberty whether the man was a Mexican or an Americano del Norte. The Mexicans indulged in a revolution against Spain, the Americanos against Mexico. Each refused to submit to domination.

Texas and California were the scenes of enormous cattle activity before the wagon trains of the pioneers ever started making ruts in the sod of the Middle West on the way to the promised land of the Pacific.

Yet, oddly enough, war whoops and the thunder of buffalo feet had exerted far more of an artistic lure at first than did the tilt of seven-foot-long horns and the sight of a rider chasing a steer. For this reason, the Plains and the Rocky Mountains "got their pictures in the papers" long before the real stamping grounds of the cattle and horses down Texas way attracted any notice at all from the men with the easels and the paintbrushes. If Texas and California could boast settlements and ranchos while the midcontinent prairies were untrodden by the feet of wagon-train oxen, the Louisiana Purchase still could claim with complete justification that it had drawn to its vast expanses some of the best artists Europe and the new United States could produce. For the most part, the sight of the Texas and California cattle and the horses with the men who rode them were so routine that they failed to stir much attention from the occasional artist who wandered that way.

In California, occasionally, a painter did put down on canvas the likeness of some notable *caballero* or ranch owner, but this was more in reciprocation for hospitality received than from any basic interest in the subject of man-on-horseback. In Texas, the subject was almost totally neglected.

Even Texas and California differed somewhat in their horse and cattle careers, just as

they did in their saddle rigging and chaps and boots and spurs. Texas was so immense and harsh that it never did experience the intimate, carefree kind of pastoral life that marked California in its more temperate clime along the ocean and in the inland valleys. The Spaniards who tried to enter Texas were met by savage resistance from someone else who prized his liberty, the native Indian. Comanches made it impossible for Texas ever to have the same kind of security and languid existence which California enjoyed in its golden era. The fiesta had little chance to flourish in a land where the scalping knife was a constant threat. San Diego might dance at its *bailes*, but San Antonio was happy just to be alive when morning came.

Yet, despite these differences, Texas and

Sketch made at the Spear Ranch, by W. H. D. Koerner. (Ruth Koerner Oliver, Santa Barbara, California.)

California shared the basic essentials for the coming of the cowboy. Charlie Goodnight and John C. Frémont were cut out of pretty much the same cloth. They encountered in their respective regions the surge and bellow of vast herds of wild cattle, heard the thunder of pounding hoofs and witnessed the sight of innumerable flying manes. Each saw the passing of an era and the arrival of a new one.

By the time when the Texas Republic was set up in 1836—California still had ten years to go before ending its Mexican era— the horses and cattle from the Rio Grande to the Red River were so numerous that no one ever attempted to count them accurately. J. Frank Dobie, the Texas historian and folklorist who came from cattle people, placed the number developed during the generation from the Texas Revolution to the outbreak of the Civil War at "millions" east of the Pecos River before the cattle ever spread out onto the plains to the north, and estimated that a third or so were never branded. The river bottoms with their groves of pecans, sycamores, cottonwoods, cedar and small oaks and brush were so ideal for the cattle that they sometimes lived their whole lives there without being glimpsed by man. The wild horses often frequented the same regions, but some ranged far and wide over the lands between the rivers.

In California, too, cattle and horses multiplied to such proportions that they became a menace. Between San Diego and Santa Ana at the Santa Margarita Rancho of 200,000 acres

"In Trouble." Pencil sketch by Olaf Wieghorst.

or more (which successively was the Don Juan Forster Rancho, the Flood-O'Neill Ranch, the Jerome O'Neill Ranch, and eventually today's United States Marine Camp Joseph H. Pendleton), the horses became so numerous that they were eating the grass needed by the cattle. The vaqueros thereupon drove them over a cliff to their deaths near the ranch house, which today serves as headquarters for the commanding general of Camp Pendleton.

Americanos del Norte who ventured into California during the pastoral era before the Gold Rush were astounded by the sight of the wild horses. William Heath Davis, who was born in Honolulu, son of a Boston ship captain, and came to California when he was only nine, in 1831, was struck with admiration and awe by the spectacle provided by the wild horses and the "mustanging" to capture and tame them.

The horses [he observed] were never stabled. They were broken for the saddle only, and were used almost wholly for herding cattle. They were divided up into caponeras, or small bodies of about 25 each, each caponera having a bell mare, which was always a yequa pinta (calico mare), having a beautiful variety of color, whom they followed—and so accustomed were they to their leaders that the different little bands never mixed; and if by chance one got into the wrong company, he would presently go back to where he belonged.

(Above) *"Old Timer." Pencil sketch by Olaf Wieghorst.*

(Right) *A sampling of brands. (L. A. Corral Westerners.)*

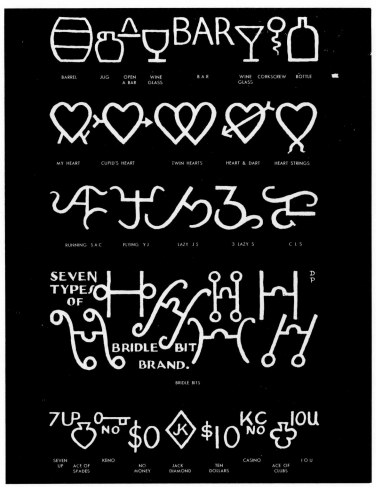

A large number of horses were needed on each rancho for herding stock, as they were used up very fast. They were numerous and cheap, and the owners placed no restraint upon the vaqueros, who rode without a particle of regard for the horses, till they soon became unfit for further use in this way. The vaqueros were continually breaking in young colts three years old and upwards, to replace those already beyond service.

There were large bands of wild horses in the Valley of the San Joaquin which at that time was entirely unsettled. At times, a few mares, and perhaps a young stallion, would stray away from a rancho and get out of reach, until in the course of time there were collected in that valley immense herds, thousands and tens of thousands of horses, entirely wild and untamed, living and breeding by themselves, finding there plenty of good feed to sustain them.

A pioneer Texas mustanger found it difficult to believe his eyes when he looked at the herds of wild horses.

I well remember when I first came to Texas, in 1847, seeing thousands and tens of thousands of mustangs running all over the western country as far as the eye or the telescope could reach [related Thomas A. Dwyer at San Antonio]. Time and again in traveling, I have had to send out my best mounted men to act as flankers in scaring away the immense masses of mustangs charging around and threatening to rush over us, by yelling and firing at them; then they would wheel and go thundering away.

Out of the war between the armies of General Sam Houston and General Antonio López de Santa Anna came not only the Alamo, Goliad, the Battle of San Jacinto and Texan victory, but also the tensions which culminated ten years later in the Mexican War. When that conflict in turn was concluded, the United States, after already annexing Texas, had acquired California and all the vast territory which later became the states of Arizona and New Mexico and stretched from sea to sea.

In the struggles, the hardy men who were to become the cowboys had tested their mettle on the battlefields against the brave vaqueros and the *charros*. Each came to respect the prowess of the other, both as soldiers and horsemen. After peace was concluded, there was a certain mingling of the former enemies in the cow camps and on the long trails of the big herds. That contest for supremacy still went on in some places, the old-time vaquero against the incipient cowboy. The term "cow boy" came into use sometime during the early part of the nineteenth century, probably around 1820. It was applied with a slight tone of derision to the counterparts of the mustangers who chased wild cattle. Gradually it came to include the American equivalent of the Mexican vaquero and, in time, was contracted to the one word "cowboy."

The third war, this time within the United States, was required as a final catalyst for the true cowboy to stand forth in typical outline for posterity. The Civil War was more than the tragedy of brother fighting brother over principles; it led to a fateful shaping of the social and economic future of the nation after it was reunited. During the war, great factories and war plants evolved in the North, and large populations flocked to the cities. Thus begun, urbanization continued after the war, as has been the case following all American wars since then.

This population, sick of wartime privations and now beginning to be swollen too by a vast new tide of immigrants from Europe, shared a common longing.

It was hungry for beef.

Now was the hour of the cowboy.

On the immense plains of Texas and in the river bottoms roamed longhorns in uncounted numbers, each packing on his lean and ornery carcass a certain number of pounds of beefsteak. At this very moment, while a potential market was licking its chops in New York, Boston, Philadelphia, Washington and numerous other centers, the transcontinental railroad, so long a mere dream, was stretching in a reality of steel rails west of the Mississippi onto the plains of Kansas and to the rough new towns springing up along its route in the wilds. These rails provided, for the first time, mass transportation at cheap cost funneling into the big cities.

Supply and demand, beef and appetite were ready to supplement each other. The Chisholm and Goodnight Trails and railhead towns like Abilene and Dodge City began to function to bring the other elements into contact.

Amid the slush, mire, sleet, northers, stampedes, dust, gunplay, heat, rustlers, misery and greed of the Goodnight and Chisholm Trails, the cowboy was born. He had come up to his full stature, ready to ride, fight, herd, love, play, gamble and kill. He had created for himself an image, part real and part fictional, which attracted the painters and the sculptors, those inevitable chroniclers who perceptively sensed that beyond mere picturesqueness here was a breed destined to live forever in story and legend, and to help shape the whole idea of the American man.

5
LURE OF THE WILDS

Conquistadors of the Cortés period, 1519

Most of the two hundred million or so Americans now living and able to talk, if asked to name the greatest painters of the cowboy and Western range scene, would reply almost automatically with two names: "Charlie Russell and Frederic Remington." This answer is so expected, and indeed so justified, that it is almost as if it were vacuum-packed and totally standardized. The emotional appeal and technical proficiency of the Russell and Remington portrayals are so overwhelming that they tend, in a sense, to create this vacuum atmosphere. Many people, looking at their work, seem to regard the creators of the masterpieces as shining statues on some high pedestal, encased and shut off from the world, marble men on a granite base. Fortunately, on the contrary, they were human beings. Each endured the privations of all pioneers in the West, felt the blast of northers biting into

their bones, endured desert heat and thirst, were galled by long hours in the saddle, suffered love and sorrow, felt the sting of frustration and disappointment, got grumpy, "fought" their pictures to make them come out right, were buffeted by a boisterous and tempestuous world and went through changing and often baffling times.

Neither ever knew a sheltered or "vacuum" existence. They fought their way up amid the surge and fluctuation of masses of humanity in lusty, growing America. They lived among soldiers, Indians, river men, drunken cowboys, church folks, riotous miners, gun slingers and fancy ladies on the local scene and in an ever-changing panorama of vast events shaping the future of the unfolding United States.

Painters were part of the everyday world, gawking like other mortals at the new wonders

"The Burial Horse," by Friedrich Kurz. (Van Kirke Nelson, M.D., Kalispell, Montana.)

of science, swayed by political passions, terrified in the midst of successive wars, subject to lashing by the elements, and beset by hunger and thirst and the necessity of appeasing these wants.

This universality, this sharing of the emotions of friends and neighbors, gave eventually to the painters, both European and American, the depth of character and discernment which would, in turn, fire all those who might see their work.

Almost from the moment of the Louisiana Purchase—itself born out of the fervor, excitement and persistence of Thomas Jefferson—the curiosity of the public was stirred by what might lie out there in the vast and mysterious region stretching toward the west. The

initial explorations of Lewis and Clark merely whetted this curiosity. When, a few years later, the government in Washington decided to obtain more definitive information about the whole enormous territory, public interest was so keen that artists were sent along to portray the native people and the places visited.

The 1819–1820 expedition under the command of Major Stephen H. Long for the War Department took with it a Philadelphia painter, Samuel Seymour, and a younger artist, Titian Ramsay Peale, who, although he was only twenty, was notably talented and deeply imbued with the spirit of Western adventure. He knew something about wild life, too. Zebulon Pike, of Pike's Peak note, had

This cattle-drive scene by James Walker is supposed to be set in the San Fernando Valley, now in the City of Los Angeles. (California Historical Society, San Marino, California.)

brought back to the Peale family from "way out there" two grizzly-bear cubs, and Titian Peale had grown up with them until they became too rough to keep as pets. Now he and Seymour penetrated into the wilderness which had produced the bears. Peale drew notable pictures of buffalo, among the first by any American artist, and Seymour was credited with a "first" in picturing the Rocky Mountains, also complete with buffalo in the foreground. The whole array of art work by the two painters captivated the attention of the American people, and stimulated other artists to go see and depict for themselves the Indians and interesting animals of the seemingly illimitable hinterland.

These artists constituted a veritable procession. In the process of their travels, they contributed to the creation of the first "art center" on the frontier, in St. Louis. All journeys toward the Great Plains and the Rockies funneled naturally through the Missouri city on the bank of the Mississippi. There or thereabouts came every sort of fellow with easel

and paints and his rapt gaze fixed on the western horizon. St. Louis, even by 1819 when Major Long started out exploring with Seymour and Peale, was only fifty-five years old, having been founded in 1763–1764 by Pierre Laclede and René Auguste Chouteau as a fur-trading post, but it was becoming for the United States the symbol of westward expansion. It was settled by the French only five or six years before California, on the West Coast, was colonized by the Spanish, yet by 1820 it was recognized as the outpost of the American push toward the Far West. When Seymour and Peale were passing through, a firebrand lawyer, Thomas Hart Benton, transplanted to the Missouri frontier from his native North Carolina by way of Pennsylvania and Tennessee, was just being elected United States Senator and becoming the lifelong champion and spokesman of Manifest Destiny, the two words epitomizing United States expansion to the Pacific.

The artists who went forth from St. Louis are linked with the visual history of the

West, which they produced in their paintings. Among the first was Peter Rindisbacher, a Swiss lad who at fifteen came to Canada and, in the early 1820's, trekked overland to Minnesota and Wisconsin, drawing and painting on the way. He gained notable success, but died when he was only twenty-eight. Youthfulness, indeed, was an attribute of many of the painters. They needed it. Stamina, endurance and courage were essential in the wilderness, whether a man carried a gun or a paintbox.

In addition to the Indians and the buffalo, the hardy breed of horses acquired by the aborigines from the Spaniards attracted the painters because of their picturesqueness and, in many cases, their bizarre color. The strain later known as Appaloosa was observed, and so were many paints and pintos. They made good subject matter for paintings, particularly with Indian riders in a buffalo chase.

Some of the artists could not paint horses very well, but they tried anyway. One of these men, whose extraordinary talents have made his name endure, was George Catlin, of Wilkes-Barre, Pennsylvania, member of a family of fourteen children. His chronicles of Western life, in paintings, were so vivid and for the most part so authentic that they rank as almost incomparable in the annals of pioneer America. Yet Catlin's horses are, somehow, imperfect, ethereal creations rather than realities. This defect, though, cannot dim the luster of his portrayals when he was in his thirties, of Indians and their surroundings, which were, even then, beginning to change rapidly.

John Mix Stanley, born in Canandaigua, New York, almost at the time of the War of 1812, grew up with a passion for the West and, at twenty-five, began painting it. Alfred Jacob Miller, four years older than Stanley, went from his native Baltimore into the Indian country and portrayed the red men and their horses with suspense and drama, as in his "Threatened Attack." A youth inspired by Catlin, Charles Deas of Philadelphia went out to the West about 1840, and began to paint with such assurance that his horses and riders are almost flamboyant. Charles Wilmar, a young German, was so enamored of the Indians and their horses that he depicted buffalo-hunting scenes as if he were an actual participant. Friederich Kurz, an accomplished artist in his native Switzerland before he came to this country, went to St. Louis and beyond in his quest for the spectacular and unusual, and found them.

The drawings and painting of the successive artists met various fates. Some were acclaimed, and endured. Others gained little attention. Some were lost or destroyed.

Seth Eastman, an Army officer, depicted the scenes around him at the military posts where he was stationed. Karl Bodmer, a Swiss, penetrated to remote fastnesses where Indians and buffalo formed a phantasmagoria he could never have imagined in his homeland. Felix Octavius Carr Darley went out from Philadelphia and became one of the portraitists of the bison. William Ranney viewed the horses of the Indians and left faithful depictions of them. Ernest Narjot, a Frenchman, also painted horses in action, most of them slender and dainty as if straight out of an Arabian dream. Arthur F. Tait, an Englishman, and Henry Farney, an Alsatian, went eagerly into the wilds to become chroniclers of a life that stirred their artistic fervor. George de Forest Brush of Tennessee left the domain of Andrew Jackson for the land where Senator Benton was proclaiming, "Forward march!" Charles Christian Nahl, who was in his early thirties at the time of the California gold discovery, went to the land of the Golconda as a miner, but remained to become an artist, catching the flavor and spirit of the gold camps, complete with the horsemen who formed so much a part of the whole scene.

Col. William F. Cody—"Buffalo Bill." (Roscoe E. Hazard Museum, San Diego, California.)

Self-portrait, by James Walker. (California Historical Society, San Marino, California.)

Nostalgia already was entering into the Western scene before the tide of artists abated. Alfred Bierstadt, a German-born painter who later became known as "the portraitist of the Rockies," was fifty-nine—he had been born January 7, 1830—when he painted a giant canvas symbolic of the fading of the old West. He titled the spirited scene, which depicted an Indian on a white horse spearing a buffalo amid skulls and slaughtered animals, "Last of the Buffalo." It was turned down for the Paris Exposition of 1889 but today is considered a masterpiece. Some of the artists, such as Thomas Moran, the British-born younger brother of the famous Edward Moran, dwelt more upon the scenic grandeur of the Rockies and Yellowstone than on the Indians and horses and buffalo. Still, the works of all these artists combined to give Americans a new insight into the western region. Each was depicting the ingredients from which the cowboy and his Western range were evolving.

The lives of many of these artists bridged an incredibly varied series of happenings, in which they necessarily were participants as well as observers. These years saw the election of Andrew Jackson, signalizing the advent of the rule of the common people in the United States; the Texas Revolution and the Alamo, Goliad and San Jacinto; the Mexican War and the acquisition of California and of the vast region embracing Arizona and New Mexico; and the California '49er Days. It was a period marked by the inventions of anesthesia and of photography, of the telephone and of the telegraph, as well as by that brief innovation, the Pony Express, and the completion of the transcontinental railroad. The artists shared in the agony of the Civil War and suffered the shock of the assassination of Abraham Lincoln. They witnessed, later on, the flamboyant entrance onto the international stage of Buffalo Bill Cody and his Wild West Show. Meanwhile, war played a great part in shaping the career of one notable foreign artist of the West.

It must have been an amazing transition for James Walker to have come from the England of the Charles Dickens era and to be plunged into the throes of the Mexican War in Mexico City, where he became a fugitive. Walker's career from the time of his birth in England in 1819 to his death in Watsonville, California, seventy years later, was almost as varied as his paintings. By coincidence, his birth came in the same year as the first journey from St. Louis into the American West by two artists, Samuel Seymour and Titian Ramsay Peale, who stimulated interest in Western art, a feat also accomplished by Walker in his maturity.

Before Walker arrived in Mexico City in the middle 1840s, he had lived for a time in New York with his parents and then, as a young man, traveled on to New Orleans. When the war between Mexico and the United States broke out in 1846 Walker disregarded a Mexican edict prohibiting all Americans from approaching nearer than three hundred miles to the Mexican capital. He hid for six weeks, and then escaped to the American lines where he served as an interpreter with the United States Army. This service included the battle for the Valley of Mexico, the storming of Chapultepec Castle and the American occupation of Mexico City.

After an absence of eight years he returned to New York at the end of the war in 1848, and, led on by his interest in Latin-American affairs which had been engendered by his stay in Mexico, he went to South America. Later, he set up a studio in New York. At this time his work was centered primarily on large battle scenes, such as the battle of Chapultepec and the battle of Lookout Mountain.

The call of the West summoned him to California at about the three-quarter mark in the nineteenth century, and there he found the opportunity once again to express his

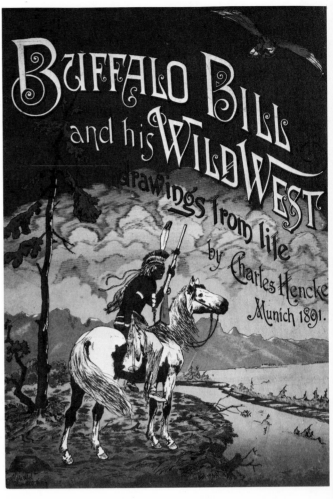

Drawing from Buffalo Bill and His Wild West, *by Charles Henckel, Munich, 1891. At this time, Buffalo Bill's tours in Europe brought him great popularity. (Roscoe E. Hazard Museum, San Diego, California.)*

interest in Spanish and Mexican subjects. Although California had been under American rule for approximately a quarter of a century, Walker still found subject matter from the pastoral period of the region to appeal to his imagination. He painted Spanish grandees, the roping of grizzly bears, wild horse hunts and the cattle which roamed in untold thousands on the hills. He visited famous ranches, such as the El Tejon, owned by General

Cowboys riding and taming bucking horses—a page from book of Buffalo Bill drawings by Charles Henckel reflecting the showman's popularity attributable to his European tours. (Roscoe E. Hazard Museum, San Diego, California.)

Edward F. Beale (one of the heroes of the battle of San Pasqual in the Mexican War), and there and in the San Fernando Valley painted some of his famous cattle scenes.

His paintings give today glimpses into a romantic period such as are provided by no other artist with a California background.

However, a fresco painter who provided a cultural touch to Southern California in the 1850s was Henri Penelon, who left a notable equestrian painting of Don José Andrés Sepulveda, a grandee of the Spanish-Mexican period. This 1856 painting hangs in the Charles W. Bowers Memorial Museum in Santa Ana. Penelon added ornamental touches to the old

Plaza Church in Los Angeles when it was renovated.

Hazards were part of the career of any artist going into the turbulent West during the middle and even the latter years of the nineteenth century. Theodore R. Davis, born in Boston in 1840, discovered this in startling fashion when he was only twenty-five. He had become an artist for *Harper's Weekly* at twenty-one and, in 1865, was sent on an assignment to Colorado. The coach taking him to Denver was attacked by Indians, but he escaped with his life, depicted the incident for his publication, and went on to become a pictorial chronicler of the Indian wars.

WHERE THE TALL STORIES GROW

A special type of pungent and laconic "tall story" emerged in the cow country where men were lonely and had time to mull over little incidents that sometimes grew into full-fledged anecdotes. Ace Powell, the Montana painter, in his book *The Ace of Diamonds* (edited by Van Kirke Nelson, M.D., Kalispell, Montana, 1965) relates one of these under the title:

You Can't Fool Me

One spring I was breaking a few horses on a ranch where old George was working. The boss brought in a farm kid about nineteen years old, from Alberta. This kid tells me he's only been twenty miles from home, and the only town he's been in is Cardston. He don't know much, but he ain't too ignorant, either.

One night old George, this kid, and me are having a little bull session out in the bunkhouse.

George makes the comment, "The queerest thing I ever seed was in the Yellerstone. It was a buffalo eating grapes and climbing trees."

"Aw! George," says the kid, "you can't fool me. A buffalo can't climb trees."

"Kid," says George, "you never can tell what a buffalo will do when he's eating grapes."

6
REMBRANDT OF THE LONGHORNS

Mexican brand-registration era, 1530

Into the Land of the Big Distance came one bright morning, in the heyday of the cowboys, the "Rembrandt of the Longhorns."

He was out of place, with his Irish soul and his artist's eyes fastening on the landscape, because he had just entered a hell-roaring, gun-toting, body-busting, dust-scattering stampede known by the name of Texas. All around him swirled the cowboys and the cow critters, one as mean as the other, and none of them paying one damn' bit of attention to anybody but themselves. It was in the midst of the cattle drive days when millions of bawling, balking, bull-tough brutes were being jounced up the long, long trail to the railroad in Kansas and the beef-hungry city masses in the East. The War—the War between the States, that is—was just eleven years over, and U. S. Grant and his cigars were in the White House, and Reconstruction was

still a pain in the guts to the South, of which Texas, besides being West, too, was so much a part.

Still, Texas cattlemen and Texas cowboys, a lot of them Confederates out of uniform, were willing to take the dollars of Yankees in exchange for beef and hides. The cattle flowed one way, north, and the dollars flowed the other way, south. It was a long sight better than Confederate paper.

So this Irish boy with his parents, jostling in a wagon over the prairies, was seeing for the first time the great tide of history going by the term "longhorn." His name was Frank Reaugh—a contraction of the old-time Irish "Castlereaugh" and pronounced simply "Ray" —and he was sixteen years old when the family moved by covered wagon and ox team from Jacksonville, Illinois, where Frank had been born December 6, 1860, to the Texas wilder-

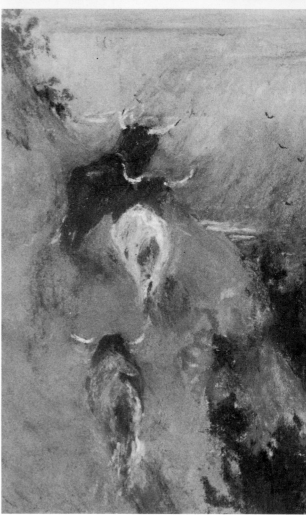

(Right) *"Longhorns," by Frank Reaugh. (Panhandle-Plains Historical Museum, Canyon, Texas.)*

(Below) *Sketches of longhorn cattle heads, by Frank Reaugh. (Panhandle-Plains Historical Museum, Canyon, Texas.)*

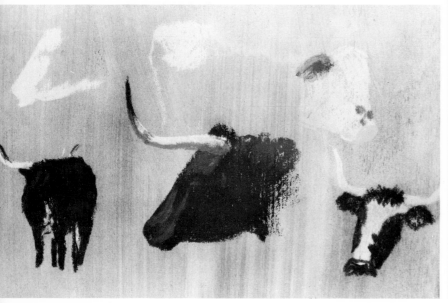

ness. From the moment they crossed the Arkansas River at Van Buren and moved on toward a ranch homesite near Terrell, Texas, Frank was deeply stirred by the illimitable distance where "all around was open range; wild and free."

In this vast, strange domain, he began to develop a "fondness for painting Texas cattle in their natural wildness." Immediately, he found a favorite, and in words and paint proclaimed "the Longhorn to be the noblest and most beautiful of all." At first he sketched only in black and white, but he yearned for a more effective means of artistic expression. Before he was able to venture into color, he wandered over the range lands from the Cross Timbers to the Staked Plains. He saw the rangy brutes being driven up the Chisholm Trail toward the railroads in Kansas. He absorbed the cowboy life of the rough men in charge of the herds. He camped in canyons and on the prairies, watched the dawns and

the sunsets, and finally knew that he must learn to depict it all in color.

When he was twenty-four, he saved enough money to go to the St. Louis School of Fine Arts for a series of lessons, his first formal training. His venture into the art realm was so exciting to frontier Texans that, upon his return to Terrell, the women of the community organized the Frank Reaugh Art Study Club. From this time on he knew he must have additional training, and four years later, in 1888, he sailed for Europe, where he studied in Paris and in the Netherlands, becoming totally enamored of pastels as a medium of expression. Back in Texas the next year, he began the work in pastels which resulted in his most lasting fame, going out always into the wildest country he could find for his rugged bulls, elusive steers and their backgrounds of creeks, mesquites and oaks.

The tragedy of progress came into Frank Reaugh's life when he was thirty years old.

Cover for one of Zane Grey's books, by W. Herbert Dunton. (Mr. and Mrs. William B. Davis.)

Frank Reaugh, who has been characterized as the "Rembrandt of the Longhorns."

This was in 1890, the year selected by most historians as marking the end of the "true cowboy" period. The longhorn was disappearing. The vast herds that had roamed over Texas during and after the Civil War had been so depleted that the cattle drives and their original picturesqueness were a thing of the past. Of course, there were some longhorns left and some cattle drives, but, as the nation moved into the 1890s, the building of railroads into remote areas and the introduction of new, heavier breeds of cattle such as the Herefords began to result in a new kind of cattle business. Barbed-wire fence and gateposts began to signify that the open freedom of the range was ending. With it went an era, the era of the longhorn.

Frank Reaugh sensed this change, and in response to it sadly moved from the region where he had been so close to the longhorns of yore and went to Dallas. He built a studio of sheet metal, and it was promptly dubbed

"Old Ironsides." J. Evetts Haley, who has written a charming monograph on Frank Reaugh, relates that Reaugh built another studio which was called "The Vault" because of the storage space he built beneath it for his pictures. Haley recounts that because of Reaugh's exacting demands he "compounded his own colors and molded his own crayons."

To his many students, Reaugh spoke in glowing terms of nature and its creatures, compressing into his remarks his own philosophical approach to the subject. He was always sentimental about the open spaces.

> My pictures have always been reminiscent [he reflected]. I like the Texas I saw in my youth. I like the old long-horned steer; the steer that made Texas famous. . . . I like to sleep under the stars far away on the Western prairie . . . far away from man and his civilization. I like to be where the skies are unstained by dust and smoke, where the trees are untrimmed and the wild flowers grow. I like the brilliant sunlight,

Sketch by Harold Bugbee. (Panhandle-Plains Historical Museum, Canyon, Texas.)

Harold Bugbee. (Panhandle-Plains Historical Museum, Canyon, Texas.)

and the far distance. I like the opalescent color of the plains. It is the beauty of the great Southwest as God has made it that I love to paint.

He spoke clearly and perceptively of what art should mean:

Art should be taught with the view of training both the vision and the mind, and especially the mind. No faculty is more used or more capable of development than the sense of sight—the practice of art renders it more accurate and enduring. No intellectual attainment is more valuable than the power of judging the fitness of things as to form, color and proportion. This power is the essential of art. Mere manual dexterity follows as an incident.

To this he added, as if in benediction,

A painting . . . if based on nature . . . should not violate nature's laws. Nature's beauty of design is matchless. Man's invention compares with it as much as his feats in engineering compare with the motion of the stars. But nature's design is that of species. To man is given the fine arts. In their enjoyment, free from all selfishness and

lust, man is at his best. Inspired by nature's motifs and guided by nature's laws he creates beautiful works of art, and therein approaches most nearly to the image of his God.

His views were so decided that when he sat down to write his will May 16, 1940, he left specific instructions for the disposition and care of the pictures he was bequeathing. In the will it was stated:

. . . The foregoing paintings . . . are donated by me to the Southwest at large. I request my Trustees to see that the intent of my will is carried out and that the control of the collection shall not be allowed to fall into the hands of any merely political, municipal or business organization. . . . The curator shall not be a radical of any kind, but shall be able and willing to point out the good qualities of conservative painting.

In accordance with his instructions, the trustees of his estate presented five hundred of his paintings to the Panhandle-Plains Historical Museum at Canyon, Texas, and two hundred to the Texas Technological College library at Lubbock.

"Law West of the Pecos," showing Judge Roy Bean holding court. (Roscoe E. Hazard Museum, San Diego, California.)

At eighty, when he wrote his will, Frank Reaugh had become the patriarch of the Texas longhorn period. His legacy was not in his pictures alone. He left in the hearts and minds of his students an inspiration which carried them forward in the tradition of Texas art. Some of his students were Edward G. Eisenlohr and Reveau Bassett, both of whom were honored by being made members of the National Academy.

Other great names in Texas art include that of W. H. Huddle, who did the monumental series of the presidents of the republic and the governors of the state for the capitol in Austin. Later, Harold Bugbee, who was born August 15, 1900, in Lexington, Massachusetts, came to be recognized as a modern master of Texas cattle scenes. His artistic stature became so great that he was prevailed upon in 1951 to join, on a part-time basis, the staff at the Panhandle-Plains Museum. Bugbee continued to paint, and the agreement was so pleasant that it was stated by officials of the museum that "the historical society has been extremely fortunate in the arrangement, for each year Bugbee has prepared far more art for the museum than that institution could have purchased from him at his established prices." Bugbee died March 27, 1963.

To this day, despite the passing of the longhorn era, Texas has continued to exert its spell upon artists. Some of those who have painted it have included Julian Onderonk; Porfirio Salinas, the distinguished painter who lives in San Antonio; Larry Chittenden, Harold Cook, Will Crawford, Chuck de Haan, of Fort Worth; Warren Hunter of Helotes; Tom Lea of El Paso; Bill Leftowich of Pecos; R. L. McCollister and Clay McGaughy of San Antonio; Ben Carlton Mead of Dallas; Richard Moore of Fort Worth; B. D. Titsworth of Denver; Charles Banks Wilson of Miami, Oklahoma; Donald Yena of San Antonio; Jim Bob Jackson of El Paso; and Bob Tommey of Dallas.

To the artist, Texas has in reality been more than a republic, a state, mesquite lands and rivers, vast stretches of prairies and mountains. It has been the personification of a romantic period echoing the tramp of longhorn hoofs.

A HERITAGE OF WESTERN SONGS

Horses and horsemen and their companions of the wilds, the burro prospectors, have given to the lore of America their own quaint examples of language and a lasting heritage of songs.

Two Western artists of great distinction also have become noted as composers of songs of the open range and the prospecting country. They are John W. Hilton and Emil (Aim) Morhardt of California, both on the board of directors of the Death Valley '49ers.

Hilton, born in a sod house near Carrington, North Dakota, September 9, 1904, was taken to China as a boy by his missionary parents, received art lessons from a Chinese master painter, later became a gem merchant, and then in 1930 went out into the California desert to learn to be a professional artist. He since has earned a reputation as a leading desert painter. He is an author (*Sonora Sketchbook*, 1947), guitarist, raconteur, plant scientist and historian. He has known many "single blanket jackass prospectors" who always expected to hit it rich, and wrote the song "The Last Bonanza" in their honor.

The Last Bonanza

Stake me a claim on the crest of a hill
    where winds of the desert march by,
Where time as it passes brings days that are still
    and sunsets that flame in the sky.
        CHORUS
I'll find my last Bonanza with a paylead
    that never shall fail.
I'll find my last Bonanza where I'll rest
    to the end of the trail.

        2

I'll mine me my wealth from the sunset's pure gold
    that glows on the threshold of night.
I'll mine from the moonbeams their silver untold
    and gems from that starry blue height.

        3

There would I rest till that last judgment day
    away from life's noises and pains,

On the warm rounded breast of the desert I'll lay
    where the hand of sweet solitude reins.

Aim Morhardt has been a teacher and musician, and is a water-colorist and oil painter. One of the most popular of the many songs he has written, a yearning expression of desert-ranch philosophy, is "My Ranch."

My Ranch

My ranch is one lone cow,
A well gone dry and a broken plough.
My ranch is one lone cow
And a thousand acres of nothing!

One hundred miles of fence,
The feed's no good but the view's immense.
Ten million tons of sand
And a thousand acres of nothing!

My old cow just had a calf,
Now I've got me a cow and a half.
I've got the range and sun
And a thousand acres of nothing.

My cow's got a wistful face
Staring across at my neighbor's place:
I'll be a cowboy yet
On my thousand acres of nothing.

7

HOME CORRAL

Francisco Coronado expedition, 1539

Where is the home corral?

To almost every human being comes the feeling, at one time or another and in a totally strange place where he has never been before, "I have come home!"

The surroundings may be different from anything he has ever known before. The scenery may be foreign, the landscape unfamiliar, yet there is an instantaneous recognition of something comforting and welcoming, intimate and warm. It is as if the harshness of the world is shut out and the glowing hearth of homecoming is awaiting the returned traveler.

So, I think, it must be with the artists who have been attracted to certain regions by their impulse to paint man on horseback with a rope in his hand in pursuit of an elusive steer. Portions of the West have acted as magnets to painters from far away, who, upon

their arrival, have exclaimed, "I have come home!" The high plains of Texas have one kind of magnetism, the mountains of New Mexico, the highlands of Colorado, the purple peaks of Arizona, the valleys of Wyoming and Montana, the coastal ranches of California another. Yet all have a great quality in common. This is the irresistible spell each exerts upon the individual who has responded to its particular appeal.

The strangest thing of all is that, although the cowboy era supposedly ended two long generations ago, about 1890, its influence is just as strong upon the painters of cowboy life today as it was three-quarters of a century ago. This recognition by the modern painters of the enduring fascination embodied in Western range life has given validity and permanence to their work. To them, too, must go the credit for recognizing and stimulating the

"Kickover of Morning Coffee Pot," by Charles M. Russell. (Hammer Galleries, New York.)

Wash drawing by Charles M. Russell

enormous resurgence of popular interest in "cowboy art." For a long while after 1890, except in limited circles which appreciated Russell and Remington, the cowboy era was too close at hand to have much appeal. Its toil and sweat were too real to have taken on any aura of romance. Some time had to pass before it could enter the realm of national legend and folklore.

Even when a propitious moment did arrive, after the passage of the years, it required the efforts of writers as well as of painters to create a "cowboy" impact upon the public mind. When, in 1902, Owen Wister wrote *The Virginian* and hinted broadly at "son-of-a-bitch" as an unprintable epithet of the Western range, he was, it may be said, paving the way for the modern painters to respond to newly aroused interest in the cowboy subject. With words, Wister and Zane Grey made it possible for Herbert Dunton and Frank Tenney Johnson to depict cowboy life at the same time with paints. When Dunton and

Johnson created book jackets for Western classics, they were not merely illustrating for a segment of readers but were pointing to the broad trail of art which their successors were to follow.

As the cowboy era receded in time it came into focus, like some magic lantern illuminating the fabled West. The cowboy and his horse assumed a new meaning, not only in history but in the inner consciousness of the American people, as a manifestation of national character impossible anywhere else on earth. It was unique. It was a fusing and molding of innate and indigenous qualities peculiar to a region and a fleeting moment in the progression of the ages. The cowboy flourished most luxuriantly in a single generation, but his long shadow lay upon future, unfolding centuries.

He was the American on horseback.

To those artists who felt the urge to depict him, the magnetism of the various regions where he had flourished became a vital

"Changing Outfits," bronze by Charles M. Russell. (National Cowboy Hall of Fame, Oklahoma City, Oklahoma.)

force. It has mattered not at all to the "cowboy artists" what their own points of origin had been. They adapted themselves spontaneously to the surroundings in which their compelling interest lay.

To others, the home range always kept calling them back, even though they might have wandered far in search of some new region which might seem more congenial than their place of birth. They, as human beings, experienced those sentiments described by J. Frank Dobie in his book *Some Part of Myself* (Little, Brown and Company, Boston; copyright 1967, by Bertha Dobie) as applying to horses:

Charles M. Russell. (Harold G. Davidson, Santa Barbara, California.)

When my father began ranching, he raised horses, traded horses, and drove a herd or two to Kansas. I used to hear talk by him and other men about mares trailed northeastward from our country to Arkansas or some other faraway land that showed up in the spring to have their colts on the ground where they had been raised and had raised colts of their own—to their querencia. This was before barbed wire fenced the country. The instinct that is in me is the instinct that was in those homing mares. . . . The brush country of Southwest Texas is my querencia. *

The "cowboy artists" have belonged to

*From *Some Part of Myself* by J. Frank Dobie, reprinted by permission of the publisher, Little, Brown and Company.

one of the two categories: those who found their true range in distant parts, and those who wandered but returned to their *querencias.*

The pair recognized as the greatest of American "cowboy artists," Frederic Remington and Charles Marion Russell, belonged to the group which, despite their birthplaces, discovered the land of their liking in the West. There they said, "I have come home!" and proved it by their paintings.

In the public mind, as I have stressed, two men stand out as pre-eminent. The place of Russell and Remington is secure, and it is impossible for me in a book of this nature to attempt biographies worthy of them. The literature on both is monumental, with notable recent and definitive contributions being *Charles M. Russell* by Frederic G. Renner (University of Texas Press, Austin, 1966) and *The Frederic Remington Book* by Dr. Harold McCracken (Doubleday and Company, Garden City, New York, 1966).

The fact that both Russell and Remington were born during the Civil War, grew up in Reconstruction times, were attracted to the frontier, and mingled with cowboys, hunters and soldiers placed them in the right place at the right time for their enduring American characterizations.

Frederic Sackrider Remington was born in Canton, N. Y., on October 1, 1861. His ruggedness and virility led him to become, in the West, a participant in the wild life of the outposts as well as a chronicler of the people and the region. His artistic success was so great that he became not only a popular figure but the friend of President Theodore Roosevelt and an illustrator of his books. He had reached the heights when he died, after an emergency appendicitis operation, on December 26, 1909, at the age of 48.

Charles Marion Russell, admittedly less cultured in the academic sense than his contemporary, was born on March 19, 1864, in Oak Hill, near Webster Groves, in the outskirts of St. Louis. The wilds of Montana became his chosen home. Even when success came and he lived for a time in New York, selling his paintings for big prices but eating Mexican beans by choice in the studio of his friend Ed Borein, he always longed for Montana. In his later years he loved California, too, and was building a new home, Trail's End, in Pasadena when death came to him in Great Falls on October 24, 1926.

To their successors, Russell and Remington left both a legacy and a challenge.

Yearning for a distant region made itself felt in strange places. The siren call of the West sometimes singled out individuals who lived far away, in crowded cities.

Out of sickness and failure, an Eastern youth who longed for the vastness and drama of the West forged the elements of character and artistic ability which suddenly catapulted him to an almost undreamed-of pinnacle of success. The life of Charles Schreyvogel was made up so long of poverty and frustration that it was difficult for him to realize his own attainment when he finally won recognition. He became the friend of a President, was an honored guest at the White House, and his work won top awards at home and abroad.

He was a contemporary of Remington and Russell, and is considered to be equal to both in his artistic depictions of Western subjects, but his output was relatively small and he has not, for that reason, attained the public recognition awarded to the others.

Charles Schreyvogel was born in New York City on January 4, 1861, just a few months before the birth of Remington. He grew up amid poverty, and was a newsboy and errand-runner in New York and Hoboken, New Jersey, where the family moved. All the while he was possessed by an insatiable desire to draw, and in his spare moments he sketched continually. He worked his way up and became a lithographer. His proficiency

"The Seventh Cavalry," by Frederic Remington. (Albert K. Mitchell collection.)

"He Gave Us the Wild Old West for Keeps"— a fanciful picture of Frederic Remington by Harold Von Schmidt. (Courtesy John Hancock Mutual Life Insurance Company.)

attracted the attention of H. August Schwabe, president of the Newark Art League, and Dr. William A. Fisher, and they made it possible for him to go to Munich to study. After three years he returned, but he was so ill that he was unable to paint.

At this point, when he was about thirty, Schreyvogel made a fortunate friendship. He met Buffalo Bill, who, despite later criticism of his ebullient mannerisms, was always a discerning sponsor of young artists. Colonel Cody gave Schreyvogel the run of the Wild West showgrounds so that he might have cowboy, Indian and buffalo models. It was good medicine. Schreyvogel was so interested that he began to regain his health, and soon was able to make his long-anticipated trip to the West.

From then on he went west whenever he could and, in time, became a foremost in-

terpreter of Army life in pictures. He spent time in Arizona, too, living on a ranch and painting cowboys and cattle, but his chief interest became the Army, that small group of hardy souls attempting to guard advancing civilization against Indian raids.

From this interest grew his greatest triumph. He submitted a painting to the 1900 exhibition of the National Academy, when he and his wife could muster only a few dollars now and then from an occasional sale. This was "My Bunkie," showing a trooper being carried on a horse by a companion during a battle. Then he forgot about it in the press of his financial woes. The picture won the grand prize in the show, but nobody knew Schreyvogel and he had to be hunted down to be informed of his good fortune.

During the next twelve years, Schreyvogel

(Above) *"Sign of the Buffalo Scout,"* by Frederic Remington. *(Albert K. Mitchell collection.)*

(Right) *"Arizona Cowboy,"* by Frederic Remington. *(National Cowboy Hall of Fame, Oklahoma City, Oklahoma.)*

visited many Army camps and painted numerous pictures showing the life of the troopers. President Theodore Roosevelt honored him with commendation and an invitation to the White House.

In the midst of his successful career, Schreyvogel was striken with blood poisoning and died on January 27, 1912.

His fidelity to an ideal and his transcendent ability shine out of his canvases. In the home of his daughter, Mrs. Archie D. Carothers in Santa Ana, California, are three of his major paintings: "The Hot Trail," done in 1900, and "Going into Action" and "The Border Patrol," both painted in 1912; a number of other paintings, and some of his celebrated bronzes, including the rare "White Eagle" and the celebrated "The Last Drop," showing a trooper sharing water with his horse.

"'Going into Action' was the last picture he painted," Mr. and Mrs. Carothers recall. "'The Hot Trail' won wide acclaim after it was put on exhibition in 1900."

Schreyvogel's legacy of paintings was small in number but eminently high in quality.

California's appeal to Western artists, contrary to the belief of many persons, continued long after the spectacular events of the Gold Rush. One man who proved this thesis was Carl Oscar Borg, who was born in Grinstad, Sweden, in 1879, and came to California by freighter when he was only twenty. Although the Gold Rush was fifty years in the past, Borg found in the Golden State so many subjects for paintings that he was apparently unaware that he had missed what might have been considered the most exciting period.

His talents became apparent when he was quite young, and attracted the attention of Mrs. Phoebe Apperson Hearst, the mother of William Randolph Hearst, the publisher. Mrs. Hearst consequently sent Borg to Europe for five years of study. When he returned to California, he had attained the technical proficiency that permitted him to launch his re-

"The Border Patrol," by Charles Schreyvogel. (Mr. and Mrs. Archie D. Carothers, Santa Ana, California.)

(Above) *"The Last Drop," bronze by Charles Schreyvogel. (Mr. and Mrs. Archie D. Carothers, Santa Ana, California.)*

(Below) *Charles Schreyvogel, portrait. (Mr. and Mrs. Archie D. Carothers, Santa Ana, California.)*

markable career. Borg lived in Santa Barbara during a prolific period from 1914 to the end of the 1920s. The entire Southwest called to him. He painted not only horses and cowboys and cattle, but Indian ceremonials all over the Southwest, and landscapes which contain evidence of his sympathetic appreciation of the beauties of nature. In Santa Barbara, he was a close friend of Ed Borein, who specialized almost entirely in cattle, horses and cowboys.

Despite his birth abroad, Borg became imbued with a great interest in California history. Millard Sheets, the designer, painter and muralist of Claremont, California, recalls a joint project with Borg and Dr. Eugene Bolton, the director of the Bancroft Library of the University of California more than a third of a century ago. The three—Borg, Sheets and Bolton—teamed up to produce a series of California historical depictions entitled "Cross, Sword, and Gold Pan," showing the history of the state in pictures and text. This first appeared in "Touring Topics," now "Westways," publication of the Automobile Club of Southern California, and was made into a book in 1936.

When Borg died in 1947, he had bridged

Carl Oscar Borg, portrait by Troy Kinney of New York. (Desert Southwest Art Gallery, Palm Desert, California.)

"The Race," by Carl Oscar Borg. (Read Mullan Gallery of Western Art, Phoenix, Arizona.)

almost half a century of California history, and had contributed not only to chronicling events in the state he loved so much, but also had left indelible impressions of the life of the entire Southwest.

California's discovery of gold had been made only six years before the birth of Herman Wendelborg Hansen in the tiny town of Tellingstat in Schleswig-Holstein on the German-Danish frontier in 1854. The little boy growing up there could not, of course, have any idea that it was in California he would be recognized as a great artist and be hailed as the "Frederic Remington of the West Coast." His father, who was a fine draftsman, recognized the boy's talent and sent him to Hamburg when he was sixteen. When he was in his early twenties, Hansen went to London and, as a student, became acquainted with the famous paintings at the Royal Academy and at the art galleries there.

When he was twenty-three, he sailed to America and studied in New York and Chicago. A commission by the Northwestern Railways gave new direction to the course of his life; he was sent to the end of the line in the Dakotas to paint advertisements, and produced a transportation series that contained not only a locomotive but also a canal boat towed by mules, and a stagecoach. This glimpse of Western life in the raw led him onward eventually to California. At the age of twenty-eight he settled in San Francisco, where he became acquainted with William Keith, the landscape painter, and Maynard Dixon, who was achieving renown for his Southwestern portrayals.

Cowboys and cowboy life particularly attracted Hansen in his medium of water colors —he seldom used oils—and in this chosen form he managed to get, as one critic said, "The life of it, the hurrah in it, the mad gallop, the smell of dust and the ringing of cheers."

Edgar S. Paxson. (William Edgar Paxson, Whittier, California.)

Mural by Edgar S. Paxson. (Missoula County Courthouse, Missoula, Montana.)

He was so historically accurate that, as one observer said, "His Pony Express riders were men of the Old West accoutered exactly as were the riders of that day. He knew his men and his animals, inside and out."

Some of the titles indicate the kind of thing that appealed to him: "Wild Riders and the Vacant Land," "A Running Bucker," "Ambushed," "Cowboys Roping Cattle" and "The Escape."

A frontiersman who deliberately went to the most dangerous and turbulent portions of Montana in the days when the Old West was still very much alive, gathered from his experiences the material which has placed him on the list of the foremost artists of America. Edgar Samuel Paxson, born in East Hamburg, New York, in 1852, felt the call of the West so insistently that, at the age of twenty-five, he went to Montana. He became a scout and Indian fighter, and from his experiences dis-

tilled the scenes which later gave him lasting fame as an artist.

He became infused with the ambition to leave a lasting record of great historical events. As a result, he executed six great murals in the House of Representatives of the state capitol at Helena, Montana, and Lewis and Clark expedition murals in the Missoula County Courthouse.

For generations of Americans, though, his most celebrated painting is the gigantic "Custer's Last Stand," which is ten feet long and six feet wide. Paxson took eight years to complete it. He was fortunate in being able to have six of the Indian chiefs who had actually participated in the Battle of the Little Bighorn pose for him. He spent twenty years of research before he embarked upon the picture, and its two hundred figures in combat reflect the prodigious amount of work that went into it. This painting now hangs in the Whitney Gallery of Western Art in Cody,

Wyoming, which is presided over by Dr. Harold McCracken, the Western art authority.

Paxson, with his long hair in frontier style, his heavy mustache and goatee, was the embodiment of the daring Americans who settled the West in an era when violence and bloodshed were almost a daily occurrence. His talent permitted him to perpetuate not only great historical events but the characters around him.

If the Mississippi has been the writer's river of Mark Twain and Tom Sawyer and Huckleberry Finn, so the "wide Missouri" has been, in a similar sense, the painter's river. Its presence in some of the most romantic country associated with the Western story has given to the river a living character, as if it had absorbed much of the spirit of the adventurous events taking place on or near its banks. "The Big Muddy" cast its spell immediately upon a fifteen-year-old immigrant boy from Denmark. Olaf Seltzer—with the same first name as his distinguished successor in the same field, Olaf Wieghorst, also from Denmark—went to the wilds of Montana from the sophisticated city of Copenhagen in 1877 with his mother. He already had been an art prodigy, having been admitted to the Art Institute of Copenhagen at the age of twelve. Now he was in a totally new realm—one of vast distances, strange Indians, horses, cattle, ranch life, through which the wide Missouri rolled—and it was a region that began to fascinate him from the moment he entered it.

Seltzer began to work for the Great Northern Railroad in Great Falls. But, despite the long hours prevailing on all sorts of jobs in the 1890s, he still managed occasionally to steal a few hours for the thing that he liked best. He strolled and sketched along the Missouri River toward old Fort Benton, which was laden with history.

The turning point in Olaf's artistic life came when he was only twenty. He made a trip into Alberta, Canada, and was encouraged there by a kindly patron, Fred Downer. Up to this time Olaf had been making mainly pen-and-ink sketches. Now, for the first time, with Downer's encouragement, he tried oils. His first painting in this medium was of an Indian war party on the trail in Sun River Valley. Soon, too, he began experimenting in water colors, and before long was at home with either medium.

For the next twenty-five years he painted steadily and began to win wide recognition. He turned out hundreds of paintings. Finally, he was encouraged by his success to go to New York, and he moved East when he was forty-nine. Almost immediately he made a contact which resulted in his going back the following year to Montana. Dr. Philip G. Cole, of Tarrytown, New York, became so enthusiastic that he commissioned Seltzer to paint a panorama of Western life. This came to include a transportation series and characters of the Old West.

At this point, Seltzer conceived an idea which was to add to his fame but to threaten his eyesight. He began portraying the historic events of the Western region in five- by six-inch oil paintings. To paint these, he had to peer through a reading glass in order to be sure that he was applying the brush strokes properly. He turned out more than one hundred of these paintings, which became prizes of collectors throughout the world, but in the process his eyes suffered so severely that from then on he could paint for only a few hours in the mornings.

In all, Seltzer turned out more than two thousand five hundred paintings. One of the prize collections, 234 paintings from Dr. Cole's collection, was acquired by Thomas Gilcrease, and now is in the Gilcrease Institute of American History and Art in Tulsa, a testimonial to the lasting quality of Seltzer's creations.

From the rhythm of nature Maynard Dixon absorbed the living spirit that ani-

(Above) "A Mountain Trail," water color by Olaf Seltzer. (Read Mullan Gallery of Western Art, Phoenix, Arizona.)

(Above right) "War Party," by Olaf Seltzer. (Trailside Galleries, Jackson Hole, Wyoming.)

(Below right) Olaf Seltzer. (Carl C. Seltzer, Great Falls, Montana.)

mates his paintings. His horses, steers, hills, clouds and rocks all became a part of a pulsating fragment of the universe. He lived so close to nature that he was able to reflect her moods in creatures or landscapes.

As a cowpuncher, Dixon knew the heave and thrust of a bucking bronc, the smell of a piñon campfire, the sight of greasewood and cat claws, and the laconic nature of the men who lived in the West and punched cattle for a living.

He never dwelt upon his own aristocratic background, which dated to the Dixons of Randshaw Hall in Durham, England. He came from American Revolutionary stock and from a distinguished Virginian family which had moved to the West. He was born in Fresno, California, in 1875, in a region of vast sandy flats in the San Joaquin valley, seemingly lacking in artistic inspiration for a young painter. Still, from the time he was seven, Maynard Dixon began working toward a career in art. By the time he was sixteen he was proficient enough to seek the advice

(Above) *Maynard Dixon. (Edith Hamlin, San Francisco, California.)*

(Above left) *"No Trail," by Maynard Dixon. (J. W. Halliday Estate.)*

(Below left) *Self-caricature done by Maynard Dixon, showing him leaving his studio after the 1906 San Francisco earthquake and fire.*

of the great Frederic Remington, who was only fourteen years older. Remington's encouragement led Dixon to go to San Francisco to attend the School of Design.

He was restless, however, while learning formal painting. It did not satisfy him. He set out to lead the only kind of life he wanted, free and alone, painting nature as he saw it in the wilds. To make a living he became a cowpuncher, and wandered all over Arizona, New Mexico and southeastern California punching cattle, observing the wranglers, getting acquainted with the Indians and forever sketching. At the same time, too, his contemplation and reflection began to emerge in the form of verse, also attuned to the rhythm of the natural world about him. The pithy

poems of Maynard Dixon began to express what he said, too, in his paintings, both a combination of simplicity, perceptiveness and graphic portrayal.

As he was entering his early twenties, Dixon encountered a "cowboy without a horse" who helped guide a number of artists who later stirred America with the romance of the Western country. This friend was Charles Fletcher Lummis, who, by 1898 when Dixon was perfecting his art, was editing the magazine *Land of Sunshine* in Los Angeles. Dixon's career is intertwined with the life of Lummis.

Charlie Lummis walked where others rode, but he was so full of vim that he sounded like a cavalry charge. He even gave

*"Coming Out," water color by Maynard Dixon.
(Edith Hamlin, San Francisco, California.)*

a name—which it had never had before—to a whole region of desert and mountains and grassy plains and cow ranches. The term "The Southwest," now well-established, was thought up and first used by this strange and lonely word-artist who tramped all over California, Arizona, New Mexico and elsewhere in the region which he lumped together under this designation.

It was a strange quirk with him in a time when everybody rode horses that he insisted on walking everywhere he went. He was reared in Ohio and learned the newspaper business from printer's devil on up. When he was in his full manhood, he obtained a job, by correspondence, as City Editor of the distant *Los Angeles Times*, which was being run in 1885 by fiery Lieutenant Colonel (later General) Harrison Gray Otis. Charlie Lum-

mis then started walking across the continent, writing his experiences as he went and sending them on to his prospective employer. After grinding down a lot of foot leather and wearing dozens of pencils to the nub, he finally arrived in Los Angeles, and began a tempestuous career which was to bring him to the attention of tens of thousands who either loved or loathed him. Having served as City Editor of the *Times*, he became Los Angeles City Librarian, and founded the Southwest Museum.

The *Land of Sunshine* venture permitted Lummis to give full expression to his appraisal of artists and writers. He was particularly impressed with twenty-three-year-old Dixon, and said in an article that Dixon was "beginning to knock with some confidence at the door of the future." The Dixon drawings which illustrated this article were indicative of the distinctive style that he was to make his own in the years ahead.

Dixon's love of cowboy life was reflected always in his paintings. He lived in the region he loved best, rotating from Tucson, Arizona, to Mount Carmel, Utah, and in the winter spending time in the Colorado Desert of California, where he stayed at a small camp six miles east of Mecca near the Salton Sea. The camp was close to the main line of the Southern Pacific Railroad. It was here that Dixon painted one of his most famous canvases, "Destination Unknown," showing a tramp walking down railroad tracks into the distance.

When Dixon went into painting murals, he indicated his basic interests by the titles he chose for the four panels of the railway station in Tucson. These were "Cattlemen," "Apache," "Miner," and "Irrigation," and reflected his appreciation of the men and the elements making up the vast desert region he was depicting.

Maynard Dixon was married in "El Alisal," the home of Lummis in Los Angeles, and to Lummis he often sent poems for consideration. In a few words Dixon summed up his own philosophy of painting: "My object has always been to get as close to the real nature of my subjects as possible—people, animals and country."

Despite his residence in the desert, he was continually having to fight a deadly enemy—asthma. This finally conquered his body in 1946, when he died, although his rugged spirit had continued to sustain him in his painting until the very last.

He had in all his works "reached the best of my endeavor."

Great courage and a passionate conviction about the possibilities of "American" art when almost everyone else was following the popular "European" trend stamped William R. Leigh as a pioneer among Western painters. He spent many years as a young man studying art in Europe but he declined to follow the easy path of slavish copying of Continental styles. Instead, he conceived the radical idea that in the American West—which he had not yet seen—there existed virgin material for painters. When he tried to get sponsors for such an artistic innovation he was met with scorn and ridicule.

He was forty years of age before he was able to overcome his poverty and go West to satisfy his longing to paint scenes which so far had existed only in his imagination. After that, he dedicated his life to the depiction of every facet of the West, from wild horses to Navahos and from wolf hunts to burro trains.

Critics said he painted "purple horses with yellow bellies" but he defended his brilliant colors and persisted to the end of his days in presenting the West as he saw it.

Late in life, when he was still actively painting in his eighties, he began at last to receive the acclaim which the quality of his work deserved.

William Robinson Leigh was born in Virginia in 1866 during the same decade in which Russell and Remington were born, and he always retained a courtly manner associated with the storied land of his nativity. He was a big man with big mustaches and a goatee and an enormous energy to carry out his tasks which took him not only all over the American West but to Africa. His African backgrounds in the Carl Akeley Hall at the American Museum of Natural History demonstrate one facet of his talent.

After Mr. Leigh's death, his entire studio was offered by his widow to the Thomas Gilcrease Institute of American History and Art of Tulsa, Oklahoma. The matter was arranged by the then-director of the Institute, Dean Krakel, who later became the director of the National Cowboy Hall of Fame. The Leigh collection in the Leigh studio-gallery was opened to the public in Tulsa November 7, 1964, with 534 oils, 344 charcoals, and many pen-and-ink and pencil sketches on display.

An artist who has been "discovered" a quarter of a century after his death in 1938 is steadily gaining new stature. This strange lapse in public appreciation of the Western paintings of William Henry Dethlep Koerner was due in part to the fact that he was considered primarily an illustrator in the East and also because his tremendous and powerful canvases have been kept almost entirely within the family. Only in the period since 1962 have a number of important exhibitions aroused interest in his work, and caused him to be evaluated anew as one of the most accomplished of the artists depicting the West.

Koerner, born in Nunn in Schleswig-Holstein on November 19, 1878, was brought to this country as an infant. He grew up in Clinton, Iowa, apparently a community not calculated to nurture a Western painter, but Koerner from an early age was determined to have an art career of some sort.

The training he received as the result of this compulsion gained him the technical proficiency which later stood him in good stead

(Above) *W. H. D. Koerner. (Ruth Koerner Oliver, Santa Barbara, California.)*

(Left) *"Welcome for the First Trail Herd," by W. H. D. Koerner, from "North of '36" by Emerson Hough, in The Saturday Evening Post, 1923. (Ruth Koerner Oliver, Santa Barbara, California.)*

in New York as a magazine and book illustrator. When he was sixteen, he went to Chicago and got a job on *The Tribune* as a staff artist, serving in the capacity that would be filled by a staff photographer now. In those days, however, the quick-sketch artist was sent to all sorts of news events to make his drawings, which were reproduced in the newspaper prior to the general use of photoengraving. The skill he gained in his job was supplemented by attending art classes at the Chicago Art Institute. He became so proficient as an illustrator that he began to teach, and one of his students was Lillian M. Lusk, whom he subsequently married. Soon Koerner and his wife moved to New York, pausing on the way for a brief editorship of an art publication, *The Pilgrim*. In New York he became a student of George Bridgman at the Art Students' League and then studied with Howard Pyle in Wilmington, Delaware, for four years between 1907 and 1911. He and his companions, who also were students of Pyle—N. C. Wyeth, Harvey Dunn, Frank Schoonover, and Anton Otto Fisher—began to attain national attention as magazine illustrators. Koerner, like Frederic Remington, did art work for *Harper's*, and

for *Century* and *Redbook*, and then became a steady contributor to *The Saturday Evening Post*. From then on he specialized in Western subjects.

His daughter, Ruth Koerner Oliver of Santa Barbara, California, recently explained why he turned to Western subjects.

"He knew he could draw," she said. "He felt that the cow pony, the Indians, ox-drawn Conestogas, the daily existence on lonely cattle ranches as well as all of the historical power of the West had become his consuming interest and love."

As a result of this he began to make summer trips to Montana, staying first at Shaw's Camp near Cooke City and then later at the ranch of Phil Spear at Lodge Grass. He did many sketches of miners, cowboys, cabins and mountains in pencil, crayon and water colors.

"Dad used to say he soaked in all there was to hear and see of the West," Mrs. Oliver recalls. "This enabled him to understand and create the authentic paintings which are here today for all to enjoy."

Koerner's success in magazines was so great that he began to be in demand as a book illustrator for works done by Zane Grey, Ben

Ames Williams, Oliver La Farge, Mary Roberts Rinehart, and Rose Wilder Lane. He was so thorough in his research that his paintings became historical documents in themselves. He illustrated for Earl Derr Biggers' "Charlie Chan," Clarence Buddington Kelland's "Scattergood Baines" series, Joseph Hergesheimer, Thomas Beard, Don Marquis, William Faulkner, Willa Cather and Emerson Hough. Hough's *The Covered Wagon* contained twenty-one illustrations by Koerner. He also illustrated for Stewart Edward White and for Eugene Manlove Rhodes. This included art work for Rhodes's "Paso Por Aqui," considered by many to be the most distinguished of Western stories.

When W. H. D. Koerner died, the family kept his paintings intact in one collection and had no public exhibitions. When Mrs. Koerner died in 1964, the showings had just begun. Since then there have been exhibits at the Whitney Gallery of Western Art in Cody, at the Montana Historical Society in Helena, at the Kennedy Galleries in New York, the Santa Barbara Historical Society, the Charles M. Russell Gallery at Great Falls, the University of Texas and the Los Angeles County Museum of Natural History, the latter show having been held in the early part of 1968.

Mrs. Koerner once said that her husband "lived his pictures and got the very soul of his people, of his animals, of his backgrounds—treating his characters not as fiction or as puppets but as though they were really living."

In his studio at Interlaken, New Jersey, Koerner turned out the prodigious number of paintings which today comprise the collection in the home of his daughter, Mrs. Oliver. It was at his home on August 11, 1938, that he died, leaving a studio filled with oils, crayons, charcoal and water colors, his sketchbooks and notebooks, and mementos he had gathered all over the West.

Now that his work has been "discovered" anew, he has come into his own as a major factor in Western art.

A thirty-year interruption was unable to stifle the basic urge in Grey Bartlett to paint Western scenes. Family responsibilities and the need to make money did halt his artistic efforts for an entire generation. Then, after he had made enough money to permit him to do what he wanted, he resumed the sketching and painting which he had begun almost a third of a century before.

Bartlett was born July 3, 1885, in Rochester, Minnesota, but it was in another environment that he gained the aspiration to become an artist. The family moved to Colorado when he was small, and it was there that the scenery and the people gave him the motivation which lasted all his life. He became a cowboy when he was sixteen, and then, after studying at the Greely Art School and the Chicago Art Institute, he was so poor that he was compelled to go into business. It was not until 1937, when he was in his fifties, that he was able to resume painting. At that time he set up a studio in Los Angeles and another in the wild country of Moab, Utah.

"The test of a painting is truth and beauty," he said, in regard to his work. "I paint the things I like to paint. I get my ideas by traveling through the parts of the West I most enjoy to portray and living among the people whose lives I find enjoyment in depicting."

Since his death of a heart attack in 1951, his dramatic paintings have been sought by collectors all over the United States.

Rosa Bonheur a "cowboy artist"?
She was.
Even more remarkable, she put her brand on the history of the western United States through her influence on one of the most

"Indian Scouts," by Gray Bart-lett. (Read Mullan Gallery of Western Art, Phoenix, Arizona.)

flamboyant of American painters. Buffalo Bill was the cause of it all. Colonel Cody took his Wild West Show to Europe, and started literally millions of staid Frenchmen, Englishmen, Germans, Dutchmen and others talking about scalping parties, tomahawks, buffalo, quick draws and Boot Hills.

Rosa Bonheur, who is remembered by most people only for her "Horse Fair" and other, similar paintings, fell under the artistic spell of Buffalo Bill. She painted his portrait full length. To Paris at this moment for youthful impression came Robert Lindneux of New York to study at the École des Beaux-Arts. He was continuing his painting studies after having spent two and one-half years at the National Academy at Düsseldorf.

Just arrived on the Champs Élysées at the age of twenty-one, young Lindneux saw Buffalo Bill in the flesh. Then he became acquainted with Rosa Bonheur, and was so stirred by her painting of Cody that he decided to go see what the West offered to a painter.

In the United States, though, his Western adventure was delayed because of the lack of money. He went to Boston to try portrait painting in an effort to save enough for his journey. He had become an orphan before he was five, and his early education had been at the expense of an aunt who was interested in his artistic talent, but now that he was grown he felt he must be on his own. Finally, a year after his return from Paris, he saved enough for a ticket to Denver. He went there, and immediately became so delighted with Western life that he stayed three years. The farther West beckoned to him then, and he worked his way over to Billings, Montana, and from there, after making the acquaintance of Charlie Russell, joined Russell in his Great Falls studio.

From Great Falls, he traveled over the entire cattle region, observing and painting every sort of Western scene including the Indians. Within ten years he had acquired so many relics and so much horse gear that it was necessary for him to have a place of his own to store it. He set up a permanent studio in Denver in 1909 but continued his travels.

He began to be known as "the historian of the West," because of the multiplicity of subjects he painted, and he even ascribed the title to himself. He was considered by some to be an eccentric, yet he continued his zestful portrayal of the West, seemingly unmindful of the jibes of his critics.

The Bonheur painting of Buffalo Bill eventually came to rest in the Whitney Museum of Western Art in Cody, Wyoming, a reminder of the impetus given to Lindneux's career. Lindneux painted a monumental portrait of Buffalo Bill atop Lookout Mountain, where Colonel Cody is buried, as the culmination of his interest derived from the earlier depiction by Rosa Bonheur.

Buffalo Bill scored another artistic bull's-eye with R. Farrington Ellwell, just as he had with Robert Lindneux. In the case of Ellwell, the connection was much closer than it had been with Lindneux. Both budding painters had regarded the spectacular Colonel Cody, with his daredevil riders and Indians surrounding him, with a degree of hero worship. For Ellwell, the association with Buffalo Bill became an enduring reality and entered into the daily life of the artist as it had never done with Lindneux. Ellwell began sketching while still a child under the encouragement of his father, who painted marines as a hobby, and his mother, who was a musician and also sketched when she had time, but he failed to find any definite purpose until one day when he was in his middle teens.

At this particular moment, the Wild West Show of Buffalo Bill arrived in Boston for an indefinite engagement. Bob Ellwell went to the show, and the real cowboys and sure-enough Indians so captivated him that he returned for every performance and made

"Buffalo Bill on Horseback," by Robert Lindneux—shown atop Lookout Mountain, Colorado, where Colonel W. F. Cody is buried. (William Moyers, Albuquerque, New Mexico.)

sketches of the participants. As he sat one day on a bale of hay, Buffalo Bill came by and took a look at the sketch. He was so impressed that he started a conversation with Ellwell and changed the entire course of the boy's life. Colonel Cody invited Ellwell to spend the following summer at his ranch in Wyoming, promising that he could have all the cowboys, horses, and Indians he wanted in a natural environment for his sketches. This first visit resulted in a friendship which culminated in Ellwell's becoming ranch manager for many years for Colonel Cody.

He learned to work in pastels and also turned to sculpture, in which he attained great proficiency almost immediately.

In everything he did the qualities of vitality, excitement and naturalness leaped out. When Ellwell moved to Phoenix, in the midst of the land that had produced the characters and incidents portrayed in his paintings, he continued to paint with extra-

Robert Lindneux (right) in front of Mint Saloon, Great Falls, Montana, with the owner, Sid Willis. (William Moyers, Albuquerque, New Mexico.)

ordinary discernment and proficiency after he had reached his eighty-fifth birthday. Ellwell's bucking horses, roundups, cattle drives, and stagecoaches and Indian portrayals all reflect youth and vigor.

A remarkably dull old geography book was the first "sketch pad" of Ed Borein. Inside the front cover of *The Independent Course Comprehensive Geography* by James Monteith, copyright 1882, are drawings of the three subjects which later made Borein one of the most popular of American Western artists—horses, a cowboy, and a steer. The steer was depicted in the form of a longhorn skull, and two rifles were drawn in behind the skull for decoration. At the top of the page the boy who was supposed to be study-ing his geography had written his name, "Ed Borein," in flowing letters more than an inch high.

The geography is owned by Harold G. Davidson of Santa Barbara, California, col-lector of Borein material, who saved it from the trash heap when he saw it being thrown away by the former owner. It contains in the cowboy-horses-steer-guns drawing what is believed to be the oldest Borein "art work" in existence.

Borein must have been, to judge from the copyright date, somewhere around ten years old when he decorated the geography book because he was born in San Leandro, in Alameda County, California, on October 21, 1873. The drawing is a typical sample of his boredom with school. He wanted to be out punching cows, hunting, fishing and drawing pictures of cowboys instead of poring over dull books. Before he was able to satisfy this craving for wandering he did the next best thing, and sketched his favorite subjects under the light of an old kerosene lamp at home. Then, before long, he did start out on his own to study art and see the West.

While he was still in his teens he be-came a vaquero. He apparently preferred this term for himself to "cowboy" because, in a recommendation which he received in 1896, when he was twenty-two, from the Jesus Maria Rancho at Santa Maria, he was specifically listed as "vaquero" and "a young man of honest . . . habits."

In his wanderings during this period, Ed Borein decorated many a bunkhouse wall and door with his drawings, and gave many on scraps of paper to other cowboys. His first little water colors, like the drawings, were lost or thrown away although within twenty-five years after his death, a Borein water color was selling for somewhere around four thousand to six thousand dollars. In his early cowboy days he simply drew for the fun of it and attached no value to his efforts.

Still, by the time he was twenty-two, he was gaining attention for his excellent pencil and pen-and-ink drawings. One of the first to recognize his exceptional talent was the dis-cerning Charles Fletcher Lummis, first city editor of *The Los Angeles Times* in the 1880s and by 1896 the editor of *Land of Sunshine*, a literary magazine in Los Angeles. In the August 1896 issue, Lummis printed an article on "The Old California Vaquero," including descriptions of *reata* weaving by Flora Haines Loughead, and the illustrator was none other

"Oolagah," by Edward Borein. (Dr. Irving Wills Estate.)

than "Ed Borein, a vaquero on the Jesus Maria Rancho." Out of this association grew a warm and lasting friendship between Lummis and Borein. In fact, Borein, like Maynard Dixon, was married in Lummis' home, "El Alisal," by the Arroyo Seco between Los Angeles and Pasadena.

After he began to attain some success, Borein went to New York and there cemented his lifelong friendships with Jimmy Swinnerton, the painter; Charlie Russell; Leo Carrillo, the actor and film star; Irvin S. Cobb, writer and humorist; Fred Stone, the actor, who was one of the first to buy a major Borein art work; Will Rogers; and Clyde (Vic) Forsythe, cartoonist and painter.

In New York, trapped in the steel and concrete canyons and surrounded by hordes of unfamiliar faces, Borein was homesick for cattle ranches, the open country and his cowpuncher companions. To offset his homesickness, he cooked chili peppers and frijoles in his apartment and, on occasion, shocked his potential customers. Once a friend brought two lady socialites to his studio for "tea," a

ritual totally foreign to Borein's whole way of life. When one of the ladies took the lid off the sugar bowl, a full-grown cockroach jumped out, and she started to scream and flail at it with her purse.

"Hey," cried Borein with deadpan seriousness, "don't kill her, that's Margaret, our pet!" And he carefully picked up the insect, put it back in the sugar bowl and replaced the lid.

In a few years, despite increasing sales, Borein could stand New York no longer. By the 1920s, he and his wife Lucille were permanently established in Santa Barbara, and Ed was operating a studio and shop in El Paseo de la Guerra, a beautiful, rambling old Spanish home converted into a restaurant and shops. Here he turned out drawings, etchings, water colors and an occasional painting. Often, during slack times, he would sit and "doodle," drawing horses, longhorns and cowboys by the thousands. His studio became the gathering place for his cronies, including Russell, Rogers, Swinnerton, Cobb, Forsythe, Stone and some new ones, including Irving (Nat) Wills, M.D., who became the leading collector of Borein material and an authority on Borein's life story.

Borein's love of company, such as his old buddies, led to an accomplishment far re-

Bucking horses, sketches by Edward Borein. (Mr. and Mrs. Keith Atherton, San Diego, California.)

moved from the artistic field. In 1930 he conceived the idea of reviving an old Spanish custom in the ranching country back of Santa Barbara, with *rancheros visitadores* going from one rancho to another for sport, visiting and fiesta. Out of this was born the Rancheros Visitadores, which continues as an organization to this day, and each May goes on its celebrated horseback ride in traditional fashion.

For a long time Borein leaned toward etchings, at which his skill was superlative, having been aided in New York by members of the Art Students League when he was a young man. Later in life he turned more and more to water colors.

He became the subject of a portrait when he was well along in years. It was painted by the eminent Spencer Bagdatopolis and was duly hung in the Borein home atop a hill in Santa Barbara overlooking the Pacific. Soon after it was installed, Ed went out of the house for a while and while he was gone, Lucille put lovely fresh flowers in front of the painting. When Ed came back, he exclaimed:

"Hell, that ain't right for me!" He removed the flowers and in their place put sage, dry teasel and weeds. This bouquet remained in front of his portrait after his death on May 19, 1945, and until Mrs. Borein's passing in 1967.

Edward Borein. (Harold G. Davidson, Santa Barbara, California.)

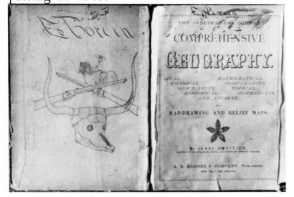

The first Borein—this drawing in his geography book, done in the 1880s when he was about 10, is regarded as the earliest-known sketch by Edward Borein. (Harold G. Davidson, Santa Barbara, California.)

At the time Ed Borein died he was working on an oil, a Western scene.

All his etchings, water colors and doodles have become tremendously—and deservedly—highly priced. They were done by a true vaquero who always remained a "man of honest . . . habits."

A former Texas ranger was so influential in the artistic life of a boy born near Council Bluffs, Iowa, that the whole panorama of the West appeared to be transmitted to the mind and heart of the student. Frank Tenney Johnson, who became internationally famous for his cowboys and his moonlight scenes on the

"Coming Up the Trail," by Frank Tenney Johnson. (Read Mullan Gallery of Western Art, Phoenix, Arizona.)

Lorenz and from other teachers with whom he came in contact, Johnson went to New York and continued his art studies. Then he felt the call of the West again, and went to a ranch in Colorado where he was able to see in reality the cowboys and cattle he liked to paint.

Before long, his work was attracting such favorable public response that he became a magazine illustrator and began doing book jackets for Zane Grey and other Western writers. Along the artistic trail he encountered Clyde (Vic) Forsythe, the cartoonist and oil painter who gave up his successful New York career to return with his wife to his native California to paint. Forsythe and Johnson became good friends because of their mutual interest in depicting the historic West, and when Johnson too moved to California with his wife, the painters shared a studio in Alhambra for many years. To the studio came Norman Rockwell, Forsythe's protégé at *The Saturday Evening Post*; Dean Cornwell, the illustrator; Charlie Russell; Ed Borein; Tex Wheeler, the horse sculptor; and actors and outdoorsmen.

The art business seemed so promising that Forsythe and Johnson became joint founders of the Biltmore Art Gallery in the new Biltmore Hotel in Los Angeles.

When Borein and others organized the Rancheros Visitadores, Johnson and Forsythe became enthusiastic participants.

Johnson by now was developing his "Johnson moonlight" technique so that his paintings showing cowboys under the stars became nationally famous. He was at the height of his career when he suddenly died in 1939. Since his death, his paintings have grown steadily in popularity and when one becomes available, it now commands a top price.

Bill Gollings, who was a working cowboy all his life, received the Western version of

open range, owed much of his perception to the teaching of the ex-ranger, Richard Lorenz, who, after his service in Texas, opened an art studio in Milwaukee.

Johnson was born on June 28, 1874, in the Iowa hamlet of Big Grove. He roamed a countryside along the banks of the Missouri River where Lewis and Clark had traveled in 1804 and had given the name "Council Bluffs" to the area because of their parleys with the Indians. Johnson, steeped in this lore, became an apt disciple when he came under the tutelage of Lorenz, whose own background during the lawless days of the Texas frontier had given him a deep understanding of the character and traits of cowpunchers, criminals, law men and sod busters.

After he had absorbed all he could from

an Olympic torch from Frederic Remington. When Bill, who was born in Idaho in 1878, was growing up as a boy on a ranch, Remington was drawing for *Harper's Magazine*. Bill's brother, Oliver, had stirred his first interest in art when Bill was only nine years old. Oliver had only a slate on which to practice, but on it he drew horses and then carefully put saddles and bridles on them. Bill Gollings admired and watched and learned.

He went only to the eighth grade in school, but while he was there he did learn something about art. He was twelve when the family moved to Chicago. After he had left school and had become a hero worshiper of Remington, he began the roaming which familiarized him with every aspect of ranch life. All the romantic names attracted him—Deadwood, Lead City, Belle Fourche, and many a little cattle town. He saw cowboys riding into saloons, heard the bark of six-shooters, saw the rambunctious Texas steers unloaded for their imminent fate and absorbed every detail of ranch life.

Then Montgomery Ward came into his life. When he was twenty-five he bought a set of painting materials from the mail-order house, and began trying his hand at some of the scenes he had witnessed. His brother, De Witt, was so impressed with the results that he took some of the first paintings to Sheridan, Wyoming. There he found a furniture-store owner, W. E. Freeman, who was willing to exhibit them. Meanwhile, Bill had taken his Montgomery Ward paints and had gone back to working as a ranch hand.

One day in the mail, a fifty-dollar check caught up with him; it was from Mr. Freeman. A painting had been sold, and Mr. Freeman said that so much interest had been aroused that he would like to have more. This so excited Bill that he quit his job, went to his brother's ranch and alternated between breaking horses and working at the easel.

Frank Tenney Johnson. (Mr. and Mrs. William Riffle, Santa Ana, California.)

From then on he was torn by his two interests. He loved the life of a cowboy, and yet the attraction of making money from paintings was a strong incentive, too. For several years he hesitated. Then, when he was thirty-one, he decided on art. Until his death (when he was only in his middle fifties), he devoted most of his time to painting the scenes in which he himself had played a part. At intervals he helped his brother on the ranch, but mostly he traveled through the range lands, and depicted them with a fidelity nurtured by his lifelong idolizing of Remington.

A premature baby who was rubbed with whisky and kept warm in the oven of the kitchen stove grew up to be one of the respected illustrators and painters of the American West. Clarence Ellsworth's extraordinary survival took place in the little town of Holdrege, Nebraska. From the time when he was old enough to hold a pair of scissors, he started cutting out horses and cattle and people from butcher's wrapping paper. At the same time, he drew so well that the guests at the Ellsworth home were amazed.

Ellsworth's lifelong interest in Indians and his friendship with them stemmed from traveling medicine shows that visited the little towns in the Midwest where the family successively lived. When he became a newspaperman in Denver, his art work (aside from that for the *Rocky Mountain News* and later the *Denver Post*), centered on Indians, Western scenes and cowboys. He sketched the Sioux and members of other tribes. At one time, he set up a stand in the Garden of the Gods at Colorado Springs and made portraits of the tourists for twenty-five cents apiece. This training led him into doing covers for *Outdoor Life* and illustrations for other Eastern magazines.

Eventually, he moved to California and went to work for Paramount Studios. In 1924, he met Iron Eyes Cody, the expert on bows and arrows and all kinds of Indian lore, who was a technical adviser for the films, and they became lifelong friends.

Iron Eyes gave Ellsworth a homesite next to his own house and posed for many of Ellsworth's paintings. Ellsworth helped to interest Iron Eyes' children in the great heritage of their people through his own personal knowledge of them. All this time Ellsworth's paintings were improving in technique. He illustrated many notable books, and did drawings for "The Brand Book" of the Los Angeles Corral of the Westerners, a group devoted to history.

As Clarence Ellsworth lay dying, he said to his friend Iron Eyes, as if his firm belief in immortality were being summed up, "Well, good night. I'll see you tomorrow."

Clarence Ellsworth with Iron Eyes Cody in 1959. (Iron Eyes Cody, Los Angeles, California.)

When it came to painting gunslingers, Lea Franklin McCarty was the kind of fellow who wanted to know where every bullet went. His paintings depicting not only the great gun fighters but also many other aspects of Western life were researched so carefully that he became a sort of literary two-gun man himself, able to write as well as paint.

First, after he had gone to Chouinard Art School in Los Angeles, he thought he wanted to be primarily a sculptor, and he did become a good one. He created the Wyatt Earp plaque in Tombstone, scene of the O.K. Corral fight, and the Jack London statue in Jack London Square in Oakland, and a bust of Robert Louis Stevenson and many others. However, he became so interested in Western history that he was not content to deal merely in sculpture. He ventured into painting to express some of his ideas.

His paintings of "The Gunslingers" in his famous series included everybody from Wyatt Earp to Wild Bill Hickok and Clay Allison to John Wesley Hardin and Doc Holliday. When he completed his research and per-

"Indian Scouts," by Clarence Ellsworth. (Iron Eyes Cody, Los Angeles, California.)

suaded friends to pose for him in the costumes of killers in his Santa Rosa, California, studio, he was such an expert on every aspect of gun toting that he might have been ready to take on almost anybody himself.

After a while, when it came to this kind of subject, he was the fastest draw in the art business.

In the long run, Jack Van Ryder failed to get very far from home. He made a lot of detours and met a lot of people, but he wound up right back in Arizona almost in the spot where he was born. His paintings nearly always tell a story of the region he knew best.

"The country I was raised in made good storytellers," he used to say. "I began my career mainly living in the cow country and I still believe in all the principles this life has taught me."

Most of the time when he was out of his native Arizona, where he was born in Continental between Tucson and Nogales, he was in some other part of the West where livestock was plentiful. When he was just a kid he shipped up to Montana with a bunch of Mexican steers and stayed around there quite a while, traveling all over the place, including the site of General Custer's defeat on the

Little Bighorn. He was a wrangler and horse breaker, and in those early days was totally illiterate. Eventually, he learned to read and write, and this seemed to help him in his art work, too. He even did a little work for the movies as an extra rider, but he got tired of that and went into the rodeo game. He won some bareback riding titles and competed in Cheyenne and Calgary and the Seattle Stampede and many other places.

Always he was painting between events, because the West had a story to tell him and he was retelling it to everybody else—and everybody else was the subject of his pictures.

Near the end of his career he was able to say, "My friends are of all classes, they are rich and poor."

Any collector who sets out to find an oil painting by Ross Santee is almost certainly doomed to disappointment. Santee paintings are so scarce that it is virtually impossible to find one. All his zest and enthusiasm went into drawings, many of them for books of his own writing, and they are so full of action and life and meaning that, although they are in black and white, they do not seem to need color to carry their full message.

The word "disappointment" might be

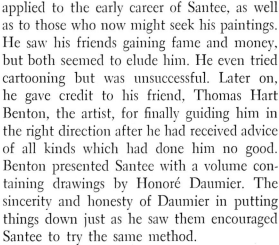

"Happy Days," by Jack Van Ryder

"The Bull Rider," by William R. Leigh. (Desert Southwest Art Gallery, Palm Desert, California.)

applied to the early career of Santee, as well as to those who now might seek his paintings. He saw his friends gaining fame and money, but both seemed to elude him. He even tried cartooning but was unsuccessful. Later on, he gave credit to his friend, Thomas Hart Benton, the artist, for finally guiding him in the right direction after he had received advice of all kinds which had done him no good. Benton presented Santee with a volume containing drawings by Honoré Daumier. The sincerity and honesty of Daumier in putting things down just as he saw them encouraged Santee to try the same method.

Santee had been born in Thornburg, Iowa, on August 16, 1889, had been reared in Iowa and had lived for a time in Illinois where he studied at the Chicago Art Institute. Then he gained practical art experience in New York, trying to get into the "big time," but failing this, went west and became a horse wrangler in Arizona when he was about thirty years old.

In Arizona he apparently found what he had been seeking all along without realizing it. The whole tenor of cowboy life there reinvigorated his artistic perception. He began to draw men, horses, cattle and landscapes, and to write about them, too. This proved to be the right approach. His books with their honest drawings—based upon his admiration for Daumier—attracted readers all over the country. The titles of his books, starting back in 1926 with *Men and Horses*, indicated the kind of thing which enthralled him: *Cowboy, The Sleepy Black, Rusty, a Cowboy of the Old West, Apache Land, Hard Rock and Silver Sage, Lost Pony Tracks* and *The Bubbling Spring*.

Sometimes Santee used water colors, but usually he preferred to draw black and white depictions of simple everyday scenes: a cowboy herding steers, a wrangler cinching up, a bucking horse, a pack animal acting up, a cook wagon surrounded by hungry cowboys. His early failures were forgotten in the satisfaction he felt in doing what he wanted to do in the way he wanted to do it.

Some artists need words to supplement and explain their paintings, but this was never the case with Ray Strang. Each of his pictures tells its own story so forcibly that a mere glance is sufficient to gain its full import. Pic-

"The West of Ross Santee," by Ross Santee. (Read Mullan Gallery of Western Art, Phoenix, Arizona.)

tures such as "Slowpoke," depicting a colt amid wildflowers declining to follow a cowboy on his horse; "Spring," an exuberant portrayal of horses in vast fields of wildflowers; "The Native's Return," showing a burro prospector in the ruins of a ghost town; "Wood Gatherers," "Water" and "Waiting for Mail" all convey their meaning immediately to the viewer.

Strang, however, did not come easily by his Western flair. He was born in Sandoval, Illinois, in 1893, and later studied at the Chicago Art Institute. His work there was interrupted by World War I, during which he was wounded. He studied at the Art Students League and the Society of Illustrators' School in New York, and then plunged into a career as an illustrator, gaining tremendous success in national magazines.

During this time he apparently thought he had gained his chosen profession, but when he went on a visit to Tucson he was so overwhelmed with the desert and the life in it he realized that his career was sterile. He de-

cided he must move to Arizona. When he did so, he began to paint the things he saw around him, and compressed each experience into a capsule of meaning. He gained, too, a placidity for himself on his sixty-acre ranch with the vast landscape forever beckoning him to come forth to find new material for his paintings.

A friend to whom Charlie Russell once said, "You're just as good an artist as I am— all you need is the name," failed to continue in the artistic vein which had won him this compliment and, when he turned to abstractionism, the world lost a possibly great Western painter. C. S. Price, a native Iowan who became a bronc buster in Wyoming, for a while excelled in cowboy-type art. Then he became enamored of twentieth century expressionism and abandoned such subjects as his celebrated "The Running Bucking Horse," painted in 1910, in favor of a mystical type of art. Price, who was born in 1874 and died in 1950, never reverted to the style which won him the Russell accolade.

A LEGACY FROM THE MIDDLE AGES

A method of artistic expression dating back to the Middle Ages has been carried on successfully in depicting horses and cowboys in the late twentieth century. Kirk Martin of Yucca Valley, California, makes wood blocks as a means of portraying the people and animals that have engrossed him since childhood.

Born in Colorado in 1906, Martin often has had to contend with ill health and adversity in striving toward his goals. He paints in oil and also uses wood blocks, the latter a facet of the prtining craft into which he was born.

Martin, a brother of Fletcher Martin, the New York illustrator, comes by his love of printing naturally. He is the son of a country printer who lived in Colorado and taught Kirk to be a printer from the time he was ten. Any printer must have patience and exactitude, and both these qualities are required in an extraordinary degree in the making of wood blocks. The technique dates back before the Renaissance. Just three things are required—a wood block; a small triangular cutting tool, the graver; and an artist.

The wood is sometimes hard to come by these days. It is laminated rock maple with the end grain up, and the surface polished to a mirror smoothness. It costs about $250 a square foot. First, the artist draws his design on tracing paper. This is then turned over and traced onto the wood surface. Then the real work begins. The cutting tool is used to create the design, with just the right depth. Martin uses a light from the side so that the shadow will help him in deciding just when sufficient cutting has been done. When the block is completed it is examined through a magnifying glass for imperfections, and if it is in proper condition, the engravings are made with ordinary printer's ink.

Martin, who was inspired to do wood-block carving by Paul Landacre of Los Angeles, creates all sorts of Western subjects, but he particularly favors horses, which he has drawn since childhood.

8

WILL JAMES: THE LONE COWBOY

Mexican vaquero, 1530–1540

Out from the drifting smoke of many a campfire down the years, the misty figure of a special man and the lasting image of a special horse emerge as part of the immortal legend of cowboys in Western art.

The man was "Will James," and the horse was "Smoky."

Together they have formed the ideal horseman and his mount for two generations of Americans who reveled in their exploits as depicted in twin mediums—the pithy vernacular of the cowhand and the visual impressions of the artist. "Will James" wrote and drew with such a balance of talent that he is unique on his home range, with the possible exception of his great predecessor Charlie Russell, who likewise could express in words some of the thoughts which animated him when he was drawing and painting. Few other artists ever have exerted so profound an in-

fluence on a single topic in prose and pictures as did "Will James."

He grappled his enthusiastic followers to him with thongs of rawhide. His written vernacular was so individualistic and, in many senses, so exaggerated that it could have been atrocious. Yet it was not. It was saved by the living, breathing essence of truth and sincerity that stemmed from his absolute and total command of the subject. "James's" language from almost anybody else would have been ridiculous. Yet, with his deep understanding of cowboys and horses and the perfection of his accompanying art work, it became a fitting and appropriate vehicle to convey his meaning, even though the reader-viewer might be totally unfamiliar with cowboy lingo. His steeping in the cowboy life went back so far that he recalled roping chickens as soon as he could walk.

WILL JAMES: THE LONE COWBOY

"James" took cow-camp jargon, and made it intelligible to everybody in America who had learned his A B C's. His language came out just the way he intended it. He refused to change his stuff once it was put down. It was a matter of principle.

"You wouldn't go to raise a steer, and then when he was full-grown, cut his head off to improve his looks," he once told an inquisitive interviewer. "Well, I write like I raise beef."

He was prideful about being able to illustrate his own books and articles, and switched easily from one mode of expression to the other.

"I jest write till I'm tired an' then spell off 'nd draw till I get tired of that," he explained succinctly.

He scorned rough drafts of his drawings and did them, like his writing, once and for all.

When he went, briefly, to art school, they put a beautiful nude girl model before him—and he drew a steer.

Tall, lean and rangy, he drawled with a slight French accent, but his writings and drawings were as American as Huck Finn and as flavorful as wild blackberries.

The fact that now it is necessary to put quotation marks around the name "Will James" is in itself an indication of the legendary status he has attained. The quotation marks signifying that "Will James" in reality was not "Will James" but somebody else, put him in a class with his own creation, "Smoky," who likewise was fictional but still holds a real and enduring place in our annals. "Will James" as portrayed by himself in his supposed autobiography *Lone Cowboy* never existed, because in actuality he was a French-Canadian named Ernest Dufault. Yet this can in no way detract from his ability as a writer and artist, despite his attempt to remain hidden behind his assumed name. The complete reason why "James" did not want his identity known must always remain a mystery,

although there are convincing indications why Ernest Dufault chose to become "Will James." In *Lone Cowboy*, published by Scribner's in 1930, "Will James" tells of two incidents involving encounters with the law. One concerned an altercation in a saloon in which "James" was held for a time as a possible murder suspect, but later was released after it turned out that the assailant was someone else and that the supposed victim did not die. The other related to cattle rustling and the experiences of "Will James" in the penitentiary making atonement for his transgression.

The first incident, which seems from the evidence to have taken place in Canada when "Will James" was still in his teens, may have been the reason for his leaving Canada for Montana and assuming, successively, the names "C. W. Jackson," "W. R. James" and "Will James." This supposition is advanced in the biography *Will James, the Gilt-Edged Cowboy*, by Anthony Amaral, a Nevada librarian, published in 1967 by Westernlore Press. In this book there is the first major public disclosure of the actual identity of "Will James" as Ernest Dufault, a French-Canadian. Amaral, however, while mentioning in passing that a few persons knew who "James" actually was fails, perhaps, to emphasize sufficiently the extent of this knowledge. It was rather widespread. I, for instance, had become aware of the facts long before I knew that Amaral's book was to be published.

Among the persons who knew that "Will James" was Ernest Dufault was L. H. Brague, of the staff of Scribner's, publishers of "Will James's" books, with whom I corresponded on the subject; Harold von Schmidt, the eminent illustrator and painter of Westport, Connecticut, who helped start "Will James" on his career in San Francisco; Joe De Yong of Los Angeles, the artist friend and protégé of Charlie Russell, who first met "James" in Montana half a century or more ago; and Bill Bender, the Western painter of Oro Grande,

California, near Victorville, where "James" spent some portion of his last tempestuous and tormented years on a ranch.

All these were acquainted with the fact of "Will James's" identity and some other aspects of his life which were not generally known, and these they imparted to me. So that I might be able to write as accurately as possible about "James" in discussing his career as author and artist, I obtained court records from Billings, Montana, where his will was probated, and thus was in possession of the name and address of his brother who inherited the estate, and also that of his mother.

Anthony Amaral, in researching his book, also, of course, studied the Billings court records and likewise baptismal and other documents in Canada. From the latter he discovered that "Will James" was born Joseph-Ernest-Nepthali Dufault on June 6, 1892, at Saint Nazaire de Acton, Quebec. His parents were Jean and Joséphine Dufault, both of whom had been born in Quebec Province. In *Lone Cowboy*, an entirely fictitious set of circumstances had been invented by "Will James" in regard to his birth. He recounted that he was born in the Judith Basin country of Montana while his parents were on a wagon-train trip, and that his mother died immediately afterwards as did his father while he was still only a small child.

"Will James" then goes on in the enthralling account of his supposed life to tell of his wanderings with a French-Canadian trapper, Jean Beaupré, to whom he had been entrusted by his father. Everyone who has read *Lone Cowboy* or who has seen the motion picture made from it will recall the graphic description of "James's" wanderings with "Bopy," as he calls his foster father, and his poignant grief when "Bopy" disappears after presumably being drowned in a river swollen by the spring thaw. Some of the things he did not spell out in detail in *Lone Cowboy* concern his marriage to Alice Conradt in 1920, his acquiring of the 12,000-acre

"Will James" at about 16 years of age. (Joe De Yong, Los Angeles, California.)

Rocking R Ranch near Billings, and his friendship with film celebrities.

The most unpleasant part of his existence, according to Anthony Amaral, was his attempt to keep his mother and his public from knowing that "Will James" was in fact Ernest Dufault. The above author says that the "private Hell" of "Will James" was this constant fear of exposure when, accepted as a literary and artistic lion, he was at the same time the witty and convivial cowboy in keeping with the hero of his book. Amaral says that "James's" mother was unable either to read or to write, and that "James" confided only in his brother Auguste Dufault and in-

"Will James" (right), William S. Hart (center), Charlie Russell (left), circa 1925. (Joe De Yong, Los Angeles, California.)

structed him never to let their mother know that he was in fact the famous American author "Will James." To attain this end, "James" is said by Amaral to have burned his papers, letters and drawings at the family home in Canada.

Two persons besides those I have already mentioned who knew all about "James's" identity were Earl and Eleanor Snook, who operated an art shop in Billings. Earl Snook became "James's" guardian and attempted to keep him under control during his sprees; on occasion he found it necessary to commit him to a hospital for recovery from these excesses. Mr. and Mrs. Snook treasured all of the work of "James" and collected his sketches and other art work because they firmly believed in its lasting value. Mrs. Snook, now a widow, is credited with having probably the largest collection of "James's" work in the country. Another notable collection, the most important items of which are being preserved permanently as a unit, is that belonging to the Desert Southwest Art Gallery in Palm Desert, California.

Some of the happiest times of "James's" erratic career came on his Rocking R Ranch, where he acquired longhorn cattle and entertained visitors by explaining the difference between modern beef cattle and the old rangy longhorns.

During the last few years of his life he particularly enjoyed interludes at the Cal Godshall Ranch on a hill near Victorville, looking out over an area where cattle grazed and fine horses were raised along the Mojave River. Cal Godshall and his wife, Joie, made "James" welcome and gave him the use of a cottage near the main ranch house. Here he participated in many of the gatherings of film celebrities who frequently came to the ranch. The guests included Wallace Beery, Bing Crosby, Jerry Colonna, Jimmy Durante, Phil Harris, Chill Wills and many others who enjoyed the impromptu rodeos, the barbecues and the talkfests with the Godshalls. To everybody at these gatherings "James" was "Bill," the name which also was applied to him at the cow camps where he had worked before he attained fame from his writing and drawing. For the Godshalls, to whom he was greatly attached, "James" inscribed books, and photographs and drawings that now adorn the ranch walls.

Mrs. Godshall told me and Bill Bender, who had suggested I visit her, many stories of "James" and his problems at the time he frequented the ranch. It was in the little cottage that "James" did some of his final writing when he was sober enough to concentrate on it. Down in Victorville, still at that time a "cow town," he was a great favorite at the old Green Spot Bar on Seventh Street, which was the main drag. Here, in the evenings, "James" would draw pictures on the big bar mirror after he had imbibed sufficiently. The bar was operated by the late John Gray, and the bartender was the late Lew Parrish, a former city editor in New York. The story is told in Victorville that after "James's" death a big black Cadillac with Nevada license plates drew up to the curb in front of the Green Spot one day and a sportily dressed stranger got out and went in to talk to Parrish.

"Is this the place where 'Will James' used to do some of his drinking?" asked the stranger.

"It sure is," answered Parrish.

"I heard that he used to draw pictures on the mirrors. We are starting a new casino in Las Vegas and we are prepared to pay ten thousand dollars for any mirror with a 'Will James' drawing on it."

Parrish smote his brow.

Every time "James" had drawn a picture, it had been swabbed off the next morning at the start of business so there would be room for another one that night. When the ten-thousand-dollar offer was made there wasn't a single "James" bar-mirror picture left in Victorville.

Toward the end, "James" went also to Palm Springs, where he tried to work on his writing and drawing, but he was continually overcome by drinking. In 1942 he was living at 6460 Ivarene Avenue, Los Angeles. Late in August of that year he collapsed and was taken to the Hollywood Presbyterian Hospital, where he remained twelve days suffering from cirrhosis of the liver and chronic nephritis. He died at 5:15 A.M. on September 3, according to his death certificate signed by Charles Warner. On the death certificate, which I have examined, his full name was given as William Roderick James, and it was stated that his usual occupation was cowboy, author and artist, and that his father's name was William James from Texas and his mother was Bonnie Unknown from California.

In subsequent court proceedings in Billings, where M. J. Lamb was executor of the "Will James" estate, it was determined in a decree settling the estate on June 30, 1944, that Auguste Dufault of 45 St. Andrews Street, Ottawa, Ontario, Canada, "is entitled to take and receive all the residue of said estate as residuary legatee."

In *Lone Cowboy*, "James" made some bitter statements about a "great man" from whom he tried to obtain advice when he was a struggling artist seeking recognition. Up to the time he began to think he might sell his art work, "James" had left hundreds of his sketches on the walls of bunkhouses and saloons throughout the West. He attached no value to them. When, after being injured by a horse, "James" became anxious to sell his art material and his writings, he was intense in his efforts to gain advice and recognition. In *Lone Cowboy* he does not specify who he is talking about in one incident, but it is known that it was Charlie Russell. As "James" recounts the story, the great man deliberately ignored him after he was permitted to enter the studio, and "James" left, feeling that he had been humiliated and snubbed.

An entirely different interpretation of Russell's conduct is given by the only living eyewitness of that meeting. Joe De Yong, of Hollywood, the protégé of Russell who lived in the Russell household for ten years, described the incident to me. He said that "James" did in fact come to visit Russell and that he was admitted while Joe was present. Joe's explanation of the situation that developed is based on his own observation and his knowledge of Russell's habits. He said that when Russell was "fighting" a picture, he became totally oblivious of his surroundings and of everyone who might be present. Joe said that Russell greeted "James" affably enough but that he was in the midst of one of his sessions with a rambunctious picture which

"In the Saddle" by "Will James" from In the Saddle with Uncle Bill. (Dale Hawkins, Billings, Montana.)

"1910 Montana Cattle Drive" by "Will James" from Smoky. (Desert Southwest Art Gallery, Palm Desert, California.)

would not come out as he wanted, and that in his concentration he forgot all about the presence of the visitor. Joe is convinced that there was no slight intended.

The way in which "James" actually was aided in obtaining his start in the art and magazine field has never been publicly told in detail, I believe. The man who knows most about it is Harold von Schmidt, because he participated actively in it. "Von" wrote out for me, at my request, his recollection of this crucial moment at a time when "James" was first trying to break into the writing and sketching game with a magazine. As "Von" tells it, this is the way it happened:

I was in my studio in the offices of Foster & Kleiser, in San Francisco, when the telephone rang. The girl at the board said, "Mr. Von Schmidt, another one of your big-hatted friends is out here. He has a letter for you."

I walked out and saw that the man was big-hatted but I did not know him. We shook hands and he said, "Mr. Field, of Sunset Magazine, asked me to bring this letter to you." I read the letter. It was from a California Senator whose name I don't recall. It said that he had seen this rider

injured in a rodeo accident and from his friends discovered that he drew a lot of the West, ranch life, rodeos, etc. I asked "Bill James" into the studio where we sat down and talked. The bronc he was riding had bucked up an embankment alongside of the rodeo grounds and tripped on some railroad ties, throwing him. He landed on the side of his head against a rail. The split ran from his forehead back along the side of his head. It took sixteen stitches to close the wound. He told me that when he raised his arms above his head his eyes went out of focus, so that he could not continue working or riding. (I thought immediately of Kipling's "The Light That Failed," when a sabre slash caused the same result.)

I asked him about the little package he carried under his arm. He untied and unwrapped it, showing me two shoe-box bottoms. On each he had drawn minutely everything that could go on at a cattle ranch —in one corner was a ranch house with horses tied to a rail in front, the rest was filled with one corral where they were branding calves; in another they were breaking horses, in the next they were shoeing them, on the other side they were bringing herds in, and below taking a herd out. In another picture they were cutting calves from the cows through a swinging gate operated by a man sitting on it. I was fascinated by the drawings and hoped to buy them later.

"James" said, "Mr. Field wanted you to call him after reading the letter."

I did. Field asked if I had any ideas on how he could use him in *Sunset Magazine*, of which he was the editor. I told him I would call him in a day or so.

Maynard Dixon, famous painter of the West, was working with us there, so I introduced him to "James." We decided to "stake" him. We brought Charley Duncan, head of the sales department, in on the deal.

"Bill," as we called him, was living in a dingy hotel on lower Mission Street. Duncan, living in Sausalito, found a small place over there for him. "Bill" came up to the studio every day, drawing pictures on letter paper. The beautiful drawings covered almost half of the page. Below he wrote letters to his friends in Nevada. He was very lonely.

Dixon and I decided to buy him a horse. I went to the sales yards south of Market Street. I have forgotten where. "Bill" picked out an iron gray and said, "Gee, he's great."

"Bill" never thanked anybody for anything.

He took the horse over to Sausalito. We didn't see him as often then.

I called Field and suggested that he let "James" have a page in *Sunset*, to make a drawing of "Western" subjects, that it could be very interesting. Field said he would try it.

"Bill" made drawings of "Western" incidents, and in a panel at the bottom of the paper wrote about the incident.

They went over big. I have most of them clipped out of the magazine. He did one every month for about a year and a half. During this time he showed up with a wife, Alice, a grand girl. She was the sister of one of his closest friends. ("Bill's" signature carried always this "|||"—one was "Bill," one stood for Alice's brother, and the last was for another buddy.)

One day after the last drawing had appeared in *Sunset*, he came to our studio and said he wanted to go to Taos, New Mexico. Dixon and I supplied the money and off he and his wife went.

He wrote, in a couple of weeks, that

"Cortés," by "Will James." (Desert Southwest Art Gallery, Palm Desert, California.)

he didn't like Taos, the artists there wouldn't help him, so he was going on to New York. Ed Springer, who had a ranch south of Cimmaron, New Mexico, gave them the money for some drawings, and off they went.

Dixon and I found this out from a letter he wrote from New York City, saying he was going to write and draw for *Scribner's Magazine*.

That closes the Western chapter in which Dixon and I figured.

With the sympathetic help of Scribner's, "Will James" went on to the heights of success, as one book after another came out. In the profound influence he exerted during the latter part of his lifetime and after his death, it mattered not in the least whether his name was "Will James" or Ernest Dufault. The message he conveyed in his drawings went beyond the necessity of a name at all. It was a universal symbol, as understandable as a child's smile, a bird's song or a mustang's neigh. He awakened in millions of Americans and people of other nations a feeling of participation in that almost mythical world of "the West," into which others like Russell and Remington, Owen Wister and Zane Grey, Maynard Dixon and Clyde Forsythe had given tantalizing glimpses, too.

In establishing this communion by word and picture with his followers, "Will James" became at an opportune moment a galvanizing force in Western art, giving such a forward thrust to popular interest in it that the surging and cumulative effects are still being felt today. When he wrote *Smoky* and *Lone Cowboy*, it still was possible to purchase a Russell or Remington painting or bronze at a relatively low price. *Smoky*, in fact, was published at the very time Russell died—in Great Falls on October 24, 1926—and Remington had been dead only seventeen years, following his tragic end from an emergency operation December 26, 1909.

In the 1920s, of course, the greatness of both Russell and Remington had been long appreciated. Yet in the public mind the desirability of collecting Western art for esthetic reasons or for investment had not become generally accepted. Aside from persons like Homer Britzman in Los Angeles and Amon Carter in Fort Worth, and the localized collectors in Russell's "home country" in Montana and Wyoming, the ordinary home owner who bought "art" acquired prints or etchings or copies of French, Italian and British masterpieces pretty much in the fashion of the 1890s and the first decade of the 1900s.

This inattention to the potentials of original oils of Western painters was part of the cultural atmosphere into which "Will James" came riding like a cowboy into a Ladies Aid meeting. The impact of his arrival was all the more dramatic because it was so unexpected. The same generation that had been brought up on the pap of "Black Beauty," a steed so genteel he presumably used cologne, suddenly was confronted with "Smoky," an honest-to-God range horse with guts and a hell of a lot of earthy character. "Smoky" captivated America. Some slow yeast had been preparing people for "Smoky." For maybe twenty years that new medium, the motion picture featuring Bronco Billy Anderson, Bill Hart, Hoot Gibson, Buck Jones and Tom Mix, had been helping to cultivate an awareness of cowboys and the frontier and the colorful background of the West, to supplement what had already been going on, first in the pulps and the dime novels and, later, in the colorful writing of Owen Wister, whose *Virginian* had come out in 1902; Zane Grey with *Riders of the Purple Sage* in 1912; Stewart Edward White and others, who were glorifying the cattle country and its men and animals.

Smoky in 1926 and *Lone Cowboy* four years later and then the films of both in 1934 capitalized upon this incipient interest. They came at a time when a necessary interim had allowed the paintings of Russell and Remington to have a stimulating effect, too, even if it was not yet generally recognized. In this favorable situation "Smoky" cantered into the limelight. His reception was spontaneous and overwhelming. He won for newcomer "Will James" the Newbery Medal "for the most distinguished contribution to children's literature published in 1926," the highest award in its field.

"Smoky" became, in a real sense, the lead horse in a stampede which caught up the American public in a still-continuing rush of Western art enthusiasm.

Russells and Remingtons, Frank Tenney Johnsons and Buck Duntons, Olaf Seltzers and Von Schmidts began to skyrocket in price. The establishment of the Amon Carter Museum of Western Art in Fort Worth featuring the Russell and Remington collection of the publisher, which previously had been hanging in the Fort Worth Club; the setting up of the Gilcrease Institute of American History and Art in Tulsa, the launching of the National Cowboy Hall of Fame, and the new attention paid to public and private collections in Cody, Great Falls, Jackson Hole, Taos, New York, Santa Fe, Los Angeles, San Diego and Austin started a price spiral.

The amounts paid for Russells and Remingtons went into five figures. "Will James" drawings and the few oil paintings he attempted have shared too in this trend and have skyrocketed in value. Present-day artists portraying the West began to benefit likewise. Top artists began to receive five thousand to seven thousand dollars per painting direct from the easel when, a few years before, they had been getting possibly fifteen hundred dollars. Perspective and the passage of time were giving to "cowboy art" a validity and acceptance based on its great intrinsic worth.

"Will James," regardless of his name or his human failings, was one of the principal factors in guiding and directing public taste in this direction. Proudly mounted on "Smoky," the "Lone Cowboy" was leading the art parade.

Bill Bender and Joie Godshall outside the cottage near Victorville, California, where "Will James" painted and wrote during the last years of his life.

GHOSTS RIDE WITH LONELY MEN

Throughout out the West the specter of the past rises to haunt the lonely men who ride the ranges or hunt the earth's treasure in mountains and desert. In a thousand distant spots the moldering ruins of human hopes attest to dead yesterdays. These are called "ghost towns." Sometimes they are inhabited only by pack rats and lizards. In a few, some doddering wreck of humanity peers with rheumy eyes at the present and looks back with longing to a distant day that can never come again. It is such a scene that William B. Schimmel, the Arizona water-colorist, has captured in his dramatic "Ghost Town" pictured here.

9

FAR PLACES

Juan de Onate expedition, 1596–1606

True art being, like all human affairs, a matter of both time and space, it is natural that regions as well as decades figure in the chronicles of Western painting.

The mere mention of certain years in the lives of notable artists is meaningless unless it is coupled with that of the location of their labors and a designation of the places which inspired them, captured their imaginations and ensnared their physical beings. In the West, some of these names leap out like signatures from the canvas of history.

They all exert a magnetism for painters. They range from Great Falls, Montana, to Mecca in the California desert, and include such widely varying locales as Sedona and Tucson and Phoenix, Arizona; Denver, Colorado; Cody and Jackson Hole, Wyoming; Carmel and Laguna Beach and La Jolla, California; Albuquerque, New Mexico; Fort Worth, Austin and San Antonio, Texas; and Oklahoma City and Tulsa.

Leading the list are Taos and Santa Fe. Their antiquity as settled habitations by aboriginal tribes long before any "civilized" settlers moved in had given them an almost tangible romantic atmosphere. They were ideally situated to appeal to discerning artistic temperaments.

It merely was a matter of slow aging, of gaining a patina of venerability, so that when the eyes of genuine artists dwelt upon them, they would constitute an immediate and irresistible attraction. The "Taos group" and the "Santa Fe group" sprang into being because of a happy combination of circumstances, when artists attuned to the public mood found in the New Mexico tradition, terrain and native inhabitants the stimulation and subject matter to cater to this popular

The Taos Society of Artists, 1927. Top row, left to right, E. Martin Henning, Bert G. Phillips, Victor Higgins, Ernest L. Blumenschein, Joseph H. Sharp. Bottom row, left to right, Walter Ufer, E. Irving Couse, Oscar E. Berninghaus, W. Herbert Dunton, Kenneth M. Adams.

craving. Along the Rio Grande, the artistic driftwood accumulating for centuries suddenly became a treasure trove for the painters.

Many of the painters who were attracted to Taos and Santa Fe, however, never painted Western subjects despite their surroundings. Still, along with those who did portray the West, they served a purpose in attracting the attention of other artists who were led to visit the New Mexico area, and some of these latter remained and in their enthusiasm did become Western artists. The Western centers soon began to become as famous as had some of

their Eastern counterparts—Woodstock, New York, Provincetown on Cape Cod, and New Hope on the Delaware River in Pennsylvania had all early attracted artist colonies.

The "discoverer" of Taos in an art sense was Joseph Henry Sharp, who was born in Bridgeport, Ohio, in 1859. When he was only twenty-four Sharp made a sketching trip through New Mexico and then, ten years later, in 1893, went back and lived for a while in Taos. When he returned to Paris for further study, Sharp interested two other young artists who soon went to New Mexico to see the region for themselves. These were Ernest L.

"Cinching Up," by Walter Ufer. (Desert Southwest Art Gallery, Palm Desert, California.)

"Shepherds Changing Camp," by O. E. Berninghaus. (Read Mullan Gallery of Western Art, Phoenix, Arizona.)

Blumenschein, born in Pittsburgh in 1874, and Bert Geer Phillips, born in Hudson, New York, in 1868. They were joined successively in the "art colony" by E. Irving Couse, born in Saginaw, Michigan, in 1866; Oscar E. Berninghaus, born in St. Louis in 1874; Herbert (Buck) Dunton, born in 1878 in Augusta, Maine; Walter Ufer, born in Louisville, Kentucky, in 1876; Victor Higgins of Shelbyville, Indiana, born in 1884; Ernest Martin Hennings, born in Pennsgrove, New Jersey, in 1886; and Kenneth M. Adams, born in 1897 in Topeka, Kansas.

Of all these, Dunton and Ufer were among the best known for having adapted themselves to Western subjects. When Dunton arrived in Taos, he was asked by the early group to join in the formation of a traveling exhibition which might serve to sell the paintings of the different artists. Out of this experience, his love of the country and his "feel" for the West, Dunton emerged as a painter of magazine covers and jackets for novels, such as those of Zane Grey. Ufer's Western

depictions also bore a stamp of great authenticity, and his horses are considered among the best drawn by anyone in the group.

At the age of 14, Frank B. Hoffman of New Orleans, later a New Mexico artist, was galloping his father's race horses in the mornings and then spending his spare moments in the afternoons and evenings drawing and sketching them. He went to Chicago where he became head of the art department of the *Chicago Daily American*. Yearning to study art seriously, Hoffman became a pupil of J. Wellington Reynolds, nationally-known portrait painter. Having been turned down by the military because of an eye injury, he went West to Montana and saw the roundup of the last big buffalo herd as it was being shipped from Alaska to Mexico. It was while he was employed at Glacier National Park that he met John Singer Sargent, the great portrait painter of Europe and America and learned a great deal from him. Hoffman then joined the Taos Art Group and went into

"Mexican Charro," by W. Herbert Dun-ton. (Mr. and Mrs. Milas Hurley, Sr., Albuquerque, New Mexico.)

commercial art and became a top-flight illustrator. For fourteen years he was an artist for the Brown and Bigelow calendar company and many of these originals are now in the private collection of this company. Hoffman stressed authenticity in his Western paintings which are sought by art collectors. He was born in Chicago, Illinois, in 1888 and died in Taos, New Mexico, on March 11, 1958.

Before artist groups evolved in Taos and Santa Fe, individual painters had traveled throughout the historic area. One of these was Thomas Moran, who had been born in 1837 in Bolton, England. He and Sharp ranged all over the West, and took particular delight in painting horses in the Indian country.

The decade of the 1890s really marked the inception of the Taos art colony, but in Santa Fe it was the ten- or fifteen-year period following 1900 that saw the greatest activity of artists there. A former seaman from California, Carlos Vierra, is credited with being the first major resident artist in Santa Fe, where he arrived in 1904. A little later came Kenneth Chapman, then Gerald Cassidy (who had been born in 1879 in Cincinnati). They were followed by Sheldon Parsons, born in 1866 in Rochester, New York; Roland Rollins; Paul Burlin, born in New York in 1886; Theodore Van Soelen; and William Pennhallow Henderson, who was born in Medford, Massachusetts, in 1877. Among foreign-born artists who came to New Mexico, two of the greatest were Nicolai Fechin, who was born in 1881 in Kasan, Russia, and Leon Gaspard, who was born in Vitebsk, Russia, in 1882. Both were such consummate artists that their fame added to the luster of Taos to which they attracted students and followers.

"Branding Time," by Theodore van Soelen. (Museum of New Mexico Art Gallery, Santa Fe, New Mexico.)

Theodore van Soelen. (Donald van Soelen, Santa Fe, New Mexico.)

Typical of the spirit which animated the artists who were drawn to New Mexico was that of Van Soelen, who found much more than fame in his adopted state.

Tuberculosis and a Southwestern tradition combined to create one of the most discerning interpreters of this ancient land. If Van Soelen, who was born in St. Paul, Minnesota, on February 15, 1890, had not contracted tuberculosis when he was about twenty-six, he might never have become distinguished as an American artist. As it was, his arrival in New Mexico transferred his artistic endeavors from Pennsylvania and Europe to the middle of the Indian country. In the process of regaining his health in the region of Santa Fe, Taos, Tusuque and Albuquerque, he also attained a remarkable artistic eminence derived from his surroundings along the Rio Grande. His innately sensitive nature—he said, "Originality is the very core of great art" and "The artist learns to live for what he is doing, believing it is worth while and convinced that if he can create something truly beautiful nothing else matters"—led him to cultivate the originality he admired as he portrayed ranch life, cowboys, cattle, Indians and the people around him in New Mexico.

Van Soelen progressed so rapidly in his art output and proficiency as his health returned that his paintings began to be exhibited in New York, Pennsylvania, Chicago, Cleveland, Washington, D.C., Boston and, of course, all over New Mexico. When he was fifty he was elected a National Academician. The great demand for his work in the East caused him to open a studio in Cornwall, Connecticut, and he commuted between there and Tusuque, New Mexico, where he established his home.

His capabilities were summed up by Henry McBride, writing about a Van Soelen show in New York, when he said, "Many pictures have come out of the Santa Fe region, but few have the allure of those of Van Soelen who actually 'sells' the place to us."

Late in life he started lithography, and exhibited in many galleries. His paintings included portraits and landscapes as well as the ranch scenes at which he excelled.

When he died, he had enjoyed more than thirty years of artistic productivity after the date he supposedly was to meet his doom from tuberculosis—a gift of life for which he thanked his New Mexico surroundings.

A KINDRED SOUL OF THE COWBOY

Kindred souls are the cowboy and the prospector. Each seeks solitude and a distant goal in his own way. Every cowboy at one time or another must have met a prospector because the horizon lures both onward, and far off somewhere is a high mountain full of hope and promise.

A song writer who has captured this feeling of kinship in words is Bob Wagoner, painter, of Long Beach, California. As a former rodeo rider and professional guitar player for whom the out-of-doors has held a special attraction, Bob Wagoner has expressed the longing of lonely wanderers in his popular TV and radio song:

High Country

High Country callin' me
Got no worries or cares.
Timber climbin' the mountains,
To heaven's golden stairs.

Soft breezes sighin' low,
Sing a song thru the trees,
And the moon lights the evenin'
With a silvery beam.
    The thunderin' waterfall,
    Sings a haunting refrain,
    And the sky answers nature's call,
    With the wind and the rain.

I hear that High Country callin' me,
To its meadows and streams,
There I'll find a rainbow,
And a mountain of dreams.

The accompanying painting, "Prospector," is a portrait of "Cactus George" Miller of Jerome, Arizona, by the San Diego artist Lenore Sherman, and belongs to Mr. and Mrs. Frank McCoy of La Jolla, California.

10

IN THE SADDLE

Hocking pole instead of rope, 1700's

Any effort to lay out the American cowboy prematurely in his coffin because his "era" supposedly was past was bound to result in the corpse sitting up, waving his Stetson and shooting out the lights of the funeral parlor.

The cowpunchers refused to punch a time clock. Their role as "colorful characters" was presumed to end about the time of Grover Cleveland, because that was when the long-horns virtually disappeared from the land. But the calculations went wrong. The twentieth century arrived and somehow made its war-torn way through the first six decades, and there the cowboy was, stronger and more picturesque than ever because he had become an object of art.

The painters and sculptors refused to be mourners at his obsequies, and helped yank him out of the coffin for a new roundup. As a result, the cowboy not only is alive and kicking but also is providing added material every day for those who portray him in his native haunts. The years have passed, it is true, yet, in his environment, speech, garb, and work with horses and cattle, the cowboy in many ways is exactly as he was in the time of Russell and Remington. This recognition of his quality of permanence has, in no small measure, been due to the artists and writers who have gloried in his individuality and striven to preserve it for the future.

From both within the United States and from abroad have come the painters attracted by the modern cowboy as a subject; they have refused to let time dim his outline. They are the "cowboy artists."

On a hilltop by America's western sea, Olaf Wieghorst has found the heights he sought from the time he was a little boy in

"Bustin' Out," by Olaf Wieghorst. (John Murchison, Athens, Texas.)

Denmark.

It took many horses to get him there.

He lives and paints on the rocky hilltop beside a corral. He needs horses around him just as he has needed them from the time he was two or three years old, because they represent the dominant interest in his life and a principal subject of his cowboy paintings, which have become internationally famous.

In the simple, earthy sincerity of the Western art of Weighorst, a universality of appeal is present. What Will Rogers, a close friend, said about the West in words, Olaf Weighorst says in paints—creating a direct colloquial link with the heart of the land, a common expression of sentiment, a direct kinship with men and horses. Rogers reduced everything, cowboy fashion, to a distillation of thought, so terse that it was instantly understandable to everybody. Wieghorst is terse in pigments. Everybody understands him, too, as is evident in the jacket painting on the front of this book, which is typical of his enormous capability.

Wieghorst's cowboys are living personalities. His horses trample the earth with the vigor of straining muscles and arching necks and heaving flanks. His wild steers reflect brute power on the open prairie or the mountain slopes.

Painting ability he has acquired through a lifetime of study and effort. His affection for horses has always been there. Because of his intense interest, as a young boy he stayed many times all night in box stalls waiting for mares to foal, an experience which gave him a feeling of kinship with all horses as he saw them coming into the world.

Olaf Wieghorst was born on April 30, 1899, in Viborg, Jutland, Denmark. His father, Karl Weighorst, a photographer and film animator, was a physiculturist who rode the horses of the Danish Dragoons with an Army instructor and believed in keeping fit all the time and in having his son Olaf do the same. Olaf had begun riding horses almost as a baby, and later he went into the most intensive training on hand stands, swinging

(Above right) *Wash drawing by Olaf Wieghorst*

(Above left) *"The Cowboy at Rest," bronze by Olaf Wieghorst. (Donald Stevning, Coachella, California.)*

(Below left) *Olaf Wieghorst*

from rings, trapeze work and pushups which made him "very muscular." By the time Olaf was nine, his father thought it was time for his professional debut, and he got the boy a job at the famous Tivoli Theater in Copenhagen where the family had moved. On the stage Olaf did a series of acrobatic stunts and soon was appearing in vaudeville all over Denmark.

His yearning to be around horses was growing stronger all the time.

"I wanted to be a cowboy, in the worst way," he recalls. He played hooky from school and spent all his spare time exercising Russian horses at a Copenhagen horse dealer's, or riding the delivery horse at the store where he worked, or pretending he was on horseback and using a clothesline lasso to rope pigs.

When he was sent to a farm during an interruption in his stage career, the arrangement for his apprenticeship—without pay— did not work out.

"I didn't want to walk behind horses. I wanted to get up on them," he explains simply.

Finally, his father permitted him to use his great skill as a bareback rider to appear in the famous Schumann Circus at night and

"On the Move," by Burt Procter. (Genevieve K. Neveau, Palm Desert, California.)

also in daring scenes for the Great Northern Film Company.

All this time Olaf was trying to learn to draw as well as attempting to become a cowboy. His subjects naturally were horses. When he was sixteen he sold his first canvas for two Danish crowns—about fifty American cents.

Finally, just after World War I, he obtained a job as a cabin boy on a steamer bound for the United States, and on December 14, 1918—only a month after the Armistice—set sail for New York through the minefields of the European coast. In New York he jumped ship and then, unable to speak any English, rode all night on the subway because he could not read the signs to ask directions to find his way to the home of an uncle he was seeking.

Olaf soon decided that New York was not what he wanted. One night, while he was in a moving-picture theater, he saw a newsreel of units of the Fifth United States Cavalry galloping across the Rio Grande to pursue Pancho Villa. This gave him an idea. The next morning he went to the recruiting station to enlist for the Mexican Border Service.

Along the Mexican border his proficiency as a rider won him immediate attention in the army. He had a way with horses, and the officers recognized it despite Olaf's handicap of being unable to speak very much English. He was assigned to a machine-gun troop and also was sent to horseshoeing school at San Antonio where he received the highest mark ever given during the four months' course.

For three years Olaf remained in the army at Presidio, Texas, and elsewhere, patrolling the Rio Grande. When he had been in the United States only six months he was granted American citizenship—"the proudest moment of my life," he says. During his army service he had opportunity to observe horses under every sort of condition.

"I've seen horses from all angles—even from underneath 'em," he explains.

While he was in the army he was attempting to correspond with Mabel, a girl he had met in New York. But there was one great difficulty; Olaf as yet could neither read nor write English. He needed someone to write his letters and read those from Mabel. One man in the outfit he felt he could trust. This was Sergeant Bud Jones, whose family lived in New Mexico. To Jones Olaf entrusted his romantic secret, and was able through him to write to Mabel and to have her messages relayed to him.

Olaf and Bud Jones, when mustered out,

Burt Procter

"White Mustangs," by Burt Procter. (Mr. and Mrs. Ed Ainsworth, Mecca, California.)

set forth for the cow country of New Mexico. They worked their way on horseback, stopping at ranches, encountering old-time sheriffs and gunmen, ex-Texas rangers, cowboys and every kind of Western character. They camped in the Sulphur Valley of Arizona, went to Wilcox in the center of the great cattle region and visited Alma Mesa, New Mexico. Olaf broke horses and punched cows, and at last came to the Quarter Circle 2C Ranch on White Water Creek, in New Mexico. This was operated by Elton Cunningham, a holdover from the days of the Old West, and a determined man.

"The old ranch house was typical of many I had seen in that region," Olaf relates. "Guns were on the wall in handy position to be seized quickly when needed. It was the kind of thing you encountered in the West during those days. Men didn't fool around. They indulged in direct action."

Bud Jones went on over to Elida, New Mexico, where he had a sister, and Olaf remained at the Cunningham Ranch. When he wasn't punching cattle he was drawing pictures and painting. When he had no paper he would heat a running iron and burn scenes on a barn wall or in a bar. All the time, though, he was thinking of Mabel and finally

decided to go on a trip to New York.

When he arrived he was wearing a six shooter, and people would stop him and ask whether he was part of the rodeo in Madison Square Garden. Olaf found Mabel, and they renewed their friendship. He knew she was the girl for him. But he had to have a job, and the first one he could find was shoveling snow at fifty cents an hour. He rose at 4:00 A.M. so as to find customers who wanted shoveling done. In the bitter cold he contracted pneumonia, but Mabel nursed him back to health, and soon they were married. As a temporary job, Olaf applied in 1924 to the New York police force. He was accepted in the mounted division, and thought he would work there for a few months. As it turned out, he remained for twenty years, a period which entitled him in 1944 to a life pension. He became recognized as the leading rider in the entire mounted force and was given many choice assignments as a result. It was at this time that he became a close friend of Will Rogers, who was working in the theaters with his lasso and his drawling comments. Will and Olaf had many a conversation between acts while Will was waiting his turn on stage and Olaf was on duty with his horse in the theatrical district.

Most important of all, Olaf began to concentrate on his art work in his spare time. One big handicap beset him. Under the rules of the police department he was not supposed to engage in outside business activities. This caused some difficulty. At that time aspiring artists were permitted to set up their pictures in the lobby at Madison Square Garden, where the crowds going to rodeos and fights and other sporting events could see them. Olaf became acquainted with Charlie Aldrich, an old-time Colorado cowboy who had once ridden the famous gray bucking horse Steamboat, and had gone to England and France with Tex Austin's cowboy show. Charlie had worked for sixteen years for Will Rogers, caring for polo horses. Frank Moore, manager of Madison Square Garden rodeos, gave Charlie Aldrich little odd jobs of selling novelties. Both Rogers and Wieghorst regarded him highly because of his honesty.

Olaf confided his problem about selling pictures to Charlie Aldrich, who agreed to "front" for him. Pete Martinez and Olaf (through Charlie) shared a twenty-foot counter, half and half, at Madison Square Garden, and there they would display their drawings. Charlie would sell those of Olaf, turning over the sketches with a thumb wet with tobacco juice for the benefit of prospective buyers, sometimes ruining half a dozen or so during an evening in the process.

Olaf sold his drawings for from fifty cents to four dollars, and put a price of three or four hundred dollars on his oil paintings although nobody paid much attention to them. Finally, to his great surprise, Olaf did sell a painting for three hundred dollars, and then another to Tom Morgan of the Sperry Gyroscope Company for five hundred dollars.

When his twenty years in the police department ended, Olaf knew that painting must be his career. He and his wife and son Roy went first to Florida and then traveled west by car, visiting the old Cunningham Ranch in New Mexico, going on to Arizona and eventually arriving in El Cajon where they settled. In his studio Olaf toiled away to gain even greater proficiency in the subjects he loved so much.

"The hardest thing was to get ideas," he says. "I would wake up at night and think of stories and incidents and from them plan a painting. I don't make as many sketches as most. Usually I do a charcoal on canvas and then proceed with the oil. Nearly all of it is in my head because of those sessions in the night. I determine always to get a spot of interest in my landscapes and, of course, these always turn out to be horses and cattle and riders."

In addition to his paintings he began doing bronzes, including such subjects as "Bucking Horse" and "Resting Cowboy."

"Oil is really my medium," he confides.

As the years passed Olaf Wieghorst began to rise higher and higher in the estimation of those who collected Western art. His paintings were bought as soon as they were completed. He hardly had time to get them off the easel.

In 1962 he and his wife went on a voyage to Denmark. The aspiring youth who had left as a cabin boy returned as a successful painter. Olaf and his wife were entertained by the King and Queen of Denmark, and were honored at the Danish-American museum at Aalborg and at a state dinner also attended by Richard Nixon.

These honors Olaf accepts gracefully. He is more intent upon satisfying his own demanding requirements of perfection than he is on dwelling upon personal aggrandizement. Amid his mementos of the West and close to his horses, he concentrates on painting the cowboys of the vast region he knows so well. The acclaim takes care of itself.

Always Burt Procter is riding on, with whip and spur, toward the next hill in the purple yonder. He is a feuding man. He has a score to settle over there. He isn't mad at anybody, his feud is only with himself. Yet it drives him incessantly forward because it concerns the whole motivation of his art.

The symbolic hill he seeks as he presses forward is perfection, the principle of combining design with realism in a coherent unit pleasing to the eye, fully organized and with the least possible compromise. In this pursuit he has been relentless with himself. From the moment he began drawing milk-wagon horses as a tiny child to the present, when his canvases are winning acclaim in exhibitions in the National Academy of Design and other leading shows, he has been constantly at war with himself.

This intensity is rarely observable by those who meet him and admire the man and his work, but, nevertheless, Procter continues to seek an ultimate attainment which may appear impossible but still will be sought to the end. Even his first drawings as a child showed some manifestations of this spirit; he drew his horses upside down as if he was challenging himself to a difficult portrayal to test his abilities. Later, his horses came solidly to the earth and he began to gain increasing fame for his paintings of them. But it took a long time for this to happen.

Burt Procter was born on June 24, 1901, in Gloucester, Massachusetts, where his father had been a reporter on the *Gloucester Daily Times* before becoming an employee of the Bell Telephone Company. His parents, who were not particularly interested in art, were somewhat amazed when Burt started drawing pictures of horses almost before he began to walk. From an early age, too, he was adept with his hands, and in later life he took pleasure in all forms of building—a car, a boat, a house, an easel.

The call of the West was so insistent that when he was seventeen Burt journeyed to the historic Little Bighorn Basin in Wyo-

U.S. Pony Express stamps designed by Harold Von Schmidt

ming, and a while later worked for the United States government at the south rim of the Grand Canyon. During this time, on his days off, he explored caves, scaled cliffs and absorbed the color and grandeur around him.

His surroundings confirmed him in his desire to be an artist. He traveled to Los Angeles and went into commercial art work, and then lived in New York where he was successful as an advertising illustrator and art director. But it was not what he wanted. In his quest for new knowledge of the West he became, for a while, a mining engineer, using his travels to increase his knowledge of the earth and its colors and composition, always with the urge to paint dominating his activities.

At one period when he was in the throes of his inner struggle, he became virtually a hermit for five years trying to perfect his art. He lived in a garret attic during that time, and rarely emerged from the continual experiments in painting in which he sought to "find himself." This self-imposed ordeal gave him a new perspective on the element he considers most important in painting. He identifies this as "design with realism," but admits that it is a "subtle business" that each artist must perfect for himself. In his own struggle to determine his ultimate capabilities he was assisted mostly by two mentors. One was Harvey Dunn, eminent teacher in New York, and the other was Pruitt Carter, the illustrator, who eventually moved from New York to Los Angeles and continued to be of help to Procter.

At present Procter's art encompasses a wide variety of subjects. He still paints the horses which seem to be coming out of the canvas at the viewer and on which much of his reputation has been based, but he is equally at home with a multiplicity of other material. In a recent National Academy of Design exhibit in New York he submitted a marine painting that was accepted. At the Allied Arts Institute in New York his painting was of a Mexican woman with clay pottery. At an Audubon Artists show his subject was Indian ponies, a manifestation of his first love.

In an effort to find what others are doing and thus improve his own approach to art, Procter and his wife Katherine, a vivacious native of Mississippi with a Southern drawl, have traveled all over the Orient and the Latin countries of South America. In Hawaii, Japan, Malaya, Thailand, Bali and Java, Procter studied paintings both traditional and modern, and was particularly struck with the thousands of wood carvings in the shrines of Bali, an art form which gripped his imagination. In South America he was attracted to the Gaucho art of a genuine Gaucho artist in Buenos Aires.

In regard to his great versatility today and his painting of portraits, marines, oriental scenes and many other subjects he admits, "I'm still making horses. I do everything, but I'm as known about as much for horses as anything else.

"In view of the fact that things seem to be so personal, it must be that there are about as many reactions to horses as there are people. In my own mind the horse is not only a sensitive, graceful and powerful animal, but also a symbol. In connection with man, it stands for the early days of western America,

a certain type of individual and a definite way of life. In fact, I have had moments when I wondered about a culture represented by cars powered with 300 or so horses, as against that symbolized by just one real horse.

"In working horses, we've heard rumors that it's better for the person to have more sense than the horse. If this is not the case, in spite of every effort, the horse finds it out. Thus it is not infrequent that we have what is known as the 'horse laugh.'"

After the original idea comes to him, his approach to the physical process of painting is meticulous. First, he creates a relation of masses with a few swift strokes on a small piece of paper. Then he repeats the process with colors dabbed on a slightly larger piece of paper. A third step is a slightly more definite application of color and form. After this, he is ready to begin the painting.

He works in a cluttered studio back of his home at Corona del Mar on the Southern California coast, amid Indian drums, saddles, pottery frames and memo cards. He eases his feet on a piece of foam rubber as he paints from a palette so encrusted with layers of paint that it appears to be something out of a colorful mineral cave. He uses simple colors, whether the subject is horses, portraits or the sea.

Looking about him at the changes taking place in art, Procter says, "We are in a transitional age." This ferment, this spirit of unrest, this striving still animates him too. The feuding within him goes on. The distant hill always leads him onward as if it were a pristine desert dawn. Beyond it Burt Procter always expects to find the attainment of his finest work.

Meanwhile, as he continues his search, those who glory in the boldness and imagination of his canvases are satisfied that he already has reached the hill of attainment.

In the enduring panorama of the West,

(Above right) *Harold Von Schmidt.* (*Courtesy Famous Artists School, Westport, Connecticut.*)

(Above left) *Illustration for* The Saturday Evening Post, 1949, *by Harold Von Schmidt.* (*By permission of* The Saturday Evening Post, *Curtis Publishing Co.*)

(Below left) *Painting by Harold Von Schmidt*

the figure of the Pony Express rider looms large. This intrepid carrier of the mails on "The Pony" engaged in his arduous task for just a short time in 1860 and 1861, while the telegraph was under construction from the Mississippi to the Pacific coast. Yet, in that short time, his bravery and endurance became a national symbol.

When the one hundredth anniversary of the Pony Express arrived, it was only natural that the United States Government should commemorate the event with a postage stamp. For this stamp it needed the finest and most accurate artistic depiction of the Pony Express rider. An artist of consummate skill was required. He was available. He was Harold

Von Schmidt—known for half a century to his friends as "Von"—and he was selected from among all the artists of America to design the stamp. Millions of Americans thereafter saw the Pony Express rider as they sent and received their letters.

Harold Von Schmidt was qualified not only technically but by experience in his artistic background for this demanding assignment. He was known as an eminent oil painter and illustrator. However, he had attained this status only through the most arduous labors and at the cost of much sorrow and striving. Von Schmidt was born in 1893 in Alameda, California. When he was only five he became an orphan, and lived

"Ben Holladay Coach-and-Six." Model by Joe De Yong scale: 1 inch to 1 foot. (The whip had silver ferrules on it.)

for a time, miserably, in an orphan asylum and then, successively, with his grandfather and an aunt and uncle. From the time he was a youngster he worked as a cowhand, lumberjack, mule skinner and as a dock hand at San Francisco. All the while, some inner urge kept driving him toward the drawing of pictures. His aunt arranged for him to attend the California College of Arts and Crafts in Oakland, where his teacher was Frederick H. Meyers. Later, he studied with Maynard Dixon, who was then at the zenith of his career, and with Harvey Dunn at the Grand Central Art School in New York. After years of working in advertising and attempting to sell his art work to magazines, Von Schmidt began to attract attention in the East. He began to illustrate for *Collier's, Liberty, Cosmopolitan, True* and, eventually, almost entirely for *The Saturday Evening Post.* He went on assignments during World War II and took his chances in combat missions of B25's and B24's and even drew pictures from the nose of a P38.

Out of all this came his nationwide fame and increasing facility. He became a teacher in the Famous Artists School in Westport, Connecticut, and in that capacity has carried on the tradition entrusted to him by Maynard Dixon. Von Schmidt was so grateful to Dixon for his help that he asked what he might do to repay him, and Dixon's reply was, "You can paint fine pictures and pass the word along." "Von" has done so.

He has been incessantly enthralled with the West, and his work as a cowboy gave him the insight for the authentic quality which has taken him to the top rank of illustrators and painters. This recognition was climaxed in 1960 when he was given the Society of Illustrators' medal and the Artist Guild Hall of Fame award.

More than this, though—he has endeared himself to many an aspiring artist and to his ever-growing audience through his sincerity and warmth. His Pony Express rider symbolically carried him toward the Western horizon of success, which he has attained and maintained.

Bucking horses carved out of a potato and pieces of soap led to the extraordinary situation in which Joe De Yong, the kid wrangler, became in later life the last living artistic link with the household of Charlie Russell.

For the last ten years of Russell's career, Joe was his camping companion and protégé, living at intervals in the Russell home and sharing in the creative throes of his friend and teacher. The paths of the two came together in Montana after they had been born exactly a generation apart in the suburbs of St. Louis, and had traveled in opposite directions. Russell—born in Oak Grove, Missouri, in 1864, during the Civil War—had gone to Montana when he was fifteen and had begun to gain fame as an artist before Joe was born in Webster Grove, Missouri, in 1894. Joe, in his turn, went early to the Indian Territory with his folks. Montana and the Indian Territory are a long way apart, but Charlie and Joe eventually teamed up.

When Joe was a boy, he had first seen Russell's paintings at the St. Louis World's Fair, and had been totally fascinated both by the technique of the artist and the subject matter. Prior to this, Joe had been aware of the work of Frederic Remington in *Harper's* and *Collier's*, but the minute he laid eyes on a Russell painting his allegiance was firmly fixed on the new idol.

Down in the Indian Territory, Joe became a friend of Will Rogers—who had, as Joe puts it, "such a high-hearted disregard of personal danger coupled with a spontaneous, remarkably original, crackling type of wit and humor, usually of an extremely deadpan sort" —and had learned fancy roping from him. At fourteen, he began "riding for wages," getting money as a rider for what he had been doing for fun anyway.

"I began riding at five, and simply took it for granted," he recalls.

When he was seventeen, Joe "got into the movies." Tom Mix, who had been chief of cowboys on the 101 Ranch Wild West

Calf roping at Los Rancheros Visitadores Rodeo, Rancho Juan y Loleta, about 1938. The horse is "Boot Legger," one of Will Rogers' favorites. Mrs. Rogers presented the horse to De Yong two weeks after Rogers' death. Photo by Joe De Yong.

Show had married Olive Stokes, a friend of the De Yong family. When Mix started making the film *Life on the Diamond S Ranch*, Joe was put in charge of the cattle. After this, he was so enamored of the films that he followed Mix to Arizona and "rode fast and furious up and down hill in groups" as a cowboy bit player.

Then came spinal meningitis, which resulted in total deafness, and, necessarily, a new kind of life to meet this drastically changed condition.

Before this period of emotional and physical readjustment, Joe had read an article by Charlie Russell in *World's Work Magazine*, in which the modeling of figures in wax to stress light and shadow was stressed as a prelude to painting. Now, during his convalescence, Joe got a potato, carved a bucking horse and followed it with horses fashioned of soap. Finally, he got up his courage to write Russell for advice on modeling.

Russell sent an illustrated letter in reply.

This sparked Joe's resolve somehow to get out West and meet Russell.

"From then on I was consumed with a stubborn determination to go to Montana," Joe relates. "More than that—an unreasoning conviction that therein lay my next move as mapped out by Fate; a move that not only was to result in my getting to know Russell and his country, but one that led to my spending the last ten years of his life working in his studio, and being at irregular intervals a member of his household."

A strange bond then united the master painter and the eager neophyte—a common interest in the Indian sign language, a matter of mere curiosity to Russell but of vital necessity to Joe because of his deafness.

It was during these days of roaming and sketching that Joe De Yong became such an expert on Indian types and clothing and weapons that it led him by natural progression, years later, to a "return to the movies" as a costume designer and technical adviser for Cecil B. De Mille and other producers, a career that has lasted until the present.

But Joe De Yong, fortified by his training with Russell and by friendships with such eminent artists as Edward Borein, Maynard Dixon, Frank Tenney Johnson and Clyde Forsythe, did become a distinguished creator of Western scenes. During the process he kept on as a bronco rider and calf roper, and became favorably known to many of the Rancheros Visitadores, a group of pioneer-minded horsemen who annually trek forth on a camping trip from Santa Barbara, California, who respected his talents both as cowboy and artist. Along the line, too, he became acquainted with "Will James," that enigma among writers and artists, whose work has become a model in this generation. Today, Joe De Yong owns priceless mementoes and photographs of "James," or Ernest Dufault.

De Yong is working on a book of his experiences to be illustrated by himself. It will form, when published, a chapter that no other person could write from such a viewpoint, of Charlie Russell and Joe De Yong, the kid wrangler, whose trails finally crossed.

Just how Plymouth Rock and the Pilgrims ever formed a family affiliation with Monument Valley and the Navahos may remain forever a genealogical mystery; but for one American artist it has been a perfectly natural kinship. He has bridged the continent with ease and grace, so that the East of his nativity and the West of his own selection have been blended in his painting.

Gerard Curtis Delano, born in Marion, Massachusetts, on the seacoast only twenty miles from Plymouth Rock, began drawing Indians on horses when he was only four years old. Whether in his childish dreams he was seeing the red landscape and the brilliant blue skies of the Far West he has never disclosed; but something within his nature was pushing him toward that land of vast distances and upreared peaks and a proud, independent race of red men, even though in his own antecedents he could boast the blood of a French cavalier who landed in Massachusetts in 1621. His great-great-great-grandfather Philippe de Lannoy sired a family that included among its descendants both the late President Franklin Delano Roosevelt and Gerard Curtis Delano.

Delano has achieved his international reputation for portraying the horses and riders of the canyon country of Arizona because of his combination of innate talent, Eastern art training and homesteading in the wild regions of Colorado:

Nothing gives me more pleasure or greater thrill than seeing in real life the

Gerard Curtis Delano   *"Get Along, Little Dogie," by Gerard Curtis Delano*

brightly-clothed Navajos against their background of magnificent canyons or the vast open stretches which are characteristic of their reservation country. Seeing them I, perforce, must paint. There is a vastness, an immensity and the peaceful hush of an enormous cathedral about Arizona's great canyons. Whoever has been within these towering walls, who has seen the flocks of sheep and goats grazed there by the Navajos, who has heard the distant tinkle of the lead goat's bell and listened to the wild and eery songs of the bright-skirted shepherdesses and who has seen in the distance an approaching rider, a tiny speck against the massive canyon walls, must yearn to perpetuate his impressions of those precious moments.

All this followed a session Jerry Delano began in New York as a textile designer and service in the Navy during World War I. The sale of a drawing, a pen-and-ink, to *Life Magazine* encouraged him so much that he started evening classes at the Swaine Free School of Design in New Bedford near his home, and worked during the day in a gun

store. Then he went to New York and studied at the Art Students League with such instructors as George Bridgeman, Frank Vincent Du Mond and Edward Dufner. His great teachers at the Grand Central School of Art included Harvey Dunn, Dean Cornwell and N. C. Wyeth.

Always the West was beckoning to him while he maintained a studio on East Fifty-seventh Street in what was known as the "Art Center," but at last he journeyed to Colorado and started to work on a cattle ranch where he learned the rudiments of riding, traveled around the country and did some painting. This experience so exhilarated him that he went back the next year and began to build a log cabin with a dirt roof on a homestead claim he filed in the mountains of Summit Country on Cataract Creek.

The real turning point in his career was his first trip into the Navaho country. Immediately, amid the solitude or among the dignified Navahos, he began to penetrate into the soul of the region that had beckoned to him before ever he saw it. The Canyon de Chelly

"Surrender of Chief Joseph," by J. K. Ralston. (Dale Hawkins, Billings, Montana.)

and the Canyon del Muerto both spoke to him in a language of color and primitive grandeur. The Indian horsemen in this setting made an indelible impression. He began to paint the Navahos and their horses and cattle and sheep as his foremost subject.

He illustrated "The Story of the West," which appeared in a Western story magazine for two years at weekly intervals. So much research was required that Delano finally moved to Colorado Springs from his homestead, and then set up a studio in Denver which he has maintained ever since. Among the first major galleries to give him recognition were the Ferargil, Anderson and Kennedy Galleries in New York, the Cyrus Boutwell Gallery in Denver, and the Desert Southwest Gallery in Palm Desert. When the Saddleback Art Gallery in Santa Ana, California, began its notable recognition of Western artists, he became one of the popular painters to exhibit there also.

His first sketches as a child, he recalls, were with water colors, using sable brushes belonging to his mother and by the light of an old kerosene lamp.

Delano says that at one period of his life he came to the conclusion that he was trying to do too much by himself and for his own good alone. He concluded that it was important to change his point of view to that of rendering a service for God. He credits this idea with having permitted him to go on to new heights in his painting: "I love my work and I am completely at peace in doing it."

Deep in the blood and spirit of artist Ken Ralston is the ardor of Montana pioneers. Out of this ferment of restlessness, inquisitiveness, imagination and wanderlust has come Ralston's power as a painter to depict the inner meaning of the rugged land in which he lives.

The signature "J. K. Ralston" on enormous and important historical paintings all

(Above) "Enemies at War," by J. K. Ralston. (Leon Kelly, Columbiana, Alabama.)

(Left) J. K. Ralston (right) and Bill Huntington, author of They Were Good Men and Salty Cusses, talking it over in Ralston's studio

over the West has come to mean not only authenticity but also the almost indefinable quality of the great artist: a fervent breathing into the subject of something of his own character, so that events appear not as a part of the dead past but as of the living present.

Ken Ralston lives and paints in his log house at Billings, Montana, in the very region where he was born and where his immediate ancestors had fought the wilderness when it was still in the throes of Indian turmoil, bloody massacres and battles destined to live forever in American annals.

His earliest memories after his birth on his father's ranch near Choteau, Montana, on March 31, 1896, concern the great Missouri River in eastern Montana just across

from the Fort Peck Indian Reservation. The Missouri, as it has done with other Western artists, surged mightily in his consciousness from the start. Here it was that Meriwether Lewis and William Clark had figured in one of the great epics of American history, after the Louisiana Purchase, when they arrived at the headwaters of the Missouri and were in desperate straits to save themselves from death in the great wilderness into which they had penetrated. Their experience later was to form one of the historical subjects of a Ralston painting, "Into the Unknown," commissioned by the National Park Service and designed for the St. Louis Museum of Westward Expansion under the 630-foot gateway arch gleaming in that city where so many

E. B. Quigley on horseback

Western adventures began.

Before Ken Ralston was to be able to sign "J. K. Ralston" on such a painting, however, it was necessary for him to breathe in and make a part of himself the spirit of Montana—the Montana in which his grandfather had settled several decades before his birth. From the time he was ten until he was fifteen, Ken Ralston was drawing pictures in pen and ink and making water-color sketches of the open range along the Missouri River. When he was fifteen he began painting in oil. Along with his painting, he was becoming a first-rate cowboy and was riding for many Montana ranches. When he was twenty-one, he went with a cattle train to Chicago, and was so impressed by the opportunities there that he stayed to study in the Chicago Art Institute.

At the outbreak of World War I he joined the Army and served in the Eighth Division, returning in 1920 to the Chicago Art Institute for additional training. After that he went back to the life of a cowboy, but he was torn between art and the active life of the range. Following his marriage, he and his wife went to the West Coast, where he became a professional artist for seven years. During this period he worked in Seattle, Spokane, Tacoma and Vancouver, as an artist in engraving plants and advertising agencies and as a free lance in newspaper illustrating, advertising drawing and silk-screen poster work. When his father died he went back to operate the home ranch, and then moved to the log cabin at Billings where he has been doing book and magazine illustrations, murals and oil paintings.

His subjects have ranged from Custer's last stand at the battle of the Little Bighorn to the meeting of Lewis and Clark with the Shoshones when Sacajawea, the expedition's guide, a Shoshone herself, succeeded in having her people rescue the explorers. The variety of his subjects has made Ken Ralston necessarily a historian as well as a painter. His knowledge in this respect is so great that he is in constant demand before historical groups.

In addition to painting he also has gone into the creation of bronzes. The Montana Historical Society of Helena has charge of the sale of the magnificent running buffalo which is one of his recent creations.

An ambitious boy who delivered newspapers on horseback and then raced the other newsboys on their ponies can thank a grandfather who taught him to draw for the beginning of his art career.

E. B. Quigley—known to everybody as "Quig"—finds that his first memories relate to his grandfather, Charles Honey, who would draw horse pictures by the hour to amuse the toddler who sat on his knee. From that time, Quig began trying to draw pictures too. He grew up to become a commercial artist and might have remained one, turning out pictures of bears and other animals for calendars and magazine covers, but a chance encounter

"Tight Rope," by E. B. Quigley

in the wilds of the Washington State cattle country changed all that.

On a hunting trip a generation ago, Quigley and a friend were traveling through the Simcoe Hills out of Toppenish. Suddenly, they encountered a bunch of cow ponies, including pintos and paints. Quigley was so delighted at the sight that he quit the hunting trip instantaneously and sat down to sketch the horses. While he was busy at this, a cowboy rode up and observed with some astonishment the artist absorbed in his task. The cowboy was L. Frank Green, foreman of the nearby Circle S Ranch. He became so absorbed in Quig's drawing that he invited him to the ranch. There he met all sorts of people, including cowboys, Indians, bronco riders and Johnnie Mennick, chief of the Yakima Indians. From Mennick he received an invitation to a wild horse roundup on the reservation. Subsequently, he turned out many of his finest paintings from the horses and events observed there. The chance encounter in the Simcoe Hills in fact turned him away from commercial art and in the new direction from which he has never deviated. He has done hundreds of oil paintings of horse and

cowboy subjects since that encounter in the early 1930's.

His boyhood in Park River—the place of his birth in North Dakota on December 20, 1895—and in Idaho had acquainted him somewhat with the "horse world," but he had never had the opportunity in his earlier years to devote time to painting horse subjects.

Always, though, he came back to expressing in oils his feeling for horsemen and Indians. The titles give an idea of the character of his paintings: "On the Prod," "Alarm," "Mired," "Remuda," "Flying Heels," "Saddle String," "Horse Heaven," "Rain of the Range," "Night Camp," "Unruly," "Cold Night on Red Hill," "Bunch Quitter" and "Trail Herds." The Merrihill Museum of Fine Arts near Goldendale, Washington, owns "Sundown on the Trail."

A simple man, Quigley uses a simple palette with only eight colors.

"Paint en masse, keep your colors loose so you can move them around, don't get bogged down with detail and small brushes, and have a real desire to master oil painting," he advises other aspiring painters.

His advice has worked for him.

(Above) *"Cool Waters," by Stanley M. Long.* (*The artist.*)

(Center right) *Stanley M. Long*

(Below right) *Robert P. (Bert) Strathearn with two of his paintings*

From stained-glass windows to bucking horses may seem a far cry for most artists, but for Stanley Long, if there's anything to all the talk about inherited talent, there may be a connection. Long has spent most of his life depicting range horses and riders in water colors, but his grandfather, George Stanley, expressed his talent in stained-glass windows for such institutions as Stanford University's Chapel and St. Mary's Cathedral in San Francisco. A wild horse may be out of place in a house of worship, and Stanley Long has had the discretion to keep his subjects in other environments, even though he obviously has shared his grandfather's artistic abilities.

Horses have been a part of his whole life.

Now, as he depicts them in every pose— running, bucking, walking, hard at work on the ranch—he reflects in the vigor and fidelity of his creations his own long-time observation and participation in Western range life. He learned while very young to break horses on the family ranch in Napa County, California, where the horses themselves appear to share the zest and sparkle of the wines for which the region has been famous for generations.

Even before he was old enough to try riding the wild horses, though, he was attempting to draw them. When he sat at the kitchen table in the ranch house at St. Helena as a child before 1900, his folks used to look at him and say, "He's going to take after Grandpa Stanley."

From the start, however, it was obvious that his subjects were never going to be saints and holy subjects in stained glass. The only thing he cared about was horses.

His family recognized his potential talent and encouraged him in his early attempts at drawing. When he was only nineteen, he gave up his favorite job of horse breaking and went to San Francisco to the Institute of Art, now known as the California Institute of Fine Art. His early effort to teach himself to draw bore instant fruit. He won a gold medal and in addition, a scholarship to the Académie Julien in Paris. After his three years at the institute in San Francisco he went to France.

When he returned, the entire West beckoned to him because it was the domain of the horse, in which he continued to be so greatly interested. Almost from the start, he found that he was more at home in water colors than any other medium.

"It's because you must get the spirit, the extemporaneous feeling, the airiness, the activity and the lightness which you just can't find in the opaque oils," he explains. "Some do very well in oils, but for me it has to be water colors—it gives me the feeling I want to create."

A tremendous influence in his artistic life has been his friendship with Fred Maxwell, the artist who for a long time has operated San Francisco's Maxwell Galleries. Maxwell recognized the special talents of Stanley Long, and began to further his career when he opened his gallery.

In the midst of his artistic career Long managed to spend seventeen years as an art teacher in Polytechnic High School in San Francisco. He now lives in San Carlos.

Few bankers are known for their "give-away" tendencies, but Robert P. (Bert) Strathearn has been different.

He has not only been a successful banker but also a cattleman, cartoonist and oil painter, and he has given away his oil paintings all over the country because he never wanted to get money for them or to become a competitive artist. Strathearn's extraordinary career—he was a banker in Moorpark, California, for many years and a Production Credit Association director for Ventura—has included not only service with *The Los Angeles Times* and *The Los Angeles Express* in the old days as a political cartoonist but also decades as a working cowboy dating back to the 1880's.

Most of Strathearn's life has been spent in Ventura County, where his father came in the 1870's with the first purebred Angus cattle in southern California. Bert grew up in the true tradition of the Western cowboy, breaking horses, driving and branding cattle and carrying on all the infinite duties of a ranch.

More than thirty years ago, Strathearn went from cartooning into other art, beginning with etchings. His work was so meticulous that a doctor friend told him that every muscle he had depicted was correct. Soon he was working in both water colors and oils. It was at this time that his generosity began to be manifest. So many people wanted his paintings because of their authenticity that he could have had many sales, but he refused. Instead, he gave away his paintings to friends who admired them.

Recently, the quality of his work was

(Above) *Ernest Tonk*

(Left) *"High Range," by Ernest Tonk. (D. K. Yorath, Edmonton, Alberta, Canada.)*

recognized, when the National Cowboy Hall of Fame requested and received several of his major paintings. Previously, Strathearn had made his most generous gift of fourteen oil paintings to the *Western Livestock Journal*, published by his long-time friend, Nelson Crow. These were hung in the office of the *Western Livestock Journal* at Anaheim.

Buffalo Bill, as in other instances, can take part of the credit for having helped start the successful art career of Ernest Tonk. The scene was Chicago, where nineteen-year-old Tonk lived, having been born in Evanston, Illinois, on November 24, 1889. The time was 1908, and Buffalo Bill told Ernest Tonk, after seeing some of the boy's drawings, that he should try to follow in the footsteps of Remington and Russell while there was still an opportunity to see some of the genuine Old West.

Tonk was so impressed by Colonel Cody's advice that he traveled west and began work-

ing as a cowhand, wrangler and logger. Always along the way he was seeking a special place which would fit into his plans to be a painter. Finally he arrived in Cashmere, Washington, and felt that this was it. Nearby were Indian reservations and ranches and fine horses. To keep himself going, Tonk operated a fruit ranch, and then, when the seasonal work was out of the way, he devoted all his time to painting. He was such a keen observer and possessed such an ability to put down what he saw in sketches and paintings that he began to attract attention far outside the borders of Washington. News of his talent traveled as far as the film colony in southern California. There, at Universal Pictures in the early 1920's, Ernest Tonk was engaged to paint action scenes from which film directors laid out their shooting plans. He moved to Glendale, California, and worked for Universal Pictures and then Metro-Goldwyn-Mayer for many years. During all this time he found opportunity for additional painting on his own. When he finally gave up most of his film work, he continued to paint all the time, rotating between southern California and Cashmere.

In Cashmere was created the Willis Carey Historical Museum, named for a friend of Tonk, and Tonk volunteered to do a mural in the building. The subject chosen was a gathering of Indians in 1879 at the mouth of the Wenatchee River for a famous series of horse races, the last involving the Methow, Chelan and Wenatchee tribes before they were placed on reservations.

Tonk's success has been so great that his talents were solicited by Walter Foster, who puts out "how-to-draw" books, and Tonk, who now lives in Garden Grove, California, wrote and illustrated one of these showing how to deal with horse and cattle subjects. Foster said, "The Old West is almost a thing of the past, but Ernest Tonk has captured it."

In the family, Dorcas Birchim is called jestingly "the little old lady cowboy artist." Actually, despite the teasing of her children, she is an extremely young-looking woman who remains feminine even while painting spirited scenes of the bull-dogging of a steer or the taming of a wild bronco. This seeming contradiction is accounted for by her environment and her familiarity with everyday details of ranch life in the Owens Valley of California near Mount Whitney. She was born Dorcas Haynes in Danville, Indiana, on December 9, 1923, and she married into a third-generation ranching family in Owens Valley, so her children are descendants of well-known pioneers of the region such as James Birchim and · Frank Shaw. The chief obstacle in her art career has been lack of time, as she has reared four children and carried on home duties. Still, in the last few years, Mrs. Birchim has turned out enough canvases for exhibits in regional shows and the annual Death Valley Encampment art show every November. She

(Top) "A Bum Steer," by Dorcas Birchim. (Dr. and Mrs. David B. Sheldon, Bishop, California.)

(Bottom) Dorcas Birchim

has also found enough time to start the Sierra-Desert Art Association, and has been its president for three years since its founding.

Dorcas began drawing at an early age, and became familiar with outdoor life by riding at the pack station at Mammoth Lakes in the Sierra. She attended the University of California at Los Angeles for three years as a psychology major, then left to join the Marines in World War II and served for almost two years. She has been successively teacher, private tutor and social worker. Her painting began only about four years ago, but she immediately showed great facility. She says she has been influenced by Andrew Wyeth and R. Brownell McGrew more than anyone else.

"Painting is essential to my own well being," she comments. "I like the challenge and the necessary discipline of painting. I have fun every day, usually quietly, and enjoy life so much that the urge to draw, paint and write to communicate my astonishment and excitement at living becomes a compulsion."

Her "astonishment and excitement at living" are communicated to her painting. They breathe action, dust, sweat, movement and all the virility of outdoor Western life.

"I never consider failure," Mrs. Birchim says. "The entire pack hasn't been dealt so there can be no failure, just the promise of change."

Her daughter and youngest son are promising artists, and she is encouraging them to carry on in this just as they are carrying on the family tradition of ranching in the Owens Valley region. They still have a long way to go, though, to catch up with "the little old lady cowboy artist."

Somehow, the ranch seemed to have been waiting there for him along the South Fork of the Shoshone River many a year, yet it had taken Bob Meyers a long time to respond to its call. He had been in New York, and it had been in Wyoming. When he finally saw it, he knew that his career in the East must come to an end and that his activities must be transferred to this region alongside Yellowstone Park.

So he packed up his wife Helen, his son Tom and his daughter Carolyn, his easels and paintbrushes and books, and took the long road to Wyoming. Since 1960, then, Robert William Meyers and the Circle M Ranch have been a unit. Meyers, before he yielded to the blandishments of Wyoming, had been a successful New York illustrator for many years. He was known to readers of *The Saturday Evening Post, American, True* and *Argosy*, and for the advertisements he had done for many national accounts. Most of these illustrations reflected his inner urge to be someplace else than New York, although he had been born there on June 17, 1919. They nearly all pictured a Western subject. He had been influenced by such artists as Harold Von Schmidt and Nick Eggenhofer, both specializing in Western paintings, and Norman Rockwell, Fred Ludekens and Donald Teague.

The Circle M has now become unique among ranches in the West because its owner not only does all the ranch work but also conducts art classes along the Shoshone River under the willow trees. When he is not instructing a ranch guest on the handling of a paintbrush, he may be out welding, shoeing, branding, castrating, doctoring a sick cow, injecting a horse against infection, building a fence, farming or driving a team. As he says, "The saddle horse is still a necessary part of ranch life where I live."

"The Old West is fast disappearing," he states. "I would like to record in painting the West as it is lived today on my ranch and in this spectacular valley."

He has exhibited at the Society of Illustrators and Grand Central Galleries in New York City, the Whitney Gallery of Western Art in Cody, Wyoming, and the Desert Southwest Galleries at Palm Desert, California. All his work reflects the intimate knowledge he has of the everyday life which goes on at a cattle ranch.

Meyers is one of the few painters who was motivated toward an artist's life by seeing Western movies when he was a boy. This was about his only opportunity for contact with the West until he was old enough to travel—and to find the Circle M, and his true home.

(Above) *"Saddle Busters," by Robert Meyers.*
(Byron School System, Byron, Wyoming.)

(Below) *Robert Meyers*

"When you start 'hearing things' out of the past, it's time to decide whether you are an artist or a medium!"

That's the wry conclusion of Melvin C. Warren of Fort Worth after an experience on one of his painting trips to west Texas. He and his wife Lucille had gone to old Fort Davis while Warren was painting a series, "The Forts of Texas." As they stepped out of the car near the historic fort which had witnessed so many stirring events during frontier days, Mrs. Warren exclaimed, "You can almost hear the bugles!" In a moment, while Warren was parking the car, his wife stopped, turned pale and cried out, "I did hear a bugle!" Warren knew she wasn't joking, but he said, "Come off it, you just thought you heard one."

He and Mrs. Warren then hiked around the area and finally went into the museum. Suddenly, Warren himself heard the loud and unmistakable sound of a bugle call. He blanched a little, too. But then, to his relief,

Melvin C. Warren

A tempestuous night is the theme of this painting by Melvin C. Warren

he discovered that on the stroke of the hour a recording plays a bugle in keeping with the atmosphere of old Fort Davis.

His presence at Fort Davis typifies his deep interest in history and his desire to chronicle it in his paintings. He admits "a creative urge to record on canvas the mood and feeling of the West." He is convinced that the ability to grasp the "feeling" surrounding a certain scene is a vital element in the efforts of any painter.

"You have to attain this in such a thing as a distant thunder shower promising to bring relief to a thirsty desert or in an electrifying stampede of frenzied cattle, with all its danger to a struggling cowboy," he has said.

From earliest childhood, Warren was heading toward an artistic career. He began riding when he was five and drawing horses at about the same age. By the time he was twelve he was experimenting in oil painting.

His contacts with cattle and horse subjects came at an early age. He was born in Los Angeles on March 19, 1919. While he was still a small child, his family moved to ranches in Arizona, New Mexico and south and west Texas. Every day he came in contact with the picturesque life of the cowboys, and

within him there grew the urge to record this life in paintings. He served four years in the United States Air Force during World War II, and after that he decided to live in Fort Worth as the center of the kind of life he wished to portray. He went to Texas Christian University and received a degree in Fine Arts in 1952. Since then he has devoted his time to art in one form or another.

At first it was a job as a commercial artist. Then, one day he went home and told his wife that she was looking at a full-time oil painter. He had decided at last to do what he wanted to do. Now he works in Fort Worth in a studio that is a replica of a ranch bunkhouse.

Warren uses earth colors—browns, reds and yellows with contrasting grays—for most of his paintings. He is so critical of himself that he is able to complete only about four paintings a month. President Lyndon B. Johnson acquired four of his paintings, and other purchasers include Governor John B. Connally of Texas, the famous King Ranch, and Southern Methodist University of Dallas. Outlets for his paintings include the Grand Central Galleries in New York and the Fort Worth Art Center.

(Above) R. Brownell McGrew astride his new Appaloosa colt

(Left) "The Dinneh" (the Navaho word for "people" and their name for themselves), by R. Brownell McGrew. (Mr. and Mrs. M. McArthur, Jr., Davenport, Iowa.)

His paintings for the book *Frontier Forts of Texas*, published by the Texan Press in Waco, illustrated the text of eight prominent historians who dealt with the most colorful of the many forts constructed before or around the time of the Mexican War.

"It's the essence of the subject that I'm after," Warren says.

This "essence" has gained so much nationwide recognition that he had been unable to keep up with the demand for his paintings.

A single goal in art has failed to satisfy R. Brownell McGrew. He keeps pressing on from one to another.

In his technique, he has sought for many years the perfection of the old masters, yet his subject matter has varied as he has changed his objectives in the upward climb along the difficult artistic path he chose early for himself. Always the wilderness called to him. He

responded. Now he lives so far out in the wilds—he and his family drive eighty miles to church on Sundays—that he is close to the land and the people he depicts. He lives in Cottonwood, Arizona, between Jerome and Flagstaff, in a region where ranching of the old Western type still continues, and where the Indians who form such a great part of his subject matter reside.

To Jimmy Swinnerton, the cartoonist and Western painter who himself has continued active painting up into his nineties, McGrew gives credit for inspiration by the subject he likes best.

"Sketching in the Indian country with Jimmy Swinnerton began my consuming interest in these magnificent people," McGrew relates of his interest in the Navahos.

He is so intent upon painting that he finds very little time for anything else except his horses. He is devoted to them.

"Everything is wasted when I am not working myself," he admits. "When I get tired of painting I can always draw."

He is one of those who did not at first recognize the lure that the outdoor West was to exert upon him. He was born in Columbus, Ohio, on September 16, 1916, and went to school in Alhambra, California, where he still was not particularly aware of the call of the desert or the Indian country. This attraction was to come later. In his early career, his goal was primarily portrait painting. During his attendance at the Otis Art Institute in Los Angeles he concentrated on portraits. Nevertheless, while he was there he won the coveted John F. and Anna Lee Stacey Fellowship in landscape painting. He accepted the scholarship and carried on in landscape painting for a time, but returned to portraits.

Then he felt another urge. This was to paint the desert. So great did this compulsion become that he moved to the Palm Springs area and devoted several years to desert subjects. These ranged from the dry beds of arroyos (with the rocks and pebbles so natural-looking that they seemed to be in the third dimension) to trees and mountains.

"There is a great difference in natural colors in the desert which you can't find anywhere else," he says.

When he moved on to a new objective in the Navaho country, he carried with him the experience gained in this desert period. His paintings now reflect a combination of enthusiasms and skills.

He thins down his paints in conformity with Renaissance and Florentine paintings, which he has studied intimately. Then, after the paintings are completed, he uses a heavy varnish to bring out anew the beauty of his original colors.

He is at home painting both large groups of Navahos and simple portraits with the fidelity which he has learned through decades of experience in portrait work.

Bill Bender

His love for horses emerges in many paintings which are filled with the typical, small, wiry horses of the Indian reservation. Of one of his own horses he says, "The palomino is my real buddy and the joy of my life."

Whether it be portrait, landscape, Indian or horse, the mastery of artistic subject matter by Brownell McGrew comes through to the viewer with such tremendous impact that there is an involuntary and automatic recognition that "this is a McGrew."

My first good peek at the world in

(Above left) *"Racing the Storm," by Bill Bender.*
(W. H. Marsh, Tyler, Texas.)

(Above right) *Sketchbook exercises by Bill Bender*

(Left) *Sketches by Bill Bender*

general was in a little town of 2,500 in California. School to me was a necessary evil, and from the first day I trotted in for my three R's I was plumb certain the only way to make a living was in the wide open spaces, astraddle an ol' pony an' drawing thirty a month as a cowboy. This I was sure didn't call for much education, but a heap of practical savvy that could only be scooped up from a different breed of person than my teachers. But law is law, so to school I went and plumb through the twelfth grade to boot.

It wasn't long after that I was adrift in the field of hard knocks, making a living by the sweat of my brow and the bumps on my body from rodeoin'. I was enjoying every minute of it till one day . . .

A vagabonding nightmare suddenly changed everything in the rodeo world of Bill Bender, who starts his life story in the above words. He was born in El Segundo, California, on January 7, 1920, and soon afterwards started drawing horses on the bathroom door as a prelude to his bronco-riding days.

He had been making the rodeo circuit when he was about twenty-one, and had left his buckskin, Smoky, in the Owens Valley of California while he was wandering up north. He had been a packer into the Sierras at Bishop and Lone Pine and had worked for the Forestry Service in addition to riding bucking horses. One summer day he came back and picked up Smoky and started riding from Bishop via Lone Pine to his old home in El Segundo several hundred miles away.

"Anything that took walking I wouldn't do," he explains.

He began riding down the Owens Valley

in the blistering heat of August. When he reached Red Mountain, a ghost town which once had been a roaring mining camp, his horse was suffering from thirst and Bill stopped and bought him a couple buckets of water, because they didn't give away water in that region. From the water seller he heard about a man who wanted a wild horse broken. Bill meandered out to a desolate little shack and found the man with the horse. He made a deal to break it for ten dollars. The horse was tied to a snubbing post in the corral. Bill settled his black Stetson on his head and started out to begin the job.

"I never even got on him," he recalls. "He kicked me in the belly and that's the last thing I remember."

When he came to, it was dark and he was lying outside the corral, his head on the saddle and his hat on his chest. No lights were visible in the house and the owner of the horse was nowhere to be seen. The whole world seemed to be reeling.

"I was sort of goofy," Bill says.

He skylined his horse and started to drag himself over to him. He discovered his ribs were broken and he took off his wide German belt and put it tightly around his chest. In his hazy condition he thought he would try to ride to Victorville where an uncle lived. The heat was a torment.

The next few days were blurry. The horse became so weak that it was necessary for Bill to get off at intervals. He would hang onto the horse's tail for support and stagger along. A rattlesnake would buzz and Bill would shoot the snake and then proceed.

At one point he crossed a highway and encountered some drunks in a car. They had no water, but they gave his horse some beer and one of the women put a wet handkerchief on the horse's nose.

Finally, Bill and Smoky wound up in a reservoir near Victorville. Bill dunked himself and the horse drank his fill, and then they made their weary way on to the edge of town, where a rancher told Bill he could sleep in a haystack. He crawled in and went to sleep.

By coincidence, it was a ranch where Bill's uncle was working. In the morning the uncle came on the job, and the ranch owner said, "If you need any help there is a bum sleeping out in the haystack." Bill's uncle went out and looked, and remarked, "That's my nephew!"

The uncle gave Bill temporary help, and then Bill went into horse trading ventures down by Los Angeles. Months went by and Bill failed to recuperate from the internal injuries he had suffered when the horse kicked him. Successive doctors put him on a diet of milk and orange juice for a year, but nothing seemed to do any good.

"It took me about ten years to get over that one," Bill explains, "and I still can't stand to drink a glass of milk!"

He was periodically laid up during these miserable months, and during these times he made attempts to write stories and illustrate them. He took some of his work to Paul Bailey, editor and publisher of Westernlore Press in Los Angeles, who gave him some frank advice.

"You can't write or draw either one very well, but if you have to do one or the other, I would suggest that you stick with the sketching," Bailey said.

This just about decided Bill to give up literature and art and go wandering to South America, but he made one more attempt with a story and sold it for thirty-five dollars. He remembered Bailey's advice about sketching, and decided that he would try to get in touch with the famous cartoonist and painter James Swinnerton, who was enjoying enormous success with his cartoons "Little Jimmy" and "The Canyon Kiddies," and also with his oil painting. Bill managed to become acquainted with Swinnerton and was permitted

(Top) CHARROS, by Ernesto Icaza, painted about 60 years ago, shows Mexico's daring riders. The spectacular competitions for which they are preparing have been traditional for centuries. (Ernesto and Blanca Alvarez, Posada Loma Motel, Fortín de las Flores, Veracruz, Mexico.)

(Lower) BIG EAT, by Joe De Yong, is a striking example of the talent of this protégé of Charles M. Russell. De Yong is uniquely distinguished in having lived in Russell's home for 10 years while absorbing knowledge of the painting of the American West. (Joe De Yong, Los Angeles, California.)

SMOKE TALK, by Charles Marion Russell, is one of the most famous paintings by the man who, with Frederic Remington, is accorded top rating among Western artists. He was at home depicting the cowboys and Indians among whom he lived. (National Cowboy Hall of Fame.)

FROZEN SHEPHERD, by Frederic Remington, shows the compelling realism of the drawings and paintings by this artist who loved Western life. (Hammer Galleries, New York City.)

(Top) TEXAS, by James Boren, is a study in quietude by a native Texan who now is art director of the National Cowboy Hall of Fame. Boren has lived in a number of Western states and has absorbed the flavor of the land, which gives authenticity to his paintings. (National Cowboy Hall of Fame.)

(Lower) PRECIOUS WATERS, by Fred Harman, Jr., catches the spirit of the pioneer period, and is a fine example of the versatility of this artist who originated and for 25 years drew the cartoon strip "Red Ryder" for many millions of readers. (Robert Schroeder, Kansas City, Missouri.)

THE LEADER'S DOWNFALL, by W. R. Leigh, has had other titles: "In a Bad Fix" in 1927 reproductions, and later, "The Master's Hand." The painting is on permanent loan to the Cowboy Hall of Fame. (Mr. and Mrs. Luther T. Dulaney, Oklahoma City, Oklahoma.)

THE PICK OF THE BUNCH, by William Moyers of Albuquerque, reflects the intimate knowledge of cowboy life possessed by this Atlanta-born painter. Moyers has been active in ranching in Colorado and other parts of the West. (Mr. and Mrs. Marvin Hoffman, Dallas, Texas.)

(Top) RIDERS AND COLT CROSSING STREAM, by Robert Meyers, embodies the painter's deep feeling for the Wyoming country, where he operates the Circle M Ranch. He was formerly a successful illustrator in New York. (Mrs. Harold G. Davidson, Santa Barbara, California.)

(Lower) STRANGER IN TOWN, by Melvin Warren of Fort Worth, catches the spirit of loneliness which at times besets all cowpunchers. It is one example of the variety of subjects handled by this artist, who is widely known for a historical series on famous early Texas forts. (John M. Gray, Dallas, Texas.)

RIDING HIGH, by Nicholas Firfires of Santa Barbara, is a sample of the virile realism of this six-foot two-inch cowboy-painter who was born in San Luis Obispo County and absorbed California lore from vaqueros on the old ranches. (Mr. and Mrs. W. Harmsen, Wheatridge, Colorado.)

(Top) THE LIAR'S HOUR, by Charlie Dye, typifies the style of this New York illustrator whose magazine covers with Western themes were familiar to most Americans. He lives on a wooded hilltop in Sedona, Arizona. (Walter Bimson, Phoenix, Arizona.)

(Lower) PAUSE ON THE WAY TO THE SING, by R. Brownell McGrew of Cottonwood, Arizona, shows the use of vivid colors and the command of figures and landscape characteristic of a painter whose works often have the high gloss associated with the old masters. (O'Brien's Art Emporium, Scottsdale, Arizona.)

(Top)   PORTRAIT OF A WESTERNER, by Robert Rishell of Oakland, is an example of the remarkable use of light by a painter whose scope ranges from portraits to horses. The subject is Don Stevning of Coachella, California. (Desert Southwest Art Gallery, Palm Desert, California.)

(Lower)   ODD MAN OUT, by Iowa-born George Marks of Albuquerque, catches the spirit prevailing before a rodeo when cowboys are matching for places. This painting hangs at the New Mexico State Fair in Albuquerque, where it won a recent annual purchase prize. (New Mexico State Fair.)

MUY PRONTO, by Frank Tenney Johnson, embodies the vigor for which he was noted. His great talent earned him laurels as a jacket illustrator for Zane Grey novels and as a painter who captured the zest of Western life. (Jamison Galleries, Santa Fe, New Mexico.)

RANGE CHUCK, by Olaf Wieghorst of El Cajon, California, is in its tranquillity in sharp contrast to the animated scene portrayed by Mr. Wieghorst in the jacket painting of this book, and reveals his versatile touch. (Mr. and Mrs. Bud Winsby, El Cajon, California.)

(Top)   TWO OF FIFTY-FIVE, by Bill Bender of Oro Grande, California, depicts a pair of the many border riders who patrol the international boundary between Texas and Mexico to prevent cattle from crossing from one side of the Rio Grande to the other. (Helen Bender, Oro Grande, California.)

(Lower)   PACKING OUT OF THE CANYON, by G. Harvey, is in a mood and tone often adopted by this resident of Austin, Texas, who has been winning wider and wider attention, including that of the White House. His full name is Gerald Harvey Jones. (Dr. and Mrs. James Cornette, Canyon, Texas.)

(Top) THE MOUNTAIN MAN, by Gerard Curtis Delano of Denver, Colorado, and Opdyke, Illinois, displays the inimitable color and authenticity of the paintings of an artist who portrays faithfully the historical West and the Indians of its plains and mountains. (Gerard C. Delano, Denver, Colorado.)

(Lower) FREEDOM ENDS, by E. B. (Quig) Quigley of Portland, Oregon, reflects the long-time concentration on Western subjects of a man whose association with cowboys and Indians has made him acquainted with every aspect of their lives in the West Coast region. (Jim Brown, Portland, Oregon.)

ROUGH GOING, by Burt Procter of Corona del Mar, Newport Beach, California, crowns a lifetime of study aimed at the artistic goal of "combining design with realism," an attainment which has made a Procter painting instantly recognizable. (Mary Stephens, San Diego, California.)

(Top) COWPUNCHERS is by John Hampton of Phoenix, who has served as president of the Cowboy Artists of America. Hampton, born in New York, was irresistibly drawn to the West, where he has become one of the outstanding painters portraying the region. (Cowboy Hall of Fame.)

(Lower) FLYING HOOFS, by Bernard P. Thomas, indicates the predominant interest of this cowboy painter. Born in Wyoming, he now makes his home in Florida, where he has made an outstanding reputation in many cities for the quality of his murals. (Tucker Gallery, Sheridan, Wyoming.)

to accompany him on painting trips. Bill wanted to paint horses and cattle and ranch scenes because those were the things he knew best, but Swinnerton discouraged him.

"Learn the subtle colors of the desert first and then go back to horses later," he advised.

As the years passed, Bill developed a style of his own. He and John W. Hilton went under the auspices of the Air Force to paint pictures in Vietnam, Thailand and the Philippines. These paintings were presented to the United States Air Force Academy at Colorado Springs for its permanent collection, which had been gathered under the direction of Lieutenant Colonel George C. (Bob) Bales, head of the Air Force art program.

From this experience and on many new painting trips into the Navaho and Hopi and ranching country of the West, he rounded out his abilities and broadened his scope, sometimes with setbacks and disappointments, but always with a questing spirit. Often he gets up at two or three in the morning and paints steadily for six or seven hours "to use the best part of the day."

Recognition at last began to come from many places. As the result of a mural painted in the Public Library of Rockport, Texas, he was made "honorary citizen of Texas" by Governor John Connally. Soon afterwards, he and his wife Helen (Li'l ol' Hel) were house guests of Mr. Justice Tom Clark of the United States Supreme Court and Mrs. Clark, in Washington, D.C. On this trip, J. Edgar Hoover personally escorted them on a tour of the Justice Department. In New York, at the Grand Central Galleries, arrangements were made for additional showings of Bender's Western horsemen paintings, which have proved extremely popular in the East. Roy Rogers in 1967 asked Bender to hang a dozen paintings in his museum in Apple Valley, California. This resulted in a "one-man gallery" based merely on a handshake-contract in the old western way.

In recent years, Bill Bender has gone back more and more to his first love, the painting of horse and cattle scenes with the technical ability he has gained through the years of struggling with color and landscapes.

People never can be sure when they see Lenore Sherman whether she is carrying a painting box or a bag of magic tricks. This painter of the West started out as a professional magician, ventriloquist and comedienne, and still continues in these pursuits despite the fact that she has become a successful artist. In both realms—the stage and the arts—Lenore Sherman displays such tremendous zest that she impresses everyone she meets with her ebullience.

She signs her art with only an initial for the first name, and many persons who meet her exclaim, "Why, I thought from the strength of your paintings that you would be a man!"

Lenore Sherman is extremely feminine despite her ability to paint vigorous rodeo scenes.

"Being an impressionist, I feel drawn to the action and color in rodeos," she explains. "There is a thrill of the pioneering spirit and courage in our West—the cowboys, prospectors and settlers. To me this suggests the spirit of America."

She is forthright in her defense of the impressionistic technique in painting cowboy subjects.

I believe that within all things are beauty and the spark of immortality [she says]. When I paint, I try to capture the essence of the subject. Great detail does not interest me. I want to put onto the canvas only the things that seem to me to be shouting to be said about that particular person, place or thing. When I am successful, my painting contains some truth about that subject.

Lenore Sherman was born in New York

Lenore Sherman in her studio with painting "Out of the Chute"

City on May 11, 1920. She refuses to think much one way or another about the passage of years.

"I'm determined to stay young all my life, especially on the inside," she insists.

When she went on the stage for a vaudeville career, she came by her talent naturally. Her father and mother had been active in amateur theatricals and met when they were playing leading roles. Lenore began to feel some leanings toward painting when she was sixteen, but she was actually about thirty before she proceeded with it. In the meantime, she had become highly successful as a ventriloquist and comedienne and with magic tricks. When she went into art work she studied with fine teachers such as Leon Franks, Egnar Hansen, James Couper Wright and Hayward Veal, the English impressionist. From them she gained the technical ability to couple her love of horses with that for the other subjects she paints, including, notably, flowers. She has won numerous awards and prizes, and her work hangs in homes all over the United States and in Canada, Australia

and Europe. Among owners are George M. Straszer, assistant to the editor of *The Los Angeles Times*, and Mrs. Straszer. Perhaps the only critics of Lenore Sherman's work are those who, looking at her bag of tricks and her paintbox, suggest that possibly she has mixed a little magic with her pigments.

A flash of sudden spiritual inspiration in a moment of despondency started a thirty-four-year-old cowboy on a brilliant art career. A. Kelly Pruitt relates that, after a lifetime of trouble and despair, he experienced an "awakening" in which his latent talents were activated for attainment of the goals he had hitherto sought in vain.

Since 1958, when this occurred, he has gained wide recognition for his Western paintings, has had one-man shows in this country and as far away as Rome, and operates his own art gallery in Taos, New Mexico. Kelly Pruitt was born on February 9, 1924, in Waxahachie, Texas. He says that he first straddled a horse when he was two, and became a working cow hand at thirteen.

My earliest memories are of the oil fields in Texas and Oklahoma [Pruitt recounts]. My father was an oil-field pipeline walker who followed the boom towns. In those days, when oil towns sprang up out of the black earth in one night, it was not easy to find houses, so many homes were nothing more than tents over dugouts. My early years were in an unsettled atmosphere —listening to the talk of knife fights and shootouts, of hop-heads, and rich oil strikes farther on. The tent pegs would come down and the scene would change, but not the smell of oil, or the talk of killings.

Then the dreadful Depression caught us in its relentless grasp. When I was six, I was pulling a cotton sack alongside my father—when the cotton could be located.

By the time I was ten, I had attended more than one hundred different schools; the embarrassment of not knowing the lesson, as I had never learned to read, and

(Above) A. Kelly Pruitt beginning beeswax sculpture to be cast into bronze, "Taking in a Wild One," 1965

(Left) "Trail Boss," by A. Kelly Pruitt. (Mr. and Mrs. Warren Yeeno, Palo Alto, California.)

the dread of the bullies, made my life miserable.

When we moved to Presidio, Texas, where my mother refused to move any more, I was pretty discouraged with school. I had seen cowboys and horses, lonely riders off in the distance, or an occasional cattle drive. I loved the sun-browned Mexican vaqueros who came up with the cattle. They were my idea of real men.

The cowboys apparently liked me and could always find a horse for me to ride. I learned quickly to speak Spanish and throw a rawhide *reata*. By the time I was thirteen I knew I was ready to try it on my own.

One day he walked out of school, never to return. He left Presidio, and for the next four years worked for some of the largest cattle ranches in Texas. Then, as World War II broke out, seventeen-year-old Kelly Pruitt joined the United States First Cavalry at Fort Bliss. He saw the last six months of the horse cavalry and shipped overseas with the mule packs to New Guinea, India, Burma and China.

In Burma he met a Buddhist monk named Singh Ye, and later, in India, studied with him in a Buddhist temple. This simple man taught Kelly many beautiful principles of life and art.

After the war, Kelly drifted from job to job, from country to country. Finally he went to sea. He did not make a good sailor. The barges stank, and he was forever seasick.

"I felt there was no place on earth for me," he recalls. "The land had rejected me, the sea refused me. One black night I stood in torment on the cliffs overlooking the Pacific Ocean."

At this black moment he experienced, without warning, an unexpected sensation of peace and tranquility and an assurance of future success through spiritual guidance. This, he says, has been borne out during the last ten years.

He soon started painting. His paintings were accepted. Now he is successful in life and in business, and has a beautiful wife who believes in him and his art. The Pruitts have a little adopted daughter, Anna Marie. They spend six months of the year in their Gallery of Western Art, in Taos, then go to Rome for the rest of the year, where Kelly is currently working on bronze sculptures. His life story has been filmed in a motion picture, *A Lamp in the West*. His writings have been published at home and abroad. He is in demand as a speaker.

His memories of the vaqueros in Presidio when he was a boy cause him to paint many Mexican cowboys even to this day. His paintings are prized by such celebrities as Jimmy Stewart, Ken (Festus) Curtis and Paul Harvey, the broadcaster, and by colleges and universities.

All his attainments he attributes to that "moment of enlightenment" in his time of travail.

The creak and bump of Conestoga wagons seem to emerge with almost physical force from the drawings and paintings of Nick Eggenhofer. The fidelity which has put him in the forefront of those who portray the wagon-train era of America has brought upon him many requests for illustrations of books. Volumes such as Ramon F. Adam's *Come and Get It* and *The Old Time Cowhand* might seem less meaningful if they lacked Eggenhofer illustrations.

The fact that Eggenhofer lives in Cody, Wyoming—the heart of the Buffalo Bill country—is appropriate. As a boy in his native Bavaria, where he learned something about horses by riding them in the fields and brushing off horseflies, his favorite game was cowboys and Indians. This resulted from the Eu-

Nick Eggenhofer

ropean craze for Western American adventure, inspired by visits by Buffalo Bill and his Wild West Show. Eggenhofer shared in this enthusiasm.

When he did come to this country it was natural for him to take up Western subjects. He has studied Conestoga wagons, horsemen, cattle and all the varied panorama of Western life for many years. His intimate acquaintance with wagons has come from personal observation. He likes to relate that, as late as 1925, he saw a ten-horse trader in New Mexico, and he remembers when mail in the outlying regions was delivered by buckboard. He has talked to Montana and Wyoming pioneers and absorbed the lore which since has gone into his faithful depictions of the wagons and the people who accompanied them on the westward trek.

"String Team," by Nick Eggenhofer. (Read Mullan Gallery of Western Art, Phoenix, Arizona.)

A boy who became a mural painter at the age of six has gone on to attain recognition as an artist in oils, whose extraordinary sensitivity in figures and portraiture is gaining wider and wider acclaim. Bill Hampton was so proficient by the time he had reached the ripe age of nine that he won a statewide contest with a sculpture titled "Water Buffalo" after having already been kept busy creating murals on the walls of the school house in his native Simi Valley, California.

Born May 10, 1925, Bill grew up on a ranch in the Simi area and started painting horses and vaqueros at an early date. His love of horses has continued through life, and now his daughters Kathleen and Susan own horses in Apple Valley, California, where Bill and his wife Alice live.

A veteran of the Navy Air Corps during World War II, Hampton tried working in the Walt Disney Studio after he returned but found that his real interest lay in other fields of art. He began the long struggle to become a professional painter.

"Bill is most content when he is working," says his wife. "He paints every day at least 12 hours and sometimes works clear through the night."

In addition to his horses and portraits of cowboys, Hampton has specialized in Indian girls and children, either nude or semi-nude, with flesh tones of such splendid quality that his work is instantly recognizable. He admires the perfections of the old masters and manages to capture an element of Rembrandt in his creations.

For fun, he does magazine covers with horses and riders and old-time sheriffs, dating back to his acquaintance with Western characters on the Tapo Ranch in the Simi Valley.

(Above) "Cowboy," by Bill Hampton. (Mr. and Mrs. William Riffle, Santa Ana, California.)

(Right) "Bucking Horse," by Bill Hampton. (Mr. and Mrs. William Riffle, Santa Ana, California.)

A tall native of North Carolina who became a New Mexico cowboy and hunted lions in the wild country outside Silver City has gone on to become a Western painter. On the artistic side he can trace inherent talent to both his father and mother but his own success has come from persistence in working toward his goal. Bill Freeman, born August 17, 1927 in Greensboro, N.C., was only three years old when his father died. The father had been a portrait painter and his wife, left with four small children, decided in desperation to try to finish portraits which he had not completed. This courageous mother in turn became the art teacher of her son, Bill.

Bill Freeman grew up at the country

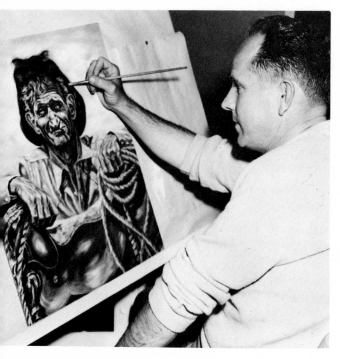

Bill Hampton

place of his mother's father outside El Paso and, between swimming in canals and exploring the Rio Grande, began trying to draw the plaster tigers, elephants, lions and bears his mother used in her art classes. After cowboying in New Mexico and Arizona and Wyoming he began painting big game animals and eventually illustrated a book on javelina by Ted Knipe. When he was 30, Bill Freeman went into fulltime painting.

He and his wife, Jackie, live in Phoenix, Arizona and also have a summer home and studio they have built themselves in the Blanco Basin near Pagosa Springs, Colorado.

"When I paint horses," Freeman says, "I try to make them appear either at work as I have known them, as pack animals or at play while running free."

A distinguished painter who has been devoting so much time to the art of others that he has had little time to paint is Paul Rossi, director of the Gilcrease Institute of American History and Art. Born in Denver, Colorado, October 1, 1929, Rossi succeeded another native of Colorado, Dean Krakel, in the Gilcrease position when Krakel became managing director of the National Cowboy Hall of Fame in 1964.

Harry Jackson, painter and sculptor who has exhibited both paintings and bronzes at the Cowboy Hall of Fame was born in Chicago in 1924. "The Stampede," "The Range Burial," and "Settin' Perty" are among his best-known works. He maintains studios both in New York City and Camaiore, Italy.

Lon Megargee, after a youth spent in the desert and mountain country of Arizona, went East to study art at various schools, such as the Pennsylvania Academy of Fine Arts, the National Academy of Design, N.Y.; Art Students League; Pratt Institute Art School of Brooklyn and the Cooper Union Art School, N.Y. It has been said that Megargee revealed in his work the "particular gift for capturing the spirit and fun of the Southwest which he loved so well." One of his works best exemplifying this quality was "Cowboy's Dream" which he painted for his friends at the Arizona Brewing Co. and which was later used as a double page spread in *The Saturday Evening Post*, Sept. 30, 1961.

Once the name "Fred Fellows" was well known for steer and calf roping on the rodeo circuit but now it has come to signify a Western artist with a growing reputation. Fellows, born in Oklahoma, became a saddlemaker in California, then went into rodeoing, and still later into advertising art.

Finally in 1964 he and his wife Jackie and their four children moved to Bigfork, Montana, where he devotes his time to painting.

"Few contemporary painters of the West are better qualified," says Van Kirke Nelson,

(Above) *"Water Stop," by Bill Freeman. (On loan to Arizona Public Service Co.)*

(Right) *Bill Freeman with his American saddle-bred mare, "Feminine Touch"*

M.D., of Kalispell, Montana, about Fellows. "People who love the outdoors and ranch life will understand."

Dr. Nelson, who has encouraged such artists as Ace Powell and has gathered a large collection of art in the Charlie Russell country, remarks that Fellows considers "color and draftsmanship in a painting as the most important things."

Fellows has had exhibitions at the Russell Gallery in Great Falls and at the Montana Historical Society in Helena, and in California, New York, Paris, Rome and London.

Many artists have specialized in some particular form of "cowboy art" or touched the perimeter of this sphere. Robert Scriver,

(Above) *"The Home Seekers," by Fred Fellows.*
(Van Kirke Nelson, M.D., Kalispell, Montana.)

(Left) *Fred Fellows*

a taxidermist of Browning, Montana, has won a reputation for the sculpturing of animals, including horses. Ernest Berke is celebrated for his sculptures in the Northwest. Andy Anderson is particularly known for his wood carvings. Down the years and in the present, those depicting the cowboy in one way or another have included Henry Balink, Henry H. Cross, Paul Dyck, Joe Grandee, Carl Runguis, Harvey Young, Robert Amick, Thomas H. Benton, Laverne Black, William de la Montagne Cary, Gilbert Gaul, Philip Good-

win, Earl Heikka, Edgar Payne, and Rufus Zogbaum. Darol Dickinson of Colorado, a member of the Cowboy Artists of America, paints horse portraits. William Hall, a Las Vegas casino worker, paints horses in his spare time.

The name of John S. Curry is associated with scenes in southern Utah. A splendid example of his work, showing cattle heading into a canyon, with a cowboy in the foreground, is in the collection of Ben Hibbs of Philadelphia, former long-time editor of *The Saturday Evening Post,* later an editor of the *Reader's Digest,* who has had special opportunities to view the work of illustrators, cover artists and painters.

A MIRAGE PAINTER IN PALM SPRINGS

Sometimes an artist paints a historic scene without realizing its portent for the future.

That was the way with gentle, poverty-stricken Carl Eytel.

This German immigrant boy, born in Stuttgart, always longed, for some mysterious reason, to be a cowboy in America. When at last he worked his way to this country in the latter part of the nineteenth century, he eventually became a hired hand on a big Miller and Lux cattle spread in the San Joaquin Valley of California. There he developed his great innate talent for drawing and painting cows, bulls and steers, catching every posture of the animals.

When Eytel became a desert painter at remote springs near the base of Mt. San Jacinto in Southern California, he attracted the attention of George Wharton James, the naturalist and author, and traveled with him by pack outfit. All this time Eytel was so poor he could not afford canvas and paints, and depended upon the generosity of such friends as James Swinnerton, the cartoonist and painter, to supply him with these.

In 1903 Eytel somehow got a large piece of canvas and painted one of his most imposing pictures.

It now has become historic.

The painting shows eight Herefords, three palm trees, and some pink and blue mountains—with nothing else except sagebrush. What makes it important is that the scene thus depicted is present-day Palm Springs, a site covered with millions of dollars worth of luxury hotels, spas and golf courses.

11
COWPUNCHERS IN CARTOONS

New-type roping, Mexico, 1700s (stage 1)

Those smells of Western sage and cattle dust travel far. Somehow they were wafted, at least symbolically, as far as Nova Scotia, Canada, Orange, California, and St. Joseph, Missouri, in at least three cases—and as a result millions of persons were entertained and their imaginations enriched. Out of the enticement of the West, felt by three boys in those widely separated spots, came the entirely fresh "art form" of the American cowboy. Previously, cowboys had been painted by famous artists who appreciated their role in the building of the Southwest, and they had been written about by authors who depicted them in words as some kind of modern knight in blue jeans and chaps. But now they were to emerge as the idols of the whole population in a new medium of public communication. This was the cartoon.

In every age the transmittal of ideas has been carried on by whatever means was developed at that time, from Babylonian mud bricks to the printing press.

In England, France and America the political lampoon came into being so that unpopular kings, prime ministers, presidents and "bosses" could be depicted in distorted, caricature form, such as that used devastatingly against "Boss" Tweed in nineteenth-century New York. However, for quite a while the idea of adapting this technique and using drawings in the public press to create fictional characters carrying on their activities every day for the benefit of newspaper readers failed to materialize.

Nobody, apparently, will ever settle the question, "Who started the cartoon strip?" but first mention must go to James Swinnerton who, in 1892, in William Randolph Hearst's *San Francisco Examiner* gave to read-

"And The Worst is Yet to Come," J. R. Williams cartoon, NEA Syndicate, April 22, 1939. (Saddleback Art Gallery, Santa Ana, California.)

ers a continuity of interest in "The Little Bears and Tigers," drawings which came to be recognized and followed from day to day. Swinnerton's "Little Jimmy" added to this feeling of kinship with the characters portrayed in the ensuing "comic strips" or "funny papers." "The Yellow Kid" of Richard Felton Outcault in the *New York World* in 1896 and "The Katzenjammer Kids" of Rudolph Dirks in *The American Humorist* in 1897 carried the continuity further. "Buster Brown," "Mutt and Jeff," "Maud the Mule" and "Happy Hooligan" also contributed to cartoon merriment.

One subject, though, was neglected. Cowboys and the open range either had not implanted themselves sufficiently in the public mind to generate a cartoon strip, or editors who passed on such matters were cold to suggestions along this line. Everybody else, from coal miners to newlyweds, had become established cartoon material before the cowboy ever got his nose in the ranch cookhouse of the cartooning fraternity.

Then, maybe late—but at any rate not *too* late—the three boys from Nova Scotia, Orange and St. Joe galloped up with a whoop and a holler and started slinging ink. They lassoed fame for their subjects and for themselves.

Out of their efforts came "Out Our Way," "Way Out West," and "Red Ryder." Each dealt with cowboys but in a different, individualistic way.

The three artists creating the strips were, respectively, J. R. Williams, Clyde (Vic) Forsythe and Fred Harman, Jr. They came to their tasks with amazingly different backgrounds, but with the one common factor of a complete knowledge of the subject and a burning desire to put it all down on paper in cartoon form. All necessarily gravitated to New York at one time or another because it was the center of their journalistic world, but none stayed to become a New Yorker; each heeded the insistent call of the West and returned there. Two eventually became distinguished oil painters in the region they loved best; and the third created notable Western bronze statuary, and could have painted too if he had not been so pressed with his cartoon work and the grind of operating a working cattle ranch.

Williams could hardly be listed as being a Nova Scotian, except that circumstance caused him to be born there because his American parents were in that region on a business assignment for a United States utilities company. When they returned to their native country, Jim Williams began the seemingly unrelated series of jobs which finally landed him in the cattle country and set him on the path he was to follow the rest of his life.

Once he got a whiff of New Mexico he knew he had found what he had been seeking. This was when he had landed on the Frank McMurray Ranch of White Sands, New Mexico. The ranch was about as far out

"Spring." Oil painting by J. R. Williams. (Saddleback Art Gallery, Santa Ana, California.)

in the midst of nowhere as could be found on the continent. It was in the rugged Dog Canyon section near the Tres Hermanos Mountains. Jim Williams' job in this vast expanse of mesquite land was to build fences, carry water to the stock and chop wood.

During this experience in the wilds under the most primitive conditions he was learning how to be a cowhand and meeting all sorts of people—wanted men fleeing the law, government mountain-lion hunters, dudes, real cowboys and squatters—and storing them all up in his memory. After a while, he drifted down to Oklahoma, helped in the roundups of the Indians' cattle, and then joined the United States cavalry and played football on the same team with George S. Patton, a lieutenant at the time and later the great general of World War II.

Here he did his first "drawing." He tatooed some of his cavalry buddies and tried a few drawings and paintings for Army raffles.

But even yet he was not really started on an artist's career. His folks in Ohio talked him into becoming a machinist, and that became his trade. In his spare time during the seven years of this period, though, he began turning out droves of cartoons, which were promptly turned down by every editor in the country. He was sticking with one kind of cartoon—the panel, or "square," as he called it—in which all of the action was compressed into one picture, rather than being drawn

J. R. Williams riding at rodeo. (Saddleback Art Gallery, Santa Ana, California.)

out in a sequence as in the comic strip of several pictures. Finally he was signed up by the NEA Syndicate in Cleveland, and began doing "Out Our Way," "Worry Wart," "Why Mothers Get Gray" and "Born Thirty Years Too Soon," for a list of newspapers which soon grew into the hundreds. Into "Out Our Way" he put the characters he had been storing up in his mind during his wanderings. It embodied the essence of all he had observed and learned on cattle ranches, the full flavor of his own personality and sense of humor. In a more serious vein, he modeled cowboys

"The Land of the Free," J. R. Williams cartoon, NEA Syndicate, August 19, 1947. (Saddleback Art Gallery, Santa Ana, California.)

and horses for bronze statuary.

From his earnings he was able after a while to make his boyhood dream come true. He bought a cattle spread on Walnut Creek in the wild Arizona country out of Prescott, and began the career with horses and cattle which always had beckoned to him. When he was not ranching, he was out hunting. In between, he did his cartoons. But, as he said, there wasn't enough time to do everything right.

He and his family finally moved to the Pasadena-San Marino area into a mansion hung with fine paintings by Nicolai Fechin and other artists, but his heart always was out on the open range. For cattle people, he held a special charm because he drew about human things appealing to everybody who was ever around livestock. In the hearts of millions there was personal sadness when he died, because to them J. R. Williams had become more than just an artist—he was the Cowboy in the Comics.

Among those of his close friends who

mourned him was his San Marino neighbor, Clyde (Vic) Forsythe, who in a different way, but also from intimate personal knowledge, translated cowboy life into cartoons, "Way Out West."

A double impulse constantly dominated the artistic career of Forsythe because he was impelled toward cartooning and Western painting at the same time.

In his blood he inherited the spirit of the O.K. Corral fight in Tombstone, Arizona—one of the classics of gunplay in the West—and a sense of humor which compelled him to express his own exuberance in hilarious drawings. Out of these twin factors, came, eventually, his fame as an oil painter of the Western scene and his equal prominence for "Way Out West," the comic feature catching the flavor of cowboy wit.

Although he was born in the new little California town of Orange, in 1885, he belonged to all of the West, and reflected it from the beginning. His father had actually been present just four years before Clyde's birth at the O.K. Corral fight when Wyatt

Trooper rescuing a companion. Bronze by J. R. Williams. (Saddleback Art Gallery, Santa Ana, California.)

Earp and his brothers and Doc Holliday had tangled with the Clanton-McLowery gang. The talk about Tombstone and other centers of the cowboy-gunman era sank into Clyde's consciousness from the moment he was old enough to listen. From earliest boyhood, he loved horses and drawing. When he started out at an early age to pursue his art career, he figuratively took horses and the West with him to New York. In New York he became an illustrator for newspapers, including the "newspaperman's newspaper," *The World*, before the era of photoengraving, and covered prize fights, horse races, murder trials and innumerable other events with his drawings. He turned out comic strips, including "Joe's Car," "Joe Jinks," "Dynamite Dunn" and, eventually, "Way Out West."

His imagination was stirred by his friendship with Bat Masterson, the Western "character" who had become a newspaper writer in New York.

Finally, the lure of the West became too much for him despite his art studies, his success, the ownership of a yacht, golf games with Damon Runyon and Grantland Rice, theater parties with Leo Carrillo, and association in the art world with Charles Dana Gibson, Howard Chandler Christy, Dean Cornwell and sculptor Jo Davidson. In 1920, at the age of thirty-five, Clyde Forsythe and his wife Cotta Owen Forsythe packed up and went to California, the home base in the West where Clyde intensified his painting. Before he departed, though, "Uncle Charlie" performed another of his acts of kindness destined to have a lasting effect in the life of a man who was later to be famous. He recognized the talent of Norman Rockwell and sent him to *The Saturday Evening Post*. This started an association which lasted more than half a century.

Once back again on his native heath, Forsythe began an extraordinarily productive career. He plunged into every phase of art

(Left to right) Clyde Forsythe, Walt Disney and Ed Ainsworth at Rancheros Visitadores near Santa Barbara about 1947.

related to cattle, horses, cowboys, the desert, and the history and lore of mining camps. He painted sunsets, burro prospectors, and ghost towns with equal enthusiasm.

He went camping with old companions such as Walt Disney and Bob Edgren. Will Rogers, Leo Carrillo, Gary Cooper and Irvin S. Cobb, the writer, were his friends. He shared a studio in Alhambra for many years with Frank Tenney Johnson. It was a big cluttered place, full of Indian rugs, cowboy hats, models of burros and horses—and visiting artists. It often was used by such friends as Dean Cornwell, Norman Rockwell and Hughlette (Tex) Wheeler, the horse and cowboy sculptor, who also was a friend of J. R. Williams.

In this studio, Clyde Forsythe's hearty laugh and sulfuric jibes formed as much a part of the surroundings as the furnishings. The "Forsythe Sky" of an incomparable blue, the "Forsythe burro" with a character all its own, became his trademarks.

He was always on the lookout, too, for

(Above) *"Mojave Bronc Rider,"*
by Clyde Forsythe. (Drs. Jerome
and Cynthia Lengyel, Albu-
querque, New Mexico.)

(Right) *"Greasewood Gus,"* car-
toon *by Clyde Forsythe from*
Desert Barnacle, *published by*
Kate and Ed Ainsworth at
Coachella, California, December
21, 1945.

new talent. Discerning as he was, he must have detected it early in the career of another cartoonist who was a much younger man coming up to join him and Jim Williams in the affections of the reading public.

Fred Harman, Jr. was one of a pair of twins—but nobody knew it, not even his parents. His "twin" was named "Red Ryder." The twins were born too late to be Pony Express riders, but they did the next best thing—considering that two generations had passed since the hardy horsemen had ridden across the continent from St. Joe, Missouri, to Sacramento, California, carrying news dispatches while the telegraph line was being

constructed across that wild and dangerous region. At least, Fred Harman was steeped in pony express lore from the moment of his birth. He was born in St. Joe beside the roiled waters of the Big Muddy at the very spot where the harried and disheveled riders had arrived some forty years before, carrying the eastbound mail from California. He did not live in St. Joe too long, it is true, because his parents decided to go farther west and settle near Pagosa Springs, Colorado, in the southern part of the state near the New Mexico border, a region about as wild as could be found at the start of the twentieth century.

In this setting of rushing streams, big

mountains, the Continental Divide, trout lakes, big game and the genuine cow country, Fred Harman and his "twin" began their real life. It was from this early experience and later adventures in the cow country that Fred Harman developed the "twin," Red Ryder, the red-headed, two-fisted cowboy of the comic strip. Before this day arrived, though, Fred Harman was compelled to ride a long, rough trail in search of the success which he was certain lay just beyond the next mountains. He crossed many a range before he came to the goal.

A borrowed nickel, a lot of nerve and a chance meeting in an Eastern business office all figured in his experiences, before he could realize his full potential in the art world in which he had chosen his life work. The borrowed nickel episode, which became a turning point in his life, took place in Hollywood when Fred Harman was in his thirties after many a year of wandering around in search of the right trail. He had become a cowboy, all right, in the Pagosa Springs setting in the big Bronco Basin where he saddled and rode wild horses, herded cattle, hunted deer and bear, fished in the ice-cold streams and did all of the chores around the roundup ground and the shipping pens. Wanderlust, though, overcame him at intervals, and he left the wild mountains for other parts of the country. On one trip, he was drawn back by some instinct to old St. Joe where he had been born.

"All I had was in a gunny sack," he recalls. But, despite his lack of earthly possessions, St. Joe proved lucky for him. There he found Lola Andrews and married her, and in St. Joe was born his only son, Fred III. Harman paid for Fred's birth by selling his first painting.

He worked in St. Joe for a while and then in Kansas City and St. Paul, Minnesota, doing commercial advertising and illustrations. At one time, he and a young man named Walt Disney, who were both doing animating for cinema advertisements, tried out a film venture in Kansas City and went broke, and each then started on paths which, in each instance, led to spectacular achievement.

Fred Harman, still without knowing that he had a "twin," arrived in Hollywood with his wife and son and no certain prospects of any secure job. He made the rounds of the newspapers trying to sell drawings, and at *The Los Angeles Times* he met the Sunday editor. At that particular moment the *Times* was starring in its Sunday magazine a Western feature series, and the editor asked Harman whether he could write a story to go with a drawing.

"Certainly," replied Harman, who had never written an article in his life.

> Riding back to Hollywood on the old Red Car, I wrote the piece on some used envelopes, copied them off neatly, did a drawing to go with the story which was titled "Packin' a Grizzly," and went back to collect the fifteen bucks I had been promised [Harman relates]. The trouble was it was a check and I didn't know where to cash it downtown, and I was so broke I had to borrow a nickel to get home.

The article and drawing appeared in the *Times* on October 8, 1933. At this time, Harman was trying every sort of gag and gimmick to "get started." He and Curly Fletcher, the rodeo cowboy, started a magazine, *Ride*, which imediately rode to a fatal financial fall despite contributors like Yakima Canute, the bronco rider, and Emmett Dalton, the ex-outlaw. Fred did a little book on "Cowboy Lingo." He invented a comic-strip character called "Bronc Peeler," who quietly passed away without even a funeral notice. He started on a project called "Southwestern Indians as I See Them," and went to New York to promote it, but nothing happened.

An incredible coincidence then changed his life. Harman went in low spirits to the office of his agent, Stephen Slesinger, who

(Right) *Fred Harman*

(Above) *"The Pride of Texas," by Fred Harman. (Leland Davidson, Midland, Texas.)*

(Above right) *"The Contrary Longhorn," by Fred Harman. (Mrs. Fred Harman, Albuquerque, New Mexico.)*

handled authors and artists like Zane Grey and "Will James." While he was there, Fred Ferguson, president of NEA Syndicate of Cleveland, came in, asking, "Where is that fellow who tried to do that strip 'Bronc Peeler'?"

"He's right here," replied Slesinger.

Ferguson, astounded by the seemingly fateful meeting, immediately suggested to Harman that he try a similar strip but change the name.

So "Red Ryder" was born. The belated "twin" of Fred Harman had arrived at last!

"Red Ryder" was an instantaneous success. During the next twenty-five years he appeared with "Little Beaver," his young Indian partner, in at least seven hundred newspapers, with forty million readers, was wildly received abroad, helped in World War II, made international tours and became an American institution, the symbol of cowboy life.

As success was heaped upon success, Fred Harman—always striving eagerly toward a new future as he had done all his life—began oil painting. At the Red Ryder Ranch in his beloved Pagosa Springs country, he began to depict the cowboy and range scenes amid which he had been brought up.

Thousands of visitors flocked to the ranch each year to see "Red Ryder"—or his twin Fred Harman—in person. Finally, after

"Red Ryder" comic strip by Fred Harman

"Red Ryder" (Fred Harman) and "Little Beaver," an Apache Indian, on parade

years of entertaining with their old piano that bore many cattle-brand marks, Fred and Lola decided they must have a quieter existence to permit Fred to paint. They moved to Albuquerque, where they now live in a rambling New Mexico-type house with a big studio. He paints with an almost feverish haste because of the intensity which has marked his activities all his life.

"Many people have asked why I would give up the highly successful 'Red Ryder' comic strip for the unknown rewards of a western painter," Harman comments. "First of all, I quit the easy returns of commercial art and struggled five years to market 'Red Ryder' because of my love of the West and naturally the large income from a syndicated comic strip. I had always painted, and in 1960, when my son and his family were successful on their own and the years were ticking by, I swapped saddles for the permanent satis-faction of trying always to do something better—just as I strive now for each canvas to surpass the last. Naturally I paint only the West because I am a westerner!"

But "Red Ryder" as the twin of Fred Harman still does exist in this country and in many other nations of the world in the form of comic books, reprints of the old strips, films and television replays.

With his mementos about him—innumerable citations, Man of the Year in Colorado, honorary citizen of Texas, saddles, bridles, drawings, cartoons—Fred Harman revels in the fun of painting Western scenes and his stature in the art world increases.

He has found that you really can't give up a twin even if you try. He and "Red Ryder" both are so deeply entrenched in the affections of the public they are galloping merrily forward together into the bright sunset there in the New Mexico studio.

"DREAMS OF LONG AGO"

Even the most confirmed Easterners are unable, at times, to resist the Western theme in their art work.

Norman Rockwell, born February 3, 1894, in New York City, confesses that one of his first ventures into the cowboy realm was something of a gag. I have a friend who owns a Rockwell painting "Dreams of Long Ago" and it has always been one of my favorites. When I started writing *The Cowboy in Art* I sent a letter to Norman, an old-time acquaintance, and asked him about the circumstances that led him to paint this particular subject.

In reply he wrote:

Dear Ed:
I painted it for *The Saturday Evening Post*. As you know, I am no cowboy artist. In fact, at the time I painted it I don't think I had been West of the Mississippi. I am afraid it was just a gag. The model for it was James K. Van Brunt, who was very proud of the fact that he was the same height as Napoleon. He had been in the Civil War and the Spanish-American war and, in New Rochelle, where he lived, they said that there were marks of his footprints as he marched forcefully and bravely at every Fourth of July celebration. He had a moustache which I once measured eight inches from tip to tip.

Cordially,
Norman

12

THE COWBOY HALL OF FAME

New-type roping, Mexico, 1700s (stage 2)

America's top hands have been signed on for the finest spread in the country by a trail boss who never wore cowboy boots. The name of the outfit is the National Cowboy Hall of Fame and Western Heritage Center down in Oklahoma City. It all happened because a fellow who made denim pants for waddies decided the time had come for this country to wake up and begin paying proper attention to the real cowboys who created the West. At the very start he lined up Will Rogers, Charlie Goodnight, Teddy Roosevelt, Charlie Russell and rodeo rider Jake McClure as the main crew, and then waved in a lot of others who were waiting, lasso in hand, for the big roundup.

Chester Arthur Reynolds of Kansas City, board chairman of the H. D. Lee Company, manufacturer of the denim pants, was the originator of the plan for the National Cow-

boy Hall of Fame, which opened June 26, 1965. It took a long time for the idea to occur to him, but when it did, his lifelong inclinations and his business training led him, despite many obstacles, to carry the project through to success. In its magnificent reality the National Cowboy Hall of Fame stands today as a fitting memorial not only to the pioneer Westerners whom it was designed to honor, but also to Chester Reynolds, who died on December 11, 1958. He lived long enough to participate in the dedication of the Hall of Fame, and to join in the selection of the first five men to be selected for the permanent scroll that is a part of the institution—Rogers, the humorist; Goodnight, the pioneer Texas cattleman; Teddy Roosevelt, the Rough Rider and President of the United States; Russell, the painter; and Mc-Clure, the rodeo champion.

The Hall of Fame's basic purpose is to honor all the cattle pioneers who helped build up the Old West, as well as any modern cattlemen and cowboys who deserve the tribute. One of its other aims is to tell America's children the truth about real cowboys and what their spirit did to build up this country—and that is why "Western Heritage Center" was added to the title "National Cowboy Hall of Fame."

Each year, the Hall of Fame makes awards for books and films and, in other categories, for contributions to an understanding of the West and the perpetuation of its traditions. In all this the work of Chester Reynolds, the founder, has been carried on by loyal associates, including the members of the Board of Trustees from the seventeen Western states; Glenn W. Faris, executive vice-president; Dean Krakel, director; and James Boren, art director. The Hall of Fame constantly is acquiring Western paintings, saddles, wagons, and every sort of memento of pioneer America for its huge buildings, built in a style that uses as it main motif the appearance of a number of tents placed together beside an immense reflecting pool. The paintings and bronzes represent the work of Russell, Remington and other noted artists.

Mr. Reynolds was already in his sixties when he began the long, arduous task of trying to bring to fruition his idea for the National Cowboy Hall of Fame, although he actually had been tending toward some such creation ever since boyhood.

He was born in Fostoria, Ohio, on August 7, 1887, but his parents moved to Kansas while he was still a baby. Soon, though, he was lifting himself, in imagination at least, into a Western saddle. Against the arching sky, the retreating thunder of ten million hoofbeats was still echoing along the Chisholm Trail when, in about 1890 in Kansas, he started yearning to be a cowboy. All the tough-legged, high-rumped cow critters that had walked the cattle trail from Texas up to Wichita and Dodge City enthralled him. He dreamed of longhorns bellowing in the night. He practiced roping white-face calves by day.

Reynolds' story is different from that of millions of other American boys who determined to be cowboys, and weren't. While he wasn't either, he got there by another direction. The National Cowboy Hall of Fame shrine now has become a reality because Reynolds got seventeen western Governors interested in the project. Then it was always Reynolds who kept the red-hot iron on the project until it was branded and fenced.

As the climax of the many years of work by Reynolds, the National Cowboy Hall of Fame's Board of Trustees built the Hall of Fame and Western Heritage Center Building on a thirty-seven-acre hillside location just outside Oklahoma City where an expressway carries the combined traffic of U.S. Highways 66 and 77, and American tourists conveniently can stop to pay tribute to the heroes of the Old West.

I first met Reynolds when he was in the formative stage of his idea in the early 1950s. He was brought to me by my longtime friend, Nelson Crow, publisher of the *Western Livestock Journal*. Immediately, I was intrigued by the whole concept. I wrote in *The Los Angeles Times* about it. Later, Governor Goodwin J. Knight of California asked me to represent him at a meeting of the National Cowboy Hall of Fame Trustees.

When Reynolds, as a wide-eyed kid with a hankering for horses and cows, was roping calves in Kansas more than seventy years ago, there was no thought by anybody of honoring "the Old West." Everybody was too busy living it. From the time he could walk, Chester was around as tough a gang of Texas and Indian Territory cowboys as ever prodded a steer up the Chisholm Trail to Abilene. Gunsmoke and cuss words, bowlegs and boot heels

National Cowboy Hall of Fame and Western Heritage Center, Oklahoma City, Oklahoma.

became as familiar to Chester as the ground he walked on. It was only natural that, as soon as he grew old enough to think about leaving home, he wanted to "go West" and homestead. He decided to try Colorado—a coincidence, perhaps, because years later it was in Colorado that his National Cowboy Hall of Fame idea really got astride the mustang of reality. He picked his homestead spot in the middle of isolation. It was in eastern Colorado, thirty-five miles in one direction to the lonely Union Pacific tracks, and twenty-five miles the other way to the equally lonely Missouri Pacific. He filed on a homestead of strictly nothing—not a tree, not a shrub, just some short grass stunted and crimped.

The wind got a free whack at him. It came howling off Pikes Peak and all the rest of the Rockies, laden with sleet that stung like birdshot and loaded with snow that went sideways instead of down. That first winter, Chester survived in a shack that kept off some of the fury of the wind but offered little else in the way of comfort. He bought a few calves at five dollars a head and a couple of cows for twenty-five dollars, and had to build them a sod shelter to keep them from starving and freezing when the snow covered the meager grass. For the full required five years, though, Chester battled it out with nature and his

Clyde Forsythe admires a print of the Charles M. Russell painting "Signal Smoke," with Governor Dan Thornton of Colorado and Mrs. Frank Bennett. Governor Thornton was influential in the founding of the Cowboy Hall of Fame.

land. Some of his calves froze in a blizzard when they got covered with ice in a gully. He promptly skinned them when they thawed out and sold the hides for two dollars apiece.

At the cracker-barrels and the candy counter in the general store at McCracken,

Kansas, Chester had begun to notice with more than passing interest a pretty girl named Cora Hicks, daughter of a local cattle raiser and buyer. He thought of his lonely days and nights at the "ranch." It gave him courage to scrape up an acquaintance with the lovely customer. So, before long, he and Cora were married just as he received, from President Woodrow Wilson, the joyous news that the United States Government formally was bestowing up Chester Arthur Reynolds the title to the homestead duly described, in the state of Colorado, U.S.A. At this moment, the prospects appeared bright for Chester and his new wife to go into the cattle business and stay. But there was a long detour.

Chester decided he needed some quick capital. He wanted to try a fling at selling, because he liked people and he had some definite ideas. At the time, the H. D. Lee Company of Salina, Kansas—a small manufacturer of work clothes—was unable to get any buyers for a new type of "mechanic's suit," a garment that completely covered the body, as contrasted with the bib-type overall of the day, and actually resembled long underwear. Mr. Lee told Reynolds he did not think anybody was going to purchase the suits because of previous failure, but Chester persisted. He was permitted to take a few leftovers on the road. They were christened "unionalls."

His first stop was Superior, Nebraska. The residents of this small community were astounded to see a young man calmly parading the streets in a "monkey suit," a garb fully as fantastic to their eyes as any creations that might pop out of a spaceship now. They were so curious that they made inquiries. Various mechanics and artisans wanted to buy. Reynolds referred them to a local store and took to the surprised owner a sheaf of signed orders. That marked the start of a commercial career and the end of a prospective cattleman. Not only did Reynolds' little venture into sell-

Casey Tibbs on "Salty," Palm Springs Rodeo, 1954

ing—"just for a few weeks," as he told his wife—last for about forty years, but he also revolutionized the Western-clothing habits of the American people. It was Reynolds who, as sales manager and advertising director, took the first full-page advertisement for cowboy clothes in a national magazine, over the protests and grave doubts of other Lee Company officials, and thereby created an unparalleled and continuing demand for denim cowboy pants. Rising to be board chairman of the big H. D. Lee Company, in Kansas City, Chester Reynolds saw his blue pants adorn not only the working butts of cowboys on Western ranches, but the tender rumps of Eastern dudes and the gently rounded fannies of America's young women.

Still, always, despite success in the business world and financial security, Chester Reynolds, the boy who had roped calves, could not get out of his mind the thought

Dean Krakel, managing director, National Cowboy Hall of Fame and Western Heritage center

Dedication of the National Cowboy Hall of Fame at Oklahoma City

The dedication of the National Cowboy Hall of Fame and Western Heritage Center. Left to right, former Governor Roy J. Turner of Oklahoma, Will Rogers, Jr., F. W. Heine, Chester A. Reynolds and Cy Faillon.

of cattle and the open range. So it happened one day that he visited the Will Rogers Memorial near Claremore, Oklahoma, as a sentimental tribute to a man who epitomized the cowboy success story. Suddenly, as he stood there, he thought, "This is just for one man. Why not pay tribute to every cowman who helped build the West?"

As a first step, he decided he must have the active interest and help of the Governors

of the seventeen western states, where most of the American cowboy legend originated.

Where should he begin? He was hearing a lot about a young man in boots and wide-brimmed Stetson who was occupying the Governor's chair in Denver, Colorado. Dan Thornton, a transplanted Texan barely in his forties sounded like the kind of cowman to fit Reynolds' needs. Thornton was the son of a tenant farmer and had grown up in 4–H work in Texas, then had gone to Colorado and developed his own strain of Herefords so brilliantly that they had emerged as a distinctive type coveted by breeders, the TT, or Thornton Triumphant.

Reynolds tackled him with the Cowboy Hall of Fame idea.

"Go to it!" said Governor Thornton with characteristic directness. "I'll help."

The only trouble was that too much enthusiasm was built up. Not only did the Western states want a Cowboy Hall of Fame; each wanted the headquarters within its own borders. To top that off, each of fifteen or twenty individual communities in each state was belligerently positive it was the sole site for the national shrine which Reynolds was proposing. Instead of Reynolds having to chase people, delegations began to chase him. He organized an executive committee and then, with real diplomacy, appointed a "Site Committee" of which he was not a member. This group was headed by former Lieutenant Governor Ray Schnell of North Dakota as chairman. Serving with Schnell were Albert K. Mitchell, one of the most famous and colorful of the nation's cattlemen and president of the Chicago International Livestock Exposition; A. M. G. (Swede) Swenson of Texas, one-time All-American football star; Fred H. Dressler of Nevada; and John D. Lewis of Utah. Working along with these, unofficially, was Nelson Crow.

These committeemen needed to be a fearless lot. More than four hundred villages, cities, camp sites, buffalo wallows and prairie-dog towns were demanding the right to house the shrine. Somehow, the list of possible sites was cut to ten amid screams and sun-fishing by the outraged losers. The ten included Cheyenne, Wyoming; Miles City, Montana; Dodge City, Kansas; Colorado Springs, Colorado; Rapid City, South Dakota; Canyon, Texas; Las Vegas, New Mexico; North Platte, Nebraska; Oklahoma City, Oklahoma; and Prescott, Arizona.

The exhausted committee went into a huddle behind locked doors and took the dangerous but necessary step of eliminating more candidates—seven this time, leaving only three in the final running. These were Colorado Springs, Oklahoma City and Dodge City. Word was sent out that each of these could present its case to the National Trustees of the Cowboy Hall of Fame at a special meeting in the Brown Palace Hotel at Denver, prior to the determining vote. The date was set.

Denver has seen some strange sights in its time, particularly during the heyday of the spectacular *Denver Post* when publishers Tamman and Bonfils were indulging in every kind of Barnumlike antic to attract attention to themselves and their city. Still, all these were but as the gambols of a newborn calf compared with the rush of a Brahman bull, when decision day came. It was an invasion. By special train, bus, horse trailer, automobile and ox cart the rivals assembled. Each contingent brought the Governor of its state. Each brought bands. Each brought horsemen in full Western regalia, with silver trappings gleaming and leather polished to a mahogany sheen. The pavements echoed to the clatter of shod hoofs as the horsemen escorted high-stepping majorettes and blaring bands to the Brown Palace where, inside, the intrepid trustees headed by Chester Reynolds huddled for the showdown. Reynolds, as chairman of the trustees, invited the Kansans, the Coloradans and the Oklahomans to come out of the chute. The delegations obliged. For hour upon hour the persuasion and the arguments went on. The lusty spirits of Bat Masterson and Wyatt Earp were invoked. Grizzled trail herders and gaunt longhorns seemed to parade there in the big room.

At last the trustees voted. Oklahoma City received twenty of the thirty-two votes and was declared the winner. Governor Raymond Gary and former Governor Roy J. Turner, who had made the presentation for their state, danced in the aisle.

First Five Nominees for National Cowboy Hall of Fame:

(Above left) "Will Rogers," by Clyde Forsythe. (Rancheros Visitadores, Santa Barbara, California.)

(Above right) Charles Goodnight

(Below left) Jake McClure, rodeo contestant

(Below right) Theodore Roosevelt

(Below center) Charles M. Russell

THE COWBOY HALL OF FAME

The offers of Oklahoma were far from niggardly. A site on a gently rolling hill just outside Oklahoma City was donated—value one hundred fifty thousand dollars—for the shrine. A pledge was made for the citizens of the state to raise one million dollars of the five-million-dollar goal for the project.

Then, at last, came site dedication day in Oklahoma, November 11, 1955. More than twelve hundred horsemen paraded down the highway and across the site, with Chester Reynolds proudly watching it all. Flags of the seventeen Western states stirred in a light breeze. A Western bedecked cowboy band played. The Norse Stars, a drill team of sixty young women from Northeast Oklahoma Agricultural College, in flashy cowgirl costumes with white boots and hats, high-stepped before the band. Trustees from each of the sponsoring states were present. They were escorted to the site by Governor and Mrs. Raymond Gary, former Governor Turner and Mrs. Turner, Mayor and Mrs. Allen Street, Oklahoma's United States Senator Mike Monroney, and Oklahoma City Chamber of Commerce president, Ray J. Spradling. Will Rogers, Jr. announced the "Pageant of Flags."

Then Dr. G. Raymond Campbell, a Pres-byterian minister, delivered a prayer that since has gone all over America in tens of thousands of reprints. He prayed:

O Thou God of the open plains, who never made a man You didn't love, we pray that You will hallow this place in the memory of men of the saddle, that the best of the past can be carried into the future.

If sometimes, someone should imagine, up here on this hill, that he has caught just a whiff of the smell of bacon frying over an open fire, or the bubble of coffee boiling over onto the coals of the fire, or the creak of a tired saddle, and the evening lowing of cattle off in the distance, we'll thank You, Lord.

It is in the memory of the men who built this West, that we ask You to dedicate this place. And, Lord, up there on the high range where the grass is always green and a man's horse never gets tired, we pray that the boys are happy with what we are doing here. Amen.

Chester Reynolds' dream was being ful-filled, and the National Cowboy Hall of Fame was on its way, in good hands. It pleases me to think that, for sure, he is wearing celestial denim pants every day as he looks down with a happy grin at his handiwork.

13

COWBOY ARTISTS OF AMERICA

California Mission vaquero, 1800

A bunch of the boys were whooping it up one June night over a sarsaparilla, or reasonable facsimile, in Bird's Bar in Sedona, Arizona. In the companionable atmosphere they suddenly got a yen to organize something.

They were all interested in one subject so it was easy to decide what it would be. Out of their enthusiasm came the Cowboy Artists of America. The fellows in the little group were among the best-known painters of cowboy and Western subjects. Their decision to form an association grew out of their mutual enthusiasm for everything involving life on the open range and its portrayal.

The date was June 23, 1965. Since then, the organization has grown in scope and membership to a point where its members are drawn from many states, and it has become increasingly important because of the annual exhibitions it conducts at the National Cow-

boy Hall of Fame in Oklahoma City. The first of these shows was held in September, 1966, and proved so popular that it has become an annual event, with the cooperation and encouragement of Dean Krakel, director, James Boren, art director, and the board of directors of the National Cowboy Hall of Fame.

The Cowboy Artists deliberately have kept their group from becoming a sales organization. The members have retained all their individuality and private ventures, and have simply banded together for consultation, fun and the annual exhibits. At the outset, the choice for president was George Phippen of Skull Valley, Arizona, the remarkably talented sculptor and painter who was rising toward a zenith of recognition and acclaim. Soon afterwards, Phippen died a tragic death from cancer.

Painting of historic stagecoach tragedy by George Phippen. (Taos Art Gallery.)

In his place, the other members elected Charlie Dye of Sedona and, later on, John Hampton of Phoenix. Phippen, Dye, Hampton, Joe Beeler of Sedona, and Fred Harman, George Marks and Gordon Snidow, all of Albuquerque, were in the early little group. They and their associates who came in later included both painters and sculptors dealing in Western subjects.

For the most part, they lived in Arizona, New Mexico, Texas, Colorado and Wyoming, the heart of the country where cattle and horse scenes abounded.

A boy who took nature's oldest art material, the clay of the earth wet by new rain, and fashioned it into the form of men and animals, grew up to become the first president of the Cowboy Artists of America. George Phippen, the fifth of nine children in an Iowa farm family, discovered early that natural clay after a rain was easier to work with than dry clay which he tried to knead to the proper consistency himself.

While the family was living in north central Kansas near Emmett, George either would be drawing or he would slip away down in the pasture to a clay bank and make models of bucking horses and riders, cows, buffaloes, coyotes and other animals.

"I don't remember ever taking too kindly to school," George reminisced. "I remember much of my time being spent standing up in front by the teacher's desk because I'd been drawing horses instead of getting at my studies."

By the time World War II broke out he was in Tucson, Arizona, trying to become an artist. He went into the Army then and was in the service for almost five years. He had been married just before being inducted, and by the time he got out of the Army he and his wife had two little boys and two others were born later.

While he was in the Army George worked on his drawing and received encour-

(Right) *"Arizona Rock Hoppers." Bronze by George Phippen. (Taos Art Gallery.)*

(Below) *George Phippen in his studio, about 1957*

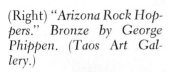

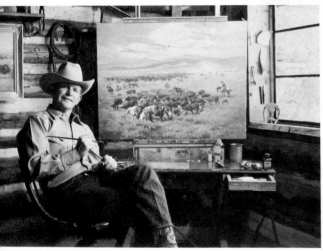

agement from artists, art dealers and collectors. This finally gave him, as he said, "the fantastic idea" of trying to get into the illustrating game, specializing on the horse and the cowboy and his surroundings, and wildlife. In his search for help in learning to be an artist he and his family went to Santa Fe, New Mexico, and there he received about three months' training from Henry Balink—"the nearest thing to formal art training I ever received." He began illustrating for small magazines and selling drawings and water colors wherever he could. Finally in 1948, he began oil painting and sold through the Taos Art Gallery of Thomas Lewis. Then his paintings were included in Christmas cards put out by Ed Trumble of Boulder, Colorado. Also he began to do calendar art for Brown and Bigelow.

It was in another realm, however, that George Phippen began to attain his greatest prominence before his untimely death. This was in sculpture. In 1958 he was commissioned by Robert Kleberg of the King Ranch in Texas to model the noted horse Wimpy P–1 for the American Quarterhorse Association. The sculpture was so splendid that it has become a standard of excellence for this type of horse art.

Phippen modeled all sorts of cowboy scenes and bull riders with an authenticity that gained him instant recognition throughout the country. He worked for a time in his studio in Prescott and then moved to the Lone Bar Ranch at Skull Valley, Arizona, where he resided until his death.

One of his sons, Ernie, now is manager of the Bear Paw Bronze Works which is casting Phippen's sculpture. Phippen's son Loren has been in the Army at Fort Myer, Virginia. His son Darrel is in high school and is a sketch artist, and a daughter, Winona, is in grade school. His studio in Skull Valley has been remodeled into a gallery for the benefit of the public.

George Phippen was so popular with his fellow artists that, when the Cowboy Artists of America was formed, it was only natural that they turned to him to be its first president.

A "big black bronc" which fell on him and sent him to the hospital started Charlie Dye on his art career.

The fall happened when Charlie was riding for old-time cow outfits in Colorado, Arizona and California. He was brought up

(Above) *"Top Hand," by Charlie Dye*

(Left) *Charlie Dye and his horse "Model"*

in the vicinity of Cannon City, Colorado, where he was born on October 30, 1906, and remembers horses, cattle and the rugged individuals who worked with them as part of the pattern of his earliest memories. He sketched almost from the time he can remember, but he says that the idea of becoming a professional artist never occurred to him.

After the bronco fell on him, though, while he was in the hospital he discovered the drawings and paintings of Charlie Russell. The ambition of portraying the life of cattlemen came to him at this time. He went to Chicago and studied at the Art Institute there and at the American Academy, and did commercial art in the daytime. Then he decided to try New York.

There he came in contact with the painter who, next to Charlie Russell, was most instrumental in shaping his future. This was Harvey Dunn, the great illustrator whose helpfulness to many artists has become proverbial. Charlie Dye persisted so purposefully that he became an illustrator for such publications as *The Saturday Evening Post, Argosy,* the *American Weekly* and *Outdoor Life.* His

magazine covers, always with a zest of their own and the feel of the subjects they portrayed, became known to millions of Americans. Although he was doing no Westerns at the time, Charlie was "the only real working cowboy artist in New York," a paradox which was about to be changed by yet another chance occurrence. He went to see a sister in California and was somewhat astonished at the relative unimportance of the Western art he saw.

"Hell, I could beat that," he said to himself, and he started out to do so. His efforts were encouraged by Jane Hyatt of the Village Gallery of Taos, New Mexico. Dye began exhibiting paintings there to pay for Western vacations and then built a studio in his native state of Colorado. He loved to go hunting and fishing to get subjects for his covers for *Outdoor Life,* but he soon found that his Western paintings were going so well that they were interfering with his magazine illustrating. Then he took another step and became head of the Colorado Institute of Art in Denver and began teaching other artists.

Once again, though, his own paintings

John W. Hampton

sold too swiftly for him to devote sufficient time to his teaching. Finally he moved to Sedona, Arizona, in 1960, and since then has devoted all his time to painting.

He and some friends own seven head of roping steers, and on Saturdays go out and amuse themselves by keeping in shape with the lasso.

I've always felt that the most beautiful animal created by nature (including man), was the horse [Charlie Dye muses]. To me every horse is just as much an individual as any person. I try to paint the truth as I know it and remember it about a life I lived as a young man. Whether or not cowboy paintings can be considered as great art does not concern me a damn bit. Such art records a time in history which interests many people, and among them are lots of old-timers who know which end of a cow eats, and I paint for that public. If a person has to be told what a painting means and what the artist intended to convey, I sure think it's a damn poor painting.

He still loves to ride and to help on roundups, in addition to roping for pleasure on weekends. He winters in Arizona, and spends the summers on the old home range around Westcliff, Colorado.

When he isn't painting, Charlie Dye likes to be out riding his twelve-year-old quarter horse, Model, using a Mexican bit which he says the horse likes.

As he looks back on his painting career, Dye likes to give credit (in addition to that going to Russell and Dunn) to his instructor, Felix G. Schmidt, in New York, who became a close friend and partner in a commercial studio.

When George Phippen of Skull Valley, Arizona, died after having become the first president of the Cowboy Artists of America, Charlie Dye followed him in office, and he in turn was succeeded by John Hampton.

The output of Charlie Dye is only about fifteen paintings a year, and this is insufficient to meet demand, but he refuses to give up the riding and other pursuits which keep him in touch with the subjects he depicts. In the 1967 Cowboy Artist Show at the National Cowboy Hall of Fame, the name on the first prize was that of Charlie Dye.

When John Hampton's mother in New York missed her clothesline rope, she would go looking for her son because she knew he was somewhere nearby roping fire plugs. John always was determined to be a cowboy. The streets of New York being singularly lacking in cattle and cow ponies, he was compelled to resort to all sorts of devices to satisfy this boyish craving. While he was still a youngster, coupled with his roping was his artistic effort. He began drawing horses as soon as he could handle pencils and crayons, and on rainy or snowy days when the fire-plug roping was out of the question he could still live in his imaginary world of the West.

When he was sixteen, *The World Telegram* conducted a contest for sketch artists. John submitted a rodeo scene. It won first prize and was published on October 22, 1935—a historic date in his life as he looks back. A little later he became acquainted with Fred Harman who had just started doing the popular comic strip "Red Ryder." Harman likes to recall that once as he was starting west, by automobile, John Hampton rode as far as Hoboken, New Jersey, just to have the feel that "he was going West, too." Soon after this, John got his first Model A Ford, and with this new mobility a thrilling idea entered his mind. He started out with his camping stuff headed west, destination uncertain. As it turned out, he landed in Silver City, New Mexico, in need of a job. He was advised that he ought to go farther out into the country, possibly to the McMillan Cattle Company ranch about twenty-five miles west of Silver City.

It was still pretty primitive out there [John recalls]. Cowpunchers still were coming through, and there weren't too many fences yet. Fencing is what has made the real change in the West. But when I started out to the McMillan Ranch I felt that I was right in the middle of all the West I had read about.

As I drove up to the ranch house and got out a small, taciturn looking cowman walked up to me and introduced himself as John McMillan. He said he'd been told about me and, "Just what do you have in mind?"

I told him I'd like to camp somewhere near water on his range and watch a cow-outfit in action while I did some painting.

He was looking me over as I talked. He looked kinda stern. I was mighty anxious to stay since I'd waited all my life for this moment and held my breath as I waited for his reply and finally he said, "Well, I guess you can camp near one of the windmills."

I was the happiest guy in the United States and tried to thank him.

"On second thought there's an old cow-camp not far away, you could stay in that. Would be better than campin' in a tent," he added.

I tried to thank him again.

"Heck," he said, warmin' up, "I just built a new bunkhouse here on th' ranch. There's an empty room next to th' cowboys that's got a wood stove and you can cook an' work in there an' be here on the ranch."

I was so overcome at this show of hospitality it durn near brought tears of gratitude to my eyes. I thought mebbe I ought to offer to pay some rent, and said so. He quit smiling and squinting at me and said, "If you're all right you can stay here for nothin' and if you're not, no amount of money will pay your way. Now go get your outfit and throw it in the bunkhouse."

It was the old West on that ranch.

Horses would be roped while it was still barely light enough to see them lining their ears up against the skyline. We'd ride out amidst joking and jingling spurs and be on a high point by sun-up. The sun was mighty welcome on those cold mornings. Many a yucca was set afire while we stood around to warm up.

(Left) *Joe Beeler*

(Below) *"Loose Cinch," by Joe Beeler. (Mrs. Joe Beeler.)*

I was at the bunkhouse when one of the cowboys brought word that Japan had bombed Pearl Harbor. Not too long after that I was in the Army.

I trained as an intelligence scout, went to the South Pacific and ended up in G-2 Intelligence and came out as a staff-sergeant. As soon as I came out I went back to Silver City, bought a small ranch on Greenwood Canyon near the McMillan ranch and near the town of Gila, New Mexico. I stayed in and around that country for twelve years before coming to Arizona.

During the ensuing years, as he was striving to attain the status of a real painter in oils, he did all sorts of other jobs. He got into the pulp magazines with drawings. He did layout for the "Lone Ranger" and "King of the Royal Mounted." All of this, though, was mere preparation for the work he wanted to undertake.

He lived at various times in Silver City and in Prescott, Scottsdale, and Cave Creek,

Arizona. Now, on Camelback Road in Phoenix he maintains his studio in his home.

When his paintings began to attract the attention of collectors, he was able to devote more and more time to this work. Soon he was exhibiting in top galleries, and one of his paintings was selected by the National Cowboy Hall of Fame to hang there permanently.

Hampton became president of the Cowboy Artists of America succeeding Charlie Dye.

His work attracted the attention of Martha McKelvie, wife of the former Governor of Arizona, and she and her publishers obtained the services of Hampton to illustrate her books, *The Fenceless Range and The Empty Sleeve.* This fitted Hampton's objectives.

"I deal mostly in Western history, which to me is the real Americana," he says.

From out in the corral by the side of the

roughhewn studio comes the sound of whinnies and nickers, as Joe Beeler paints away at his Western scenes. The horses are his, and their presence is part of the kind of life he lives. Up amid the red cliffs and great pinnacles of Sedona, Arizona, Joe Beeler lives with his wife Sharon and his young daughter Tracy and his son Joey.

The setting in which Beeler does his painting illustrates a point he likes to make in discussing the West:

> The cowboy hasn't changed much even today [he says]. Ropes, chaps, spurs, and all the gear, too, are pretty much as they used to be. It seems that everything I did when I was young pointed to this kind of thing as my subject. My family have been pioneers for generations in Missouri, Oklahoma, Kansas and Texas, and they were stock raiser, merchants, preachers, miners and even an outlaw or two. We have German, Irish French, and Cherokee blood in our veins, and all those pioneers participated in the early settlement of this country. So it isn't strange that when an artist cropped up in the bunch he would just naturally paint something as American as cowboys and Indians.

Joe was born in the southwest corner of Missouri in Joplin. He began drawing from the beginning.

"I was born with it, I guess," he comments.

When he was young, the family moved to Oklahoma where he grew up. He associated with cowboys and Indians, his own father having been part Cherokee. Because of his obvious interest, the Indians permitted him to attend powwows and to participate in some of their ceremonies. He joined in the dances with the young Indian men until he was nineteen or twenty. Having been brought up working for cow-outfits and hearing Jesse James stories and other lore of Missouri and Oklahoma, Joe Beeler became steeped in this Western tradition. It is characteristic that his own books are published by the University of Oklahoma Press, including his recent one, *Cowboys and Indians.*

He is genuinely convinced that the West of which there is so much talk still exists.

"The stuff is still going on," he remarks. "We don't live in a bunch of little pastures—this is big and rough country even yet."

His adobe home in Sedona is only a couple of minutes from the studio, and little Joey can ride his horse along with his sister Tracy down to see Daddy if they wish.

His first one-man show gave him prestige immediately. It was at the Gilcrease Institute in Tulsa, Oklahoma. Since then, he has exhibited at historical societies and museums and the National Cowboy Hall of Fame.

To keep his hand in, Joe helps with branding and the roundups in the Arizona country surrounding him. In addition to painting he has turned to sculpture, and his bronze "Sioux Warrior" won the best sculpture award at the 1967 National Cowboy Hall of Fame exhibition.

As Joe Beeler paints, the sound of his horses whinnying for him to come forth for a ride accents his sincerity and talent in portraying the West in which he was born and brought up.

On the big ranchos back of Santa Barbara lived true California vaqueros and *charros.* They came from a long line of Spanish and Mexican landowners whose way of life was devoted to raising cattle. Now, in that same region, the era of the ranchos has been brought to life anew by a man steeped in that tradition since he was a child.

Nicholas S. Firfires—"Nick" to everybody—has been so imbued with this spirit that he paints as if he were a participant in the events which shaped California.

From Santa Barbara each springtime for more than thirty years have sailed forth hundreds of men on the annual trek of the Ran-

cheros Visitadores, a trek dedicated to keeping alive the tradition of visiting from rancho to rancho as was done in the pastoral period.

Nick Firfires, as a member of the Rancheros Visitadores for almost a quarter of a century, has participated not only in this re-creation of old-time events but has added to it—in his art work and in his own experience with horses and cattle in the present century. After his birth November 10, 1917 on the Waunakee Ranch near Santa Margarita in San Luis Obispo County (not far from Santa Barbara), he spent the first twenty-four years of his life with horses. He was breaking horses at an early age, and associating with old vaqueros.

Nick began drawing so early he can barely remember it. After he had gained ranch experience he attended the Art Center School and the Otis Art Institute in Los Angeles. When World War II broke out, he served overseas with the Army Engineers, and did many sketches and paintings for Army publications, including portraits of military personnel and also water colors in Europe. Following the war, he concentrated on illustrations for Western magazines and gained continually a greater artistic proficiency. About ten years after the war, he decided to go in more strenuously for oil painting. His first show was conducted at the Biltmore Galleries in Los Angeles in 1960. Public acceptance of his work was so enthusiastic that he has devoted full time to his oil painting since then. He spends from eight to ten hours a day at his studio in Santa Barbara, although he continues to live on the Santa Margarita ranch.

The appearance of Nick Firfires, a six-foot-two cowboy who likes to wear formal Western clothes, fits the concept of an artist who knows his subject.

(Above) *A painting by Sandra Steele, only woman associated member of the Cowboy Artists of America*

(Above right) *Sandra Steele*

(Below right) *George B. Marks*

A young woman who paints with such force and power that she has been chosen as the only woman associate member of the Cowboy Artists of America has carried on a career combining art and horses. Sandra Steele —who was born in Las Vegas, Nevada, on July 18, 1938, and now lives in Van Nuys, California—has been enthusiastic about horses ever since she was seven or eight years old, even before she first became a horse owner at the age of twelve. Her father, an amateur photographer, encouraged her interest in drawing when she was very young, and she has carried this on to the point where she gained the technical ability to depict the horses in which she had always been interested. She was an art major in high school and attended Pierce Junior College in the San Fernando Valley in the Los Angeles area. Then she spent two years with the Famous Artists School and two

and a half years as an animation artist at the Walt Disney studio. Mrs. Steele's husband, George, is a wrangler at the Fat Jones Stables in North Hollywood, one of the largest suppliers of motion-picture livestock and equipment.

"Western paintings offer a challenge which I enjoy," Mrs. Steele explains. "I strive for accuracy in everything and spend as much time as necessary in research. I sometimes enjoy this as much as the painting, because I like to read history."

Mrs. Steele's seven-year-old daughter Debbie is interested in drawing, too, and shows indications of having ability. Mrs. Steele gives credit to Mrs. Kathryn Newton of Riverside who encouraged her and helped her through periods of disappointment when it seemed that the paintings would not come out right. Mrs. Steele has exhibited in the West Valley

"Riders of the N-Bar," by George B. Marks. (National Cowboy Hall of Fame.)

Artists annual shows, at the Farmers' Fair Art Exhibit, and at the Orange Show in San Bernardino.

Mrs. Steele considers her magazine work as her greatest success so far. Her work has great vigor, and there is nothing in it to indicate any feminine weakness. This capability in her rodeo and cowboy scenes led to the coveted invitation to become an associate member of the Cowboy Artists of America.

A grandfather who drove a stagecoach in South Dakota in the days of the Custer Massacre and other great Indian battles of the period influenced George Marks in the direction of Western painting. Marks is one of those attracted West by the Albuquerque "magnet"—that indefinable lure exerted by New Mexico to bring those artistically inclined within its borders.

Marks was born on September 10, 1923, in the sedate town of Conrad, Iowa, in a region more devoted to pleasure riding than

the hell-for-leather cowboy life of great cattle ranches. Still, Marks was influenced from childhood toward an adventurous cowboy career by his grandfather, George Lewis Marks, who was a cattleman and owned many fine horses.

George learned to ride even before he attained a conscious memory, and supposes that he did so with his father and grandfather as soon as he could walk. His interest in drawing also dated from earliest childhood, "ever since I was old enough to hold a pencil." By the time he was in his mid-twenties, after serving three years with the Marine Air Corps in World War II, he began formal art studies at the University of Iowa. He graduated with a B.F.A. degree and then took a year of graduate school.

At this time, the call of the West conquered. He moved to Albuquerque to continue art studies and to paint the Western scene.

"I don't suppose there is any more true

outdoorsman than the cowboy," he speculates. "His life and work are colorful and vital, and I wish to record not the make-believe aspect of it, but the factual and more interesting elements."

Marks was influenced, of course, by Russell and Remington, as so many Western painters have been, but he also greatly admires Jimmie Swinnerton, the ex-cartoonist and painter, and John W. Hilton, the desert painter, of 29 Palms, California, Buck Dunton of Taos, Peter Hurd and Andrew Wyeth. He continually haunts rodeos and ranches to get the true flavor of what he wants to put into his paintings. His initial interest in rodeos was stirred in Iowa where, at Sidney every summer, there is a great gathering of rodeo contestants.

One of his favorite painting spots is the Lee Ranch south of Magdalena, which borders on the federal Gila Wilderness Area and takes in part of the famous St. Augustine Flats. Another is the N-Bar Ranch in Montana, "where I worked with the cowboys and cattle and sketched and painted the scenes of contemporary ranch life."

He says that he has found most ranchers to be intensely interested in the modern artists who depict life on the range, and that they take pride in posing for such pictures.

Marks became a member of the Cowboy Artists of America because of his friendship with Joe Beeler of Arizona. New Mexico and other regions of the West find Marks in old clothes and with his sketching materials on the range dramatizing the life of the cowboy as he sees it today.

A living contradiction of the theory that a Western painter must have experienced some direct connection with the Old West is Gordon Snidow, who lives in the Rio Grande Valley near Albuquerque, New Mexico. He is one of the youngest contemporary cowboy artists, yet he has as definite a purpose as if he had lived fifty years ago.

"I paint things which happen every day that I can interpret—even if they seem commonplace they are worth recording because they represent the life on a cattle ranch in this period," he explains.

(Above) *Gordon Snidow*

(Above left) *"Waiting for the Herd," By Gordon Snidow*

(Above right) *Irvin (Shorty) Shope in studio*

(Below right) *"Trouble Ahead," by Irvin (Shorty) Shope. (Dr. William F. Cashmore.)*

Although he is in his early thirties, Snidow already has made an amazing record of accomplishment in output and in recognition. In the five years since he started competing, he has entered twelve art shows and has won one special award, six first, eleven second and three third places. At the 1967 New Mexico State Fair Art Show he was the subject of special attention—which he did not particularly relish. He exhibited a miniature of his painting "Waiting for the Herd." It won an award, all right, but it was stolen on the first day of the show and has never been found.

Snidow was born in Missouri on Septem-

ber 30, 1936, but lived and went to school in Texas and Oklahoma. His first "show" was in a P.T.A. exhibit in Tulsa. He began drawing horses on the farm of his grandparents during summer visits. After high school he enrolled in the Art Center School in Los Angeles, from which he graduated in the middle 1950s.

Snidow is a commercial illustrator and designer in Albuquerque, but he is devoting as much time as possible to his painting. He visits and works on cattle ranches in Arizona, Colorado, Wyoming and New Mexico. One of his favorites is the Y Ranch near the Gila

H. W. Johnson   (Above) *"When the Rocks Start to Move," by H. W. Johnson. Hypnotized from staring into darkness, the sentry imagines he sees moving shapes.*

Wilderness Area in the St. Augustine Flats of western New Mexico. At Old Horse Springs near the Slash Ranch he has joined in round-ups amid the pines and piñons, and has been able to catch fleeting moments of cowboy life.

"I feel a great compulsion to paint contemporary ranch life before it is replaced by modern technology," he comments. "I try to paint honest, fresh, new experiences happening in the West today and in which I am involved."

He and his wife, Sue, keep horses at their *ranchito* near the Rio Grande, so that his daughters Christy, eight, and Laurie, five, and his son Stephen, fifteen months, can grow up in the atmosphere of the West that inspires their father to carry on his art work.

When, many years ago, Amon Carter, Fort Worth publisher and art collector, looked around for a present for Will Rogers, he decided to give him a Western illustration by Irvin (Shorty) Shope. A third of a century later, long after Rogers and Carter have died,

Shorty Shope still is turning out the kind of drawings and paintings that appeal to all those who love the West.

Shope, born in Boulder, Montana, on May 11, 1900, has progressed continually since he first began drawing horses as a small child. His father owned a cattle ranch. As far back as he can remember, Shorty has been associated with cowboys, horses and livestock. He worked as a cowpuncher from the time he was about nineteen until he was in his thirties. He had been graduated from high school in Missoula and later attended Reed College in Portland, Oregon, then obtained a B.A. degree in art and history at the University of Montana. He studied with Harvey Dunn in New York, and later tried drawing a comic strip, "Rusty Rawlins," in Los Angeles. But he returned with his wife to Montana, which was the country he loved best.

Shope says that Edgar S. Paxson, "Will James," Charlie Russell and Dunn gave him the greatest inspiration. He has done more than twenty murals, most of them concerned

Tom Ryan

"The Ketch Hand," by Tom Ryan. Cover from Western Horse-man, *1968*

with major historical events. He has continued always to paint cowboys, and many of his paintings bear a nostalgic brand.

> My cowboy paintings are dated back a piece [he says]. They do not resemble rodeo or movie types. I do paint some modern stuff but it is from the back country where clothes look like they are worn and worked in. I do not care for the heavy quarter horse of today. I remember too well the slim trimness of half-thoroughbreds, their ability as cow horses and their capability to cover miles and miles and still be able to cut a cow or turn a herd of horses.

The authenticity of his easel paintings and his murals is based on actual experience.

> I rode when there still were neighborhood roundups with horses and cattle to which we went driving a string of horses ahead of us [he recalls]. We often rode down two or three horses a day. This was before the jeep and the trailer. I know how it feels to get off a tired horse at noon after he's

taken you 30 or 40 miles in a circle and get on a fresh one that trips along as on springs.

Shope remembers that he met Charlie Russell in Glacier Park, and that the great painter encouraged him. In 1926, the year of Russell's death, Shope sold his first painting to the Diamond A Cattle Ranch in Texas.

When the Cowboy Artists of America were formed in 1965 Shope was the only Montanan accepted for membership. In the first exhibit of the group's paintings at the National Cowboy Hall of Fame his subjects included "Wild Stallion," "Buffalo Runner," "Cowboy Roping Calf," "Mountain Men" and "Counting Cattle."

He has had exhibits all over the United States from New York to the West Coast, including the Desert Southwest Art Gallery in Palm Desert, California.

For Harvey W. Johnson the theory of inherited artistic talent must be an accepted

"The Strawberry Roan," by James Bramlett. This picture was inspired by the song by Curly Fletcher. (Jim Wilkerson, Prescott, Arizona.)

fact. His father was a sculptor and his mother a landscape painter. He has taken his own direction in art, though, and this has been definitely toward the West. The hundreds of illustrations he has done for magazines and advertisers and collectors all have in them a strong Western flavor, because that is the subject in which he is most interested.

"I've taken many a long trip throughout the West, traveling as much as eight thousand miles a year," Johnson relates. "I try to make my paintings as authentic as possible in every detail. I have a large collection of artifacts and also a large photo reference library."

His photographs include everything from tumbleweed in Texas to rock formations in Utah.

As a student, Johnson had the advantage of studying with his aunt, Mrs. Louis Saint-Gaudens, sister-in-law of Augustus Saint-Gaudens, the internationally celebrated sculptor.

Although he was born in Manhattan, Johnson lived with his parents in California until his father died. He then worked at art studios in New York City, capitalizing on the experience gained from three and one half years at the Art Students League just after World War II. The area in which he lives—New Fairfield, Connecticut—is full of reminders of Western art, because the last home-studio of Frederic Remington is nearby.

Johnson is represented in leading art galleries all over the country and continues to enjoy Western trips, although his everyday work for the past fourteen years has been as an instructor at the Famous Artists School in Westport, Connecticut.

Birth in the Abraham Lincoln country, it might be surmised, has been a formative factor in the development of the art career of Tom Ryan. His painting shows such a deep veneration for basic American qualities and

James Bramlett

(Above) *Curtis Wingate*

(Left) *"U.S. Cavalryman, 1880," by Curtis Wingate. (Mr. and Mrs. J. S. Orbeck, Odessa, Texas.)*

tendencies that it must reflect his own character. Tom Ryan was born in Springfield, Illinois, on January 12, 1922 in the city where the character of Lincoln too was molded.

Ryan has begun to reach his goals after long years of preparation and unending effort in the Lincoln tradition. He started drawing as a child, and by the time he was twenty-five he started oil painting. Service in World War II gave him the opportunity to think about a career, and he settled on art. He attended the St. Louis School of Fine Art, the American Academy of Art and the Art Students League in New York. At first, having won first prize in a contest at the Art Students League, he concentrated on Western book covers. This kind of work continued for eight years, during which he became more and more immersed in his studies of Western history. Finally, the urge was so great that he decided to "go West" both literally and figuratively. His painting began to reflect this more determined purpose as he moved to Lubbock, Texas.

"I think I do my best work in depicting the present-day cowboy in a realistic portrait type of painting," Ryan says. "My painting

'Sixty Years in the Saddle' is an indication of this kind of thing. My biggest satisfaction comes in doing oil sketches in the field."

He is so meticulous that it takes him about two months for each painting, from the idea stage to the finished work.

He traces his interest in horses to the days when his father owned a stable just west of Springfield; Tom began riding at the age of seven.

When he reached the point of exhibiting in the Grand Central Art Gallery in New York City and the National Cowboy Hall of Fame he knew that his persistence was beginning to permit satisfying achievement.

When a Western painter takes time out for a wild cow roundup, he is keeping his artistic muscles in trim. James E. Bramlett believes so firmly in this principle that he attunes his art to the workaday world of the cowboy.

"I strongly believe that a Western artist has to live what he paints in order to achieve the moods, the local color, the authenticity, the excitement and honesty of a day's work on a cow outfit," he contends.

Bramlett, who lives thirty miles north of Prescott and works on the Wine Glass Ranch, raises quarter horses and is a roper in the local rodeos. He shoes his own horses and breaks and trains his own colts, and says he favors the old California style of horse handling. Between working with his own stock and carrying on his ranch duties, he helps other ranchers on their roundups and with their calf branding. His determined efforts as an oil painter began in 1965, when he was in his early forties. So immediate was the public response that he has had a difficult time keeping up with the demand for his work. At his first show at the Saddleback Inn at Phoenix, he was completely sold out and was forced to resort to some quickly done pen and inks to have something else to hang. In addition to his gallery exhibits he has sold covers to such magazines as *Western Horseman, Quarter Horse Journal, True West, Frontier Times* and *Wyoming Wildlife.*

Raised on a ranch in southeast Oklahoma —he was born on September 6, 1932—Bramlett then turned to commercial art and was compelled by his work to be merely a "weekend cowboy" for a while. But his combined interest in horses and cattle and art now has brought him back into active ranch life where he utilizes one vocation to supplement the other.

In describing a wild cow roundup on the Yolo Ranch of 110,000 acres, he said, "This is one of the few old-time cow outfits in the country. They have some of the best cowboys you have ever seen. We were stalking cattle like you would stalk deer—and roping and tying those trotty critters on steep rock-pile mountains covered with prickly pear, saguaro and every other kind of cactus."

Bramlett believes that, now he has discovered he can paint, he should keep at it:

"If a person has any God-given talent at all, I think it would be a sin not to use it. I thoroughly enjoy painting the salty but proud old cowboys and their ponies."

An ex-Marine who had done some bronc riding in rodeos gives credit to a talented watercolor teacher, William Schimmel of Arizona, for having guided him into the life of a professional artist. Curtis Wingate of Phoenix, who is an associate member of the Cowboy Artists of America, relates that Schimmel, and John W. Hampton and the late George Phippen gave him the greatest encouragement and help. Primarily, Wingate is a watercolorist although he uses tempera and gouache too.

Born in Dennison, Texas, August 24, 1926, Wingate attributes his interest in horses and art, respectively, to his grandfather and a grade school art teacher in Austin. He says his grandfather took him for his first horseback ride when he was only five or six.

"At one time I did some bronc riding, bareback and saddle, and thought of going professional," Wingate says. "I still like rodeos and team roping events."

He has held exhibitions in California, Texas and Arizona, and the purchasers of his work have included banks and business concerns as well as individuals.

"One of the reasons that I started to paint the West of today and yesterday is that the people who buy your work are interested in the same things as yourself," Wingate remarks. "They start talking and you find suddenly that there is a common meeting ground. There is nothing that makes you feel any better than to have some old cowman or ex-cowboy look at a painting and tell you it reminds him of something that happened way back when he was cowboying."

14
ETERNAL FORMS

After the U.S. Civil War—"The Cow Boy"

Some mysterious force emanating from the alchemy of the brain must flow down the arm of the artist for the combination of spiritual and muscular animation resulting in his creations. It is a prolongation of impulses from nature, a symbolic attunement to the wave length of the universe. From it comes the thing we call art, in painting or in sculpture.

The sculptor is simply the painter in three dimensions. From the days of prehistoric clay models in Babylon, of the Sphinx and the mysterious figures of Easter Island, of the carvings in the Mayan jungles and the perfections of Phideas, the sculptor has added something special of his own to the likenesses of men and animals he has fashioned. Always he has been enthralled by horses and by men on horseback. This has carried forward to our own day. The sculptured cowboy on a horse is a lineal descendant of Egyptian, Byzantine,

Greek and Roman forebears.

Nearly every Western painter of the last one hundred years has felt at some time the urge to sculpt, to by-pass the intervening brush or palette knife, and by the direct and elemental use of the tactile faculty to feel, by actual touch of the fingers, the emerging image. Russell and Remington experienced it, and excelled in it. Some others have found fulfillment and have adopted sculpture as their mode of expression; others have experimented and returned to painting. A few have been equally at home in both realms.

This compulsion toward sculpturing has made itself felt in two generations of some American families. A notable example is that of the Borglums. Gutzon Borglum, born in Ovid, Idaho, on March 25, 1867, and Solon, Borglum, born in Utah on December 22, 1868,

(Left) "Trail Drivers." Plaster model by Gutzon Borglum. (Lincoln Borglum, Hermosa, South Dakota.)

(Above) Gutzon and Lincoln Borglum on Mount Rushmore during carving. (Lincoln Borglum, Hermosa, South Dakota.)

(Above right) "The Cowboy at Rest," by Solon Borglum. Sculptor working on the model for the statue which is sometimes called "An Easy Outlook" or "The Outlook" and which was done for the St. Louis World's Fair in 1904. (Paul A. Borglum.)

(Below right) Solon Borglum shortly before his death. (Paul A. Borglum)

sons of a Danish immigrant woodcarver who became a medical doctor in America, painted and sculptured in the West, and Gutzon Borglum's son, Lincoln Borglum, has carried on the family tradition.

Gutzon Borglum's gargantuan carvings of American heroes on Mount Rushmore is the most spectacular work of its kind in the nation and has attracted millions of visitors, and both he and Solon were so interested in western America that they excelled in depicting it, too. During the last few years,

Lincoln Borglum has been engaged on major sculpturing projects of his own, having assisted his father at Mount Rushmore and, in fact, having completed that project after his father's death in 1941.

Few persons seem aware that Gutzon Borglum was so enthralled by the Far West that he painted notable canvases of Western subjects while living as a young man in Sierra Madre in southern California. This took place before he went to Paris to study sculpting. These rare paintings are treasured by the col-

"Bucky O'Neill," by Solon Borglum. (Prescott Chamber of Commerce, Prescott, Arizona.)

lectors who obtained them after they came out of the probates of the estates of Mr. and Mrs. Spencer H. Smith of Los Angeles, his benefactors, to whom he had given them in the late 1890s in appreciation for their having sent him to Paris.

Solon Borglum, instead of being diverted into the transcendent realms to which Gutzon aspired in later life, concentrated almost entirely upon a portrayal of the spirit of the West in sculpture.

Solon, the "Cowboy of the Plains," was so filled to the bursting point with knowledge of horses and men that his statuary does not seem to repose in marble but to leap out in

Lincoln Borglum with bronze tablet of U.S. Daughters of 1812, Abilene, Texas. (Lincoln Borglum, Hermosa, South Dakota.)

action at all those who behold it. Solon Borglum could throw the lasso as well as he could ride a horse, and he did both with the superb skill of a born frontiersman. Every day of his life seemed to be filled with a fever of excitement at mere existence, and he managed to convey this in his artistic creations.

Solon Borglum's father was so filled with ambition that he left the Utah frontier when Solon was only a baby and studied medicine in St. Louis, received his degree and went to the wilds of Nebraska to practice. It was in Nebraska and later in California that Solon Borglum became a working rancher and cowboy, finally starting to study art at the suggestion of Gutzon. Solon, like his brother, lived for a while in Sierra Madre, and then in Santa Ana, and associated with Indians and outlaws in the Saddleback Mountains between Santa Ana and the desert country. When he went to study art in Cincinnati, he spent much time dissecting the bodies of horses in the city's animal repository so that he might know

every anatomical detail of his subjects. He also studied human anatomy in the city's surgical institute, and became so skilled that he could have obtained a degree if he had wished to do so, but decided instead to go to Paris. There he entered the sculpture in salon competition and attracted much attention with his "Cowboys Lassoing Wild Horses" and other sculptures.

When he came back to the West, he spent time with the Sioux Indians and in studying the cowboy and horse scenes which he had lacked in nature while in Paris. Such sculptures as "A Peril of the Plains," "The Little Horse in the Wind" and "The Little Lame Horse" all gained him new fame.

Out of one of the tragedies of the Spanish-American War in 1898 came one of his great masterpieces. William Owen O'Neill, the Mayor of Prescott, Arizona (who was known to everyone as "Bucky"), resigned his position and formed a cavalry regiment of Arizonans. He became a part of the First United

(Top) *Mustang. Drawing by Gutzon Borglum*

(Right) *Mustang. Drawing by Gutzon Borglum*

(Bottom) *Mustang head. Drawing by Gutzon Borglum*

States Volunteer Cavalry under Colonel Theodore Roosevelt, and of course was dubbed immediately one of the Rough Riders. Bucky O'Neill left Prescott on May 4, 1898, for the rendezvous in San Antonio with the Rough Riders. Then, on July 2 of that year at faraway San Juan Hill, he was fatally wounded. He was buried in Arlington, but his memory was so vivid in Prescott that it was decided to create a fitting memorial for him. This was a bronze statue done by Solon Borglum. Now the sight of Bucky O'Neill on his horse in the grass plot in the center of Prescott is a memorial not only to him but to sculptor Borglum as well.

Millions of visitors to the Panama-Pacific Exposition of 1915 in San Francisco were enthralled by a statue that became internationally famous—"The End of the Trail." Few persons paid any attention to the name of the sculptor who had created this dramatic representation of a drooping Indian figure on the back of an emaciated horse. They might not even have recognized the name James Earle Fraser had they heard it. Yet, out of the impact of an image in his mind, this man had created the symbolic figure from words which themselves carried the connotation of the statue:

The trail is lost, the path is hid, and winds that blow from out the ages sweep on to that chill borderland where time's spent sands engulf lost people and lost trails.

The first model of the statue was created by Fraser in 1894, when he was only seventeen. He had been pondering it for a long time.

As a small boy living in Dakota Territory I came in close contact with the Sioux Indians from 1880 to 1888 [Fraser recalled]. Often hunters, wintering with the Indians, stopped over to visit my grandfather on their way south, and in that way I heard many stories of Indians. On one occasion a fine fuzzy-bearded old hunter remarked with much bitterness in his voice, "The Injuns will all be driven into the Pacific Ocean." The thought so impressed me that I couldn't forget it. In fact, it created a picture in my mind which eventually became "The End of the Trail." I liked the Indians and couldn't understand why they were to be pushed into the Pacific.

When, at the age of twenty, Fraser went to Paris to study, he took the model of "The End of the Trail" with him, and won the grand prize in an exhibition of painting and sculpture by Americans.

"The End of the Trail" in its original form is in Walpan, Wisconsin. Fraser, who was born in Winona, Minnesota, in 1876, studied in Chicago with Richard Bock and also attended drawing classes at the Chicago Art Institute before going on to Paris. Some of his great proficiency came from his close association with Augustus Saint-Gaudens, with whom he worked in Paris until he was about twenty-six. He then set up his own studio in New York, and went on eventually to become president of the National Sculpture Society and to win many honors. He designed the famous buffalo nickel for the United States Mint.

The immense plaster sculpture of "The End of the Trail," which had been exhibited

"End of the Trail," by James Earle Fraser. (Visalia Chamber of Commerce, Visalia, California.)

at the San Francisco exposition, was obtained afterwards for Mooney Grove, a large park near Visalia, California, where it now stands close to another exposition statue, Solon Borglum's "The Pioneer." Just before his death in 1953, Fraser wrote a description of how he created the statue in answer to an inquiry from the Tulare County Historical Society in Visalia.

The entire studio and contents belonging to Fraser and his wife, Laura Gardin Fraser, also a famous sculptor, have been acquired for permanent exhibition at the National Cowboy Hall of Fame in Oklahoma City. The studio, valued at $400,000, has been moved from Westport, Connecticut, and includes an original model of "The End of the Trail."

"Mustangs," by Phimister Proctor. (University of Texas in Austin.)

Into the virile statuary of Phimister Proctor went all the ardor of a man who had shot his first grizzly bear when he was sixteen and his last one at eighty-six. Proctor not only depicted Western life, but he also lived it. The list of his statues is so incredibly long that it seems almost impossible they all could have been done by one person in one lifetime, although Proctor lived into his ninetieth year.

His birth—on September 27, 1860, in Bozanquit, Ontario, Canada—was just before the outbreak of the Civil War in the United States. The family soon moved to Clinton, Michigan, then to Newton, Ohio, and on to Des Moines, Iowa, where Phimister's father became an American citizen. Phimister lived until September, 1950, and thus had endured four American wars and the beginning of the fifth. It was not from war, though, that he gained his renown.

As the Proctor family traveled on to Denver when Phimister was eleven, he came into the midst of a life which shaped the trend of his entire artistic future. Around Denver he became a cowboy, staked homestead and mining claims, was a deputy in the lawless mining region and hunted all over the Indian country with his dog and horses. All this time he was sketching animals, Indians, cowboys and every facet of Western life. In later years his famous statues "Buckaroo" and "On the War Trail" were placed in Denver upon the exact spot where he had played baseball as a boy.

His desire for artistic knowledge was so great that he sold his homestead land to go to New York and study art in the Academy and the Art Students League. The influence of his Western observations was apparent even in those days, because his first bronze creations were of a fawn, a bear cub, a cub and a rabbit, and a stalking panther. He created his first horse statuary in 1892 and 1893 for the Chicago World's Fair and fashioned many animals for bridges at the Fair. After he married Daisy Margaret Gero in Chicago, the young couple went to Paris, where Proctor studied under some of the most famous teachers in France.

Proctor's career spanned such a long time that he maintained studios in New York, in Wilton, Connecticut, in Pendleton, Oregon,

J. R. Williams on "Lizard," by Hughlette (Tex) Wheeler. (Saddleback Art Gallery, Santa Ana, California.)

Hughlette (Tex) Wheeler with model of Seabiscuit. (Santa Anita Racetrack, Arcadia, California.)

in Seattle, Washington, and in Palo Alto, Los Altos and Los Angeles, California, as well as in Paris, Rome and Brussels. His statues, ranging from the "Pioneer Mother" to "Bison" and from "Bucking Bronc" to President Theodore Roosevelt, stand in honored places all over the United States.

Many consider his finest creations to be the seven plunging mustangs which he created to stand before the University of Texas Memorial Museum in Austin. He was almost eighty when he was commissioned to do this enormous piece of statuary, but he went with his family to Jim Hogg County in Texas and lived in a plank shanty beside big corrals where he studied specimens of mustangs for the sculpture. Texas historian and folklorist J. Frank Dobie had obtained the services of Proctor for the statuary, and it was Dobie who delivered the dedicatory address for the statuary in 1948.

"As I behold these glorious plunging creatures that Phimister Proctor has arrested in enduring bronze, they inspire in me a kind of release and elation," said Dobie. "I am free with them and the wind in spaces without confines."

Proctor, born in a family of eleven children, became the father of eight sons and daughters, one of whom, Gifford MacGregor Proctor, won the same scholarship to Paris which his father had received in 1893 and has become a notable sculptor himself.

A nick in the ear of the incomparably courageous racehorse, Seabiscuit, scion of Man-o'-War, caused Hughlette (Tex) Wheeler some of the worst moments in his distinguished career as a sculptor. Wheeler had been chosen from all the sculptors in America to create a life-size statue of Seabiscuit at Santa Anita Park, scene of so many thrilling triumphs by Charles S. Howard's beloved thoroughbred.

The question was: Should Wheeler show in the statue the nick which actually existed in Seabiscuit's ear, and thus preserve absolute fidelity, or should he omit it because it might confuse a viewer who would think it a defect in the sculpture.

I personally saw Tex go through the pangs of indecision on this point because he was creating the Seabiscuit model in the studio which had been shared jointly by painters Clyde (Vic) Forsythe and Frank Tenney Johnson in Alhambra, California, where I was a frequent visitor. Johnson had just met his untimely death in 1939, but Forsythe was still using the studio. Tex would debate with himself, and us, about the nick as his delicate fingers fashioned the clay. The rest of the statue was exact down to the hundredth of an inch, but Tex finally decided to leave out the nick as a favor to spectators who might argue about the reason for it. The statue was dedicated at Santa Anita February 6, 1941, with Seabiscuit present in person.

Hughlette—nobody ever called him anything but "Tex"—Wheeler also created for Santa Anita a few years later a statue of George Woolf, the jockey who was described, for his coolness and rating ability, as being able "to hold an elephant an inch away from a peanut until feeding time." Woolf was killed in a fall January 3, 1946.

Wheeler came from the little town of Christmas, Florida. He spoke with a pronounced drawl and, because he wore cowboy boots and a Western hat, he became known as "Tex."

Jim Rogers, son of Will Rogers, became convinced of Tex's great talent following the death of Will, when an equestrian statue was being considered.

"When it comes to doing a portrait in bronze, Tex was the finest craftsman of them all," Jim Rogers told me. "My wife Astrea and I were living on Jalama Ranch in Santa Barbara County along in 1940, and Tex came

"The Last War Whoop," by John D. Free. (Taos Art Gallery, Taos, New Mexico.)

John D. Free

up and stayed with us for a month or two. He modeled Soapsuds (Will's favorite riding horse) and I posed for him. It was his Seabiscuit statue that got people to talking about him. After he got married, in about 1942, I think, he lived at our old Santa Monica Ranch and started to make a life-size clay model of Dad on Soapsuds, from the ¼ size one he made first. There is a ¼ life-size plaster, hand painted by Tex's friend, artist Clyde Forsythe, in Will Rogers State Park in Santa Monica."

Apparently the large statue was never cast in bronze.

Wheeler, according to Jim Rogers, "had ridden a bit and worked a few cows." His art training took place in Chicago. "All he wanted to do was model horses and cattle," Jim recalls. "Old Tex had a world of talent but never lived long enough to take his place in the art world."

Tex Wheeler and J. R. Williams, the cartoonist of "Out Our Way," were great friends, and one of Tex's fine bronzes shows Williams on his horse Lizard.

A native Oklahoman whose grandmother was an Osage Indian started out to be a veterinarian after trying cowboying but has wound up as a sculptor in bronze. John D. Free was born in Osage County, Oklahoma, April 7, 1929, and has been moving steadily forward in his art career since a mean bronc named Pool 65 damaged him so much that he gave up a possible temporary rodeo career while studying veterinary medicine.

The fidelity of his bronze likenesses of horses and cattle has won him the privilege of having exhibitions from San Antonio to New York and recognition from the National Cowboy Hall of Fame and the Gilcrease Institute of American History and Art, both of which have permanent displays of his work.

"John Free's work in bronze may well be one of the most refreshing contributions to the field of Western art in this decade," said Dean Krakel, managing director of the Cowboy Hall of Fame. "His bronze version of 'Old Sancho,' the tortilla-eating steer from

J. Frank Dobie's book 'The Longhorns,' is outstanding. 'The Cow Boss' is another superb piece."

The popularity of Free's work is demonstrated in far places. One notable outlet for his bronzes is the Taos Gallery of Thomas Lewis in Taos.

"I decided to devote my energies to Western art because it is the subject I know best," Free explains. "I know what a steer looks like because I have followed enough of them. I have been opening and closing gates behind cows and horses since I was tall enough to lift a wire loop from a post. I am trying to document the way it is with the cowboy, his work, and the horse that helps him."

Poetry and sculpture have teamed up for a long time in the career of Wayne Hunt.

"Horses and cowboys are the only subjects I know," Hunt explains. "An artist is born with a talent. I believe he is obligated to use it. I will use mine to preserve in bronze the cowboy and horses of my era."

From the same source of inspiration, apparently, has come the poetry Hunt has written for many years. In one little poem, "Talkin' Ain't Ridin'," he starts off:

> You ornery flea bit son of a gun
> I ain't about had near enough
> You dirty pin-eared zebra dun
> I'll teach you not to get so tough. . . .

This apparently belligerent spirit in regard to a ride on an outlaw horse is not carried over into the sculpture of Wayne Hunt. He has specialized in showing the cowboy in his native environment doing the things that he traditionally does every day. As a result, Hunt's material has been exhibited at the National Cowboy Hall of Fame in Oklahoma City, at the Trailside Gallery in Jackson Hole, Wyoming, at the O'Brien Art Emporium in Scottsdale, Arizona, at the

Wayne Hunt

"Mustanger," by Wayne Hunt. (Mr. and Mrs. Keith Atherton, San Diego, California.)

Desert Southwest Galleries in Palm Desert, and elsewhere. Also, he has attracted many notable Western enthusiasts, some of whom have acquired his work. One of these, in particular, has been Keith Atherton of San Diego, whose collection of Western paintings and sculpture has become more notable year by year.

Hunt lives in the vicinity of Sedona, Arizona—in that rugged country where cattle ranching still is much the same as it was fifty or seventy-five years ago. It is a far cry from Bear Valley, Wisconsin, where he was born, May 2, 1904, but he now feels at home in the West amid the cowboys.

When Big Piney started to fall, Grant Speed knew he was in trouble and a lot of thoughts flashed through his mind in the split second before he and the rodeo bucking horse hit the ground. When the dust cleared,

Grant Speed was suffering from a broken ankle and, although he may not have known it for sure at the moment, he was headed for a new line of work. Up to the time of this rodeo at Logan, Utah, where Big Piney—one of the champs among bucking horses—fell with him, Speed had been a rodeo rider for several years. While his ankle was healing he did a lot of thinking about getting into some other occupation besides the hazardous one in which he had won many awards. The net result of the accident was that Grant Speed became a sculptor.

His background had prepared him for this new effort. In his classes at Utah State University at Provo, he had been taking animal husbandry while aiming at a ranching life. This was in keeping with his early training, because this Texan, born in San Angelo, had gone to work when he was only twelve on neighboring ranches and had begun to

U. Grant Speed

"The End of an Acquaintance." Bronze by U. Grant Speed

break horses.

After the Big Piney incident, he decided that rodeoing was becoming a little too rough, and he began teaching as a career. Then he became interested in sculpting, but he had misgivings about his ability.

"Russell and Remington were so great in their sculpturing of horses, cowboys and cattle that I was afraid I might be tempted to model my stuff after theirs," he confesses. "So from the start I have avoided copying like the plague."

When he did begin sculpting, he "built into" his models some of his own experiences—as indicated by the titles "The End of an Acquaintance" and "Doubtful Outcome." These depictions of bucking horses were linked with his own memories of some of the great outlaws he had tried to ride in his rodeo days, including Mountain Man, Rocking Chair, Polka Dot (an Appaloosa) and Indian Boy—with Indian Boy ranking as about the worst horse he ever encountered.

One of Speed's popular sculptures has been "The Bull Rider." He has had exhibitions at Scottsdale, Arizona, and at the Trailside Gallery in Jackson Hole, Wyoming.

Grant Speed married Sue Collins of Provo, and they still live there while he carries on his teaching and gives more and more time to his sculpture.

"I think a lot of horses are smarter than a lot of men."

Perhaps it is this sentiment that has brought national attention to John Henry Kittleson, a wood sculptor with no formal training who lives in Cheyenne, Wyoming.

Carving by John H. Kittelson

John H. Kittelson

Kittleson began riding horses when he was about three years old and trying to draw at about the same age. He still paints and draws cowboys and other Western subjects, but his principal interest is in wood sculpture.

"I figure that is what I know best," he explains.

He was born in Arlington, South Dakota, on July 5, 1930. He was born with skill in his hands, and because of his interest in horses became a saddlemaker, turning out his first saddle when he was thirteen. He never went to school beyond the eighth grade but started to work on ranches. He has broken horses and been a working cowboy on ranches in South Dakota, Montana, Nebraska and Wyoming. He has exhibited in notable galleries throughout the West, and his work is owned by the King Ranch in Texas, by Ilia Tolstoy in New York City and by many collectors in Arizona and other Western states.

A modern medical doctor, who was born beside the old California-Oregon Trail that led from the East in covered wagon days, has become in recent years one of the leading exponents in bronze of the era typified by the spirit of 1849. Joseph J. Shebl, M.D. of Salinas, California, was born too late for covered wagons—May 28, 1913—at Crete, Nebraska, on the Big Blue River which led to the Platte on the westward trail followed by so many pioneers. He has been a history enthusiast ever since he can remember.

A busy specialist in radiology, with degrees from Creighton University and the

"Longhorns." Bronze by Joseph J. Shebl, M.D., Salinas, California.

University of Pennsylvania, Dr. Shebl still finds time for his outside interests of studying history, collecting Western art, and creating bronze statuary. His bronzes reflect this interest in the early West. One is of a buffalo with calf dozing beside her. Others are a mare and colt, horsemen of all types, wild animals and cattle. Each bronze is limited to twenty copies. Dr. Shebl does the clay modeling, the hand-casting, the chasing, the application of the waxes. For his knowledge of horses he gives credit to Jack Swanson, the rancher of Carmel Valley who also is an oil painter.

"I fell off my first pony when I was four and was dragged forty-four miles because I was afraid I'd lose him, and I've been attached to horses ever since!" Dr. Shebl quips.

He believes that the spell of the West exerts itself everywhere. "The love of the American West has spread all over the world and I don't think we'll ever really lose it," he says. "I think we can only preserve it for ourselves and for the youngsters of the future in our books and in art."

Noah Berry, Jr. has followed in his cele-

Joseph J. Shebl, M.D., working on the wax model for "Night Wrangler"

"Geronimo." Bronze by Noah Berry

Noah Berry on his mule "Amigo"

brated father's footsteps as a successful film actor and has added the talent of becoming a sculptor in bronze. Berry, who lives in Keene, California, has been a lifelong friend of Jim Rogers, son of Will Rogers. They once tried raising buffalo together but found that their pets were too agile in jumping over high fences and devastating neighbors' ranches.

Greatest artistic inspiration in Berry's life, he says, came from Charlie Russell. Born

in New York City, August 10, 1916, Berry learned early to ride horses and has been a horseman in films nearly all his life.

His sculptured pieces have been exhibited in California, Arizona and Montana and are owned by many families throughout this country and in Canada.

Desiring, as he explains, "to hand down to posterity an image of the cowboy, who played such a major role in the development of California in the covered wagon days, already vanished, and in the operation of a major industry, cattle raising, which is being automated" Frances Sedgwick, sculptor in the Santa Ynez Valley, California, created the statue of a range rider which now stands in the Earl Warren Showgrounds at Santa Barbara. Model for the three-ton one and one-half times life-size statue was "Lefty" McPeters, local cowboy, and the horse is a composite of three quarter horses owned by Sedgwick.

Robert Macfie Scriver specializes in Western animal sculpture and casts his own bronzes in the Bighorn Foundry which he owns. He also runs the Scriver Taxidermy and Art Studio and the Museum of Montana Wildlife which are located in Browning, Montana, where he was born August 15, 1914.

Visitors to Central Park in New York probably are unaware that the powerful statue of Simon Bolivar mounted upon a mighty steed is the work of a woman. Sally James Farnham, born in Ogdensburg, N. Y., turned to sculpture after being encouraged by Charlie Russell and received the Order of Bolivar honor from the Venezuelan government for her statue of this great hero.

STRANGE BIRTH OF A STALLION

Far out in the Arizona desert one spring day long ago, on the edge of the hamlet of Chloride, I saw the strange birth of a stallion.

This was no puny foal. He was full grown at birth . . .

I was on a journey in 1939 with my friend John Hilton, the painter, and the sculptor Oskar J. W. Hansen, the Norwegian-born genius who had just completed the immense winged figures at Hoover Dam representing man's triumph over nature. Near Chloride we encountered a desert prospector with long whiskers and a gunny sack. From the gunny sack he took an object that lighted up the eyes of Hilton and Hansen as if neons had been turned on in their heads.

Let me say that, ordinarily, the desert gem turquoise comes in thin layers because during its creation in solidifying rock in the heated interior of the earth it is mashed as if by a gigantic press.

Hence a large chunk is as unlikely as a seven-legged horse.

But from the gunny sack the bearded desert rat had pulled out a chunk of sky-colored turquoise as large as the doubled fist of a man. Hansen spoke first. He bargained. He got the treasure. The desert rat left.

"My God," exclaimed Hansen. "I see the head of an Arabian stallion in this!"

Thirteen years later, in 1952, when Hansen was just completing for the U.S. government the great figure of "Liberty" for the Yorktown Monument, I went with him to the Smithsonian Institute in Washington, D.C. Just inside the gem room, in a special glass case, was something I had once seen before, at Chloride. But now it was different. It was the head of an Arabian stallion, in turquoise.

15

PERSISTENT CHARRO

Mexican charro, 1900 onward to today

In a puzzling paradox, artistic hobbles seem to have been put on the Spanish horse in modern Mexico.

The country that witnessed the arrival of the first horses on American soil in 1519 might be expected to be even more zealous in preserving in oil painting the image and tradition of these equine pioneers than its younger northern neighbor, the United States. Yet this appears not to be so. Mexico today is profoundly interested in horsemanship and horse sports as typified by the dangerous games and exhibitions of its twentieth-century *charros*, those incomparable horsemen who have managed to maintain a degree of dashing excellence dating back to medieval Spain. Conversely, Mexico manifests in equal degree a striking indifference to the horse and the horseman as subjects for paintings. This is in such startling contrast to the enormous popu-

larity being enjoyed by cowboy and horse art in the United States that the visitor from this country to Mexico is bound to notice it.

I sought in vain throughout Mexico recently on a forty-five-hundred-mile automobile trip that took me on research projects to most of its major cities for examples of contemporary "horse art." They were singularly lacking. It was a surprise and thrill to see on the wall of a hostelry in Fortín de las Flores in the state of Veracruz a spirited *charro* painting, showing horses and riders in action—because it was the first I had encountered. When I asked the proprietor, Sr. Ernesto Alvarez, about it, he told me that the painting was not contemporary at all, but done by Ernesto Icaza about sixty years ago. Icaza and G. Morales were among the leading *charro* painters in the past.

My wife and I were continually on the

"*Charro in Action.*" *(Mexican Government Tourism Department.)*

(Bottom) Brig. Gen. *William J. Fox, U.S. Marine Corps, retd., known as "the Gringo Charro," lives in San Miguel de Allende and is shown here executing a difficult roping feat in a charreada.*

(Top) Charros in action. (Mexican Government Tourism Department.)

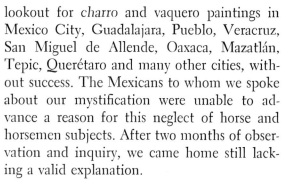

lookout for *charro* and vaquero paintings in Mexico City, Guadalajara, Pueblo, Veracruz, San Miguel de Allende, Oaxaca, Mazatlán, Tepic, Querétaro and many other cities, without success. The Mexicans to whom we spoke about our mystification were unable to advance a reason for this neglect of horse and horsemen subjects. After two months of observation and inquiry, we came home still lacking a valid explanation.

Regarding the activities of the present-day *charro*, though, we encountered unlimited enthusiasm and interest everywhere. The *charros* can be seen not only in parades and on fiesta days, in their huge hats and rigidly prescribed trousers, shirts and boots, but also on Sundays in *charreadas*, where they match skill against wild bulls and mares and against each other, lightheartedly risking their lives in the process. They can be seen riding in

Mexico City's Chapultepec Park and in Monterrey and Guadalajara and all the big cities, and in many of the smaller ones too.

The feats of *charros* are staggering in their impact upon foreign observers. Happily, also, the Mexicans are receptive to the interest of Americanos del Norte to the point of permitting them to participate in the *charreadas*—if they are worthy. In San Miguel de Allende, for example, this courteous treatment

"Mexican Charro," by Edward Borein. (Harold G. Davidson, Santa Barbara, California.)

has permitted one Americano to earn the title of "the Gringo *Charro*," and to accompany the Mexican *charro* team to Spain and Argentina. Brigadier General William J. Fox, United States Marine Corps (Retired), who has lived in San Miguel for a number of years, is termed "gringo" with affection and not with the derision the term sometimes connotes.

General Fox is the celebrated Marine flier whose legendary feats in World War II placed him in the first rank of flying officers. Later, he became director of Los Angeles County airports, and then moved to San Miguel de Allende and built a home and stables on a small hacienda at the edge of the lovely old Mexican city.

With the perspective of an Americano del Norte who has come to have a deep understanding of the Mexican people among whom he lives and to share a *simpatico* feeling, he

has been able to evaluate the enormous significance of the *charros* in their native environment.

The *charreada* and the *charro* himself, like aviation and aviator, need no exaggeration or manufactured dramatization to stir the blood of anything short of a cadaver [he states]. Both demand of the participants a dedication to an activity which is a constant challenge to their entire beings, mental and physical, and the disciplined ability to conquer with ease and certainty whatever situations and events may arise during active participation in this activity. Both are activities that are most unforgiving, and mistakes are not habit forming since the first mistake could well be the last.

I am as sure as I can be that the spiritual fiber that makes up the life of the thousands of pueblos and that intangible something that builds inspiration into the human mechanism to make Mexicans an inherently proud and contented people is involved in watching the *charros*. The *charro* in Mexico, like the *torero*, pulls something to the surface in every man, woman and child.

General Fox is familiar with the traditions, dress and terminology of the *charros* and also with the feelings of the participants in the *Charreadas*, because he is one himself. He knows the feel of the *"Death Pass"* from the back of one horse to that of a wild mare while running at full speed around the ring, the heave and pull of the steer's tail as it is seized by hand as the *charro* speeds alongside and throws the animal for a full turn in the *"Coleada."* He has practiced for years on end with the *reata*, to be able to perform the amazing feats of roping which are part of the *charro* performance.

All this personal participation has led him to an intensive study of the rigorous standards applied to the *charro's* performance, equipment and apparel, and an appreciation of the *charro's* importance in the history of Mexico.

The essence of the paradox my wife and I encountered in Mexico is that the popular interest in *Charreadas* as a sport and literary dissection of the history and importance of *charros* in Mexico seemingly fail to stimulate artists to paint the exciting scenes involved. It is a lack I cannot help but deplore. Due to my love of Mexico, I would like to see its painters awake to the possibilities around them in the day-to-day activities of the *charros*.

Americanos del Norte continue to portray the cowboy. Mexicans could do the same with the *charro*.

MIGHTY OUTLAWS IN "HORSE HEAVEN"

Many a mourner took off his Stetson in respect when they buried old Midnight on the gentle hillside.

Midnight was being laid to rest in the Arlington of horsedom, a place for heroes. Midnight, one of the greatest bucking horses of all time and ranked along with the horrendous Steamboat, and his companion Five Minutes to Midnight, both were paid unprecedented honor when they were taken to graves at the National Cowboy Hall of Fame and reburied April 30, 1966, during the National Rodeo finals in Oklahoma City. In the crowd were rodeo performers who had tried unsuccessfully to ride the champion bucking horses in their prime.

On the grave of Midnight was placed this epitaph:

Under this sod lies a great bucking hoss;
There never lived a cowboy he couldn't toss.

His name was Midnight—his coat black as coal.
If there is a hoss heaven, please God, rest his soul!

The unusual reinterment of the bucking horses from their original resting place in Colorado came about because of the imagination and zeal of Dean Krakel, managing director of the Cowboy Hall of Fame. He arranged with Mr. and Mrs. Albert D. Kurtz of Platteville, Colorado, to permit the removal of the horses' remains from their ranch, which had previously belonged to Verne Elliott, owner of Midnight and Five Minutes to Midnight. Midnight was foaled in 1916 on the ranch of Jim McNab near McLeod, Alberta, Canada, and in fourteen years as a bucking bronc was never ridden in competition. He died in 1936. Five Minutes to Midnight, also a holy terror on the circuit, was foaled in 1918 and died in 1947.

16
BIG ROUNDUP

American cowpoke, 1880–1890

In spite of hell and high water, the big roundup has come trampling and bellowing right into the last third of the twentieth century, kicking up as much dust as it did a hundred years ago when the cowboy era began. In some ways it has changed, but a mean bull's horns are just as sharp, a horse grows just as tired out in the snow, and a man still gets galled in the thighs and mighty saddle weary.

The artists who have gone right along with the herd all this time are finding as much to put down on canvas as they ever did, maybe more because the audience is so big. It is true that electric branding irons and four-wheeled trucks and feed lots have come along, but none of them has been able to dim the enthusiasm of the painters and their customers for what the West has to offer

today in the way of action and drama and color.

In the array of artists portraying horsemen and the West it sometimes is difficult to differentiate between those wearing the brand of "painter" and others of "illustrator." In many cases they overlap, or one category moves into the realm of the other. It is almost impossible, as a consequence, to define exactly who should be included in a book like this. Because it deals primarily with Western painters specializing in the cowboy and his environment, generally with on-the-scene observation or participation, some notable illustrators in the East necessarily will be omitted, not because their work is deficient but, on the contrary, because they do not quite fit into the exact classification being used here. Many illustrators have gone on to become "Western" painters in a precise sense, or have taught with such great insight that their students with a flair for the West have climbed to the heights as oil painters in the cowboy sphere.

Howard Pyle, the dean of American illustrators, who was born in 1853 and lived until 1911 ranks at the top as one of those who inspired his followers. At his school in Chadd's Ford, Pennsylvania he gave freely of his talent and counsel to those whom he considered worthy. An example of his influence is that he taught Harvey Dunn who taught so many others, including Harold Von Schmidt, who has carried on the tradition. It is a worthy progression.

Near the head of any list including both illustrator and painter in an individual must be N. C. Wyeth of the family which has produced so many notable names in American art. Newell Convers Wyeth was born in 1882 and before his tragic death in a railway crossing accident in 1945 he had exerted enormous influence on many talented students. He idolized his teacher, Howard Pyle, and was idolized by those who, in turn, felt his galvanizing influence.

The circumstances under which prospective students came into the sphere of the teachers who apparently were best fitted to stimulate their best efforts have involved strange variations. One notable contemporary is an example.

Memories of a windmill etched against the cobalt of the New Mexico sky and of pink and lavender bluffs along the Pecos became so strong in the mind of a West Point cadet that he abandoned a military career to become an artist. The Army lost a potential general, but the world gained a modern master. His name is Peter Hurd.

For Hurd, the inborn affinity for his native New Mexico was strong enough to call him back after twelve years in the East where

"El Mocho," by Peter Hurd. (Art Institute of Chicago, Watson F. Blair Purchase Prize.)

he gained artistic stature studying with N. C. Wyeth, married Wyeth's artist-daughter, Henriette, and began to attain his great reputation with the use of tempera. Peter Hurd was born near Roswell, N. M., February 22, 1904. As a child he roamed the countryside swimming, fishing and collecting Indian relics, never giving a thought, as he recalls, to the possibility of becoming an artist. Nevertheless he was greatly attracted to articles in Scribner's illustrated by N. C. Wyeth, a name which at the time held no particular significance for him.

He attended the New Mexico Military Institute and from there was appointed to the U.S. Military Academy at West Point.

Then a box of oil paints changed the course of his life.

The box contained hints on painting by an anonymous author and, with these to guide him, Hurd turned out his first artistic works.

"To say that the resulting labors were

"Horse Trade," by Peter Hurd. (Artesia First National Bank, New Mexico.)

Peter Hurd

crude and without distinction would be a great understatement," he said in later years, "but I was ensnared—my enthusiasm was unbounded and from that time to this, painting has been my life."

This enthusiasm resulted, to the dismay of his father, in his leaving the academy at the end of his second year, in 1923. By fortunate chance, Hurd then met the very same N. C. Wyeth whose illustrations he had admired in *Scribner's*. He became Wyeth's private student for six years at Chadd's Ford, Pennsylvania, and during that time lived in an old barn which had been Wyeth's studio many years before. Wyeth never charged his students a cent.

"I worked at landscape and still life painting in oil, figure study and imaginative compositions in charcoal," Hurd recalls. "In later years I moved from oil technique to egg tempera and water color."

Once a week the little group studying with Wyeth would gather and listen to the master's criticism and discussion.

Hurd was enormously impressed with the depth of meditation and the scope of inquiry in Wyeth's comments.

"There was always a yeasty atmosphere wherever his influence penetrated," Hurd comments. "He realized that in art truth is a growing, changing factor as man progresses."

Young Hurd and Wyeth's daughter Henriette fell in love and were married in 1929. She was a fine painter then and has continued to paint alongside her husband during the years. At first the Hurds lived near Chadd's Ford. But deep within him, Peter Hurd was feeling by now the insistent call of the vast spaces and the brilliant landscapes of his native New Mexico. In the

John Meigs

"Riding Out," by John Meigs. (Baker Gallery, Lubbock, Texas.)

1930's he and his family—by now there were two children, with a third born later—moved to San Patricio, fifty miles west of Roswell on the way to the White River Apache Reservation. There, amid the foothills along the Rio Hondo, the family settled on thirty acres. They are still there, although the ranch has grown in acreage and there is a cluster of buildings to accommodate the family, ranch workers, and numerous visitors.

Hurd's successive techniques have been a dramatic attestation to the validity of the Wyeth concept that "truth is a growing, changing factor as man progresses." Until 1935, Hurd painted largely in oil. Then he went to egg tempera and gained an international reputation in the use of this ancient medium. Of more recent date, his watercolors with influence of the English painter Joseph Mallord William Turner have shown anew his masterful versatility. The spirit of the West emanates from his creations.

A remarkable exhibition of the works of both Peter Hurd and Henriette Wyeth at

the Columbus, Ohio, Gallery of Fine Arts in 1967 was an example of the powerful techniques of both, exemplifying their individual talents and their combined impact on the art world.

Peter Hurd goes forward daily gaining new stature in the land of the great sky and the rainbow landscape of New Mexico, with his beloved windmills of boyhood memory adding their touch of nostalgia in the realm of confidence and achievement in which he moves.

Something about the San Patricio countryside must provide special inspiration for artists because another notable Western painter also makes his home there. He is John Meigs, a former Los Angeles newspaperman who has gained distinction in the art world. His admiration for the work of Hurd caused Meigs to take a leading role in arranging the Columbus exhibition.

Environment has been an important factor in Meigs' life since 1951. In San Patri-

Robert Lougheed painting on Bell Ranch, New Mexico, at roundup time.

"Gathering at the Buyeros Corral," by Robert Lougheed. Buyeros means "ox team" in Spanish. Scene on the Bell Ranch, New Mexico.

cio that year he turned to full-time painting under the guidance of Peter Hurd. He credits Hurd and Henriette Wyeth Hurd with having influenced him greatly in his artistic trends. While he was in Paris for a year studying and visiting art galleries he came under the spell of the old masters.

Meigs was born in Chicago, grew up in San Antonio, and learned ranch life at his grandfather's place in Oklahoma.

When he left newspaper work and settled in San Patricio he became infused with a new spirit.

"Living in the Southwest has inspired me to look hard at the people as well as at the landscape," Meigs relates. "I am not concerned with the cowboy in action as I am in the cowboy as a man. These individuals are the backbone of today's Southwest ranching, and while they may ride a pickup instead of a horse, and herd cattle by more modern means, the spirit of the man of the West is still closely related to that of the cowboy who preceded him. My object is to record the West through its people, its buildings, its landscape and to preserve, as artists have for centuries, some small part of 'how it is in your own time'."

Meigs also has prepared a book of the complete lithographs of Peter Hurd "which will give the public a deep insight into the talent of this major American artist."

From paintings of Hernando Cortés and the early horses of America to a series on equine blue bloods in the *National Geographic Magazine* is an easy transition for Robert Lougheed. Lougheed's depiction of the West and Mexico has ranged all the way from covers for Western and adventure magazines to calendars and drawing for *The Reader's Digest.* He camps from the Canadian Rockies to the Mexican border, and particularly haunts cattle roundups in the western states.

Lougheed, born in Canada, was so attracted from his childhood to Western themes that, when he went to New York,

"The Social Hour," by William Moyers. (John W. Taylor, Enid, Oklahoma.)

it was easy for him to go into the type of art work which has occupied his attention ever since. He studied with Frank Vincent Du Mond, and credits this teacher with having opened up a new world for him. Since he started doing drawings for a mail-order catalog when he was nineteen, he has progressed steadily toward his goal of depicting the West. It was at this time, when he was an extremely young man, that he began spending his summer months in the outdoors in the West.

Lougheed has exhibited his paintings all over the country, and has one outlet, the Blair Gallery in Taos, New Mexico. His work is so highly regarded that five of his paintings hang in the National Cowboy Hall of Fame.

Hero worship has been so much a way of life for William Moyers that even now, when he is a successful painter himself, he continues to idolize those artistic giants who have best portrayed the West. His idols have ranged from "Will James" to Harold Von Schmidt, and from Frederic Remington and Charlie Russell to Nick Eggenhofer, the illus-

trator. This absorption with the artistic aspect of the West dates from the time Bill Moyers was fourteen. It was then he went to Alamosa, Colorado, in the midst of a region noted not only for its natural beauty but also for its ranches and cowboys. He learned to break horses and to be a good working ranch hand.

A fixity of purpose has kept Moyers on the path to his goal for many years. His art training includes a major at Adams State College in Colorado and additional work at the Otis Art Institute in Los Angeles, but, over and above formal training, he had contacts with many famous artists whose careers, unlike his own (he was born on December 11, 1916), stretched back into the nineteenth century. His father and grandfather were attorneys in Atlanta, Georgia, and to this day Bill Moyers retains something of the accent of the region where the hero worship of great figures in the history of the South has been an accepted tradition. His father moved to San Angelo, Texas, and later to Amarillo because of a love for the West, and then settled in Alamosa, which proved to be a fortunate choice for Bill, too.

(Above) *William Moyers*

(Right) *"The Strawberry Roan," by William Moyers. Bronze.*

Moyers became a successful illustrator in New York, and this led him into the pursuit of oil painting and sculpture. He began exhibiting at the Taos Art Gallery, owned by Thomas Lewis, and has continued with this gallery as his sole outlet.

"I believe that art is the communication of the experience of one human being to another human being in a form that pleases both," Moyers says.

His greatest enjoyment has come from being associated with cowboy life. His remarkably accurate observations make his portrayals so vivid that they meet the rigid standards that he himself sets for communication with the viewers of his paintings.

One of his greatest thrills as a young artist came while he was still a lieutenant in the army during World War II. He heard of a competition by the Limited Editions Club for drawings to be used in a reissue of Owen Wister's *The Virginian*. He immediately mustered all his imagination and skill derived from knowledge of range life, and submitted his drawings. In competition with the finest illustrators in the country, he was

declared the winner, and his illustrations did then appear in the Limited Editions issue of *The Virginian* which came out in 1951. Moyers recently received back the original drawings that he had submitted more than fifteen years before.

Moyers gravitated from Alamosa and New York to Albuquerque, New Mexico, as another center of range life. In his home on a quiet residential street he treasures many paintings which he acquired during his New York days, including those of Frederic Remington, Olaf Seltzer, Bert G. Phillips, and many others. He is a successful sculptor, and one of his bronzes, "The Last Arrow," is in the Gilcrease Institute in Tulsa. He has been impressed by the helpfulness of other artists to him. In particular, he remembers that when he was a young man visiting New York he got up his courage and called Harold Von Schmidt at his home in Connecticut. He inquired whether Von Schmidt would permit him to come out and ask advice. Kindly Von Schmidt said, "I'm coming into New York for a meeting of the Illustrators' Society tonight and I will come by your hotel and

Bill Chappell at the easel

cowboys, however, go hunting with a gun in one hand and a paintbrush in the other. Still, figuratively speaking, that is just about what Bill Chappell does. If you encounter Chappell in the wild mountains of Colorado, New Mexico or Texas, he may seem to be intent only upon hunting, but this is an illusion. Actually, he is searching for painting material as much as he is for game.

"Much of my work has been inspired while hunting deer and elk," Chappell admits.

Chappell hunts a good deal because he needs time to think about art in two separate mediums. He was brought up in the leather business—the making of saddles and bridles and many other articles—and later on he became such an accomplished leather carver that he branched out into art objects. Then, too, he began oil painting when he was in his thirties and now combines both leather work and the creation of pictures.

He has been a hard worker most of his life. Born in 1919 in Van Zandt County in Texas, he began working with his parents on hand tooling bridles and belts when he was only ten. At that time he worked with crude, homemade tools created from wood and nails. Since then, he has made more than five hundred saddles and thousands of other objects in leather, including beautifully carved boots. In leather, his most ambitious undertaking was the creation of a life-size portrait of Will Rogers, now in the National Cowboy Hall of Fame.

In recent years Chappell has been drawn more and more into painting, as he seeks to capture "the feel" of range lands of the kind in which he lived as a boy. Previously, though, he had to take time out for making a living. After his marriage to Faye Martin in Seymour, Texas, Bill served two years in the Navy, and then went back to Seymour and started a saddle business. Finally, the Chappells were attracted to southern Colorado and settled on a ranch near Alamosa. It was in this setting,

pick you up." He did so, and introduced Moyers to the eminent artists there. Moyers is passing along such courtesy by being notably kind to aspiring artists.

In his own family, Moyers notes artistic talent in his daughter Joanne, who, at sixteen, became so proficient that she began painting New Mexico scenes which she was able to sell "on her own."

Moyers is surrounded in his studio by all sorts of mementos and gear including old saddles, rifles, bridles and bits, some of which belonged to famous artists. Moyers still hero worships, even including a mythical cow horse.

"I used *Smoky* by 'Will James' as a textbook when I was breaking horses," he remarks in recollection.

It is part of a spirit which invests all his paintings with enthusiasm and warmth.

Many a cowboy goes hunting for wild game, and, in the old days, most had to be good shots if they were going to have anything to eat out on the open range. Not many

Bernard Thomas

"Heading for the Mountain Range," by Bernard Thomas. (Tucker Art Gallery, Sheridan, Wyoming.)

where Bill could feel that he was in his favorite kind of country and in the center of cattle operations, that, in the mid-1950's, he began painting.

Most Western painters mention Russell and Remington as their main inspiration, but Bernard P. Thomas gives his first allegiance on a personal basis to another cowboy painter, Bill Gollings of Sheridan, Wyoming.

I was only a kid when we moved into Sheridan from the ranch to go to school and lived in a house near Bill Gollings [Thomas recalls]. Bill was a loner and though I didn't realize it at the time was continuously experimenting with colors. He never gave me a single art lesson but he did let me watch him, and just watching him in his little clobbered-up studio was all a kid needed. Bill died when I was thirteen and I felt the loss deeply. It was then that I determined that some day I too would be like Bill Gollings, a cowboy artist.

Naturally, too, Thomas was influenced

greatly by the Russell and Remington tradition, because he was, as he says, "working in the shadows of these two great leaders of Western art."

Thomas combined practical experience on the home ranch, where he was born August 9, 1918, with his desire to paint.

Most of us kids growing up on the ranch rode before we could walk, just as soon as we had strength enough to rein a horse [he remembers]. The desire to paint cowboy life has been with me always. I rode with the old-time top hands, I slept on the ground and ate my grub with them—and I choked in the dust while hollering like hell at the poky one in the drag. I am most fortunate to have worked with the cowboys of the past. Nothing gripes me more than a Western illustration done by an Eastern illustrator who by his workmanship proves that he doesn't know straight up about a cow, a cow pony or a cowboy and his rigging.

Everybody has to have a "first picture," and Bernard Thomas recalls that his was a

Robert Rishell

"Light and Shadow," by Robert Rishell. (Mr. and Mrs. Donald J. Will, Piedmont, California.)

copy of an elk from the label on a vegetable can. From this humble beginning he has gone on to become one of the leading mural painters of the country, not to mention his work on Western canvases. At present he lives at Boynton Beach, Florida, after his early years spent with his family on the homestead, farm and ranch. Thomas is credited with the largest three-dimensional mural ever painted by one artist, the "Autorama" on the Gold Coast in Florida. He has an eighty-foot Western mural depicting the history of the Black Hills of South Dakota in the American National Bank at Rapid City. The Yellowstone Bank in Laurel, Montana, has another Western mural. One of Thomas' notable paintings is the large "Attack on the Overland Stage," which is owned by R. H. Whitney of Bel Aire, California.

For many years now I have spent my summers painting ranchscapes [Thomas says]. These are paintings of a ranch, usually the ranch buildings being a part of the background. I try to capture the color and lay of the land, some distant landmark and something personal in the foreground. I blend these into one painting and as some of the old timers retire they still have the old ranch hanging on the wall at a single glance.

From atop his high hill, Bob Rishell can look out over the vista of San Francisco Bay and see Mount Diablo and the hills and valleys of seven different counties, and at the same time he can watch the horses he delights in painting. That combined view is symbolic of the versatility of Rishell. His talent ranges from the portrayal of a horse to that of an old barn and from the painting of a portrait of a noted Californian to a mural of Father Junípero Serra, the founder of California.

From the moment he started drawing as a child he has never been "typed." When he was in the second grade, he won the attention of the teacher by drawing a leaf in a twisted form so that the viewers could see both sides at once, a device so mature that it immediately stirred unusual interest. A little later, he had progressed far enough to win his first prize of any consequence, with a drawing of King Arthur of the Round Table.

Robert Rishell, born in Oakland where he still resides on a twelve-hundred-foot hill next to a large regional park, had shown so much artistic talent by the time he reached junior high school that his parents sent him to art school for his first formal lessons. When he was leaving high school, he won his first scholarship. Out of this award came a remarkable influence in his life. He met Xavier Martinez at the California College of Arts and Crafts in Oakland, at that time the only accredited school of its kind in the country. Martinez, a descendant of the Aztecs, was a traditional artist of the old school who had studied in Paris, wore a flowing red bow tie and was extremely strict with his students. Bob Rishell became only the third student in thirty-one years to get an "A" from Martinez. While he was in art school, Rishell met Dorothy Olsen, a petite blonde artist, and married her. Since then, they have traveled extensively all over the West and in Mexico, painting together. Rishell is noted for four specialties in his oil-painting work—portraits, trees, landscapes and horses. For horses he has a particular fondness. His extraordinary use of light, whether on a cowboy's hat brim or a tree trunk, is a distinguishing feature of his work. It has been said that Rishell loves horses as Degas loved ballet dancers; he certainly portrays them with a similar sympathetic understanding.

Horses are such individuals that they have as much character as people [Rishell explains]. The old ones, the young ones, the Indian ponies, every one has its own individuality. I like to paint a horse in repose rather than in violent action. Trying to stop a horse in action is like trying to stop a wave in action. People have said to me, "Why don't you go to Europe to paint?" but I find that I prefer the American West

"The Observers," by Robert Rishell. (Desert Southwest Art Gallery, Palm Desert, California.)

and in the West the horse is as much a part of the scene and history as is man.

Rishell's wife, who has watched the reaction of many persons at his art shows, says, "People love his horse paintings so much that they say, 'That is my old horse!'"

Rishell has plenty of opportunity near at hand to study his horse subjects because there is an English riding establishment within two blocks one way and a Western riding establishment two blocks the other way. Back of him, too, in the East Bay Regional Park area he can see hunters, jumpers and Western riders constantly. His portrait painting has not been confined to humans. He has done portraits of such immortals as Seabiscuit, the race horse, and many jumpers.

In their travels throughout the West now, the Rishells are able to take their daughter Lynn, who also shows artistic promise and is interested in horseback riding, too. Rishell's combination of talents is shown in his recent paintings of Indians. The Navahos and their horses appear vividly alive on the canvases. He finds an inexhaustible supply of subjects for his art wherever he goes, and gives to each one his special touch.

(Bottom) *Don Perceval*

(Top) *"Fence Rider," by Don Perceval. (Mrs. Don Perceval, Montecito, California.)*

A special artistic brand has been burned on history's hip by Don Louis Perceval.

Art and authenticity have been welded in the life and works of this painter and illustrator. His interests and skills, born of his Irish lineage and his devotion to Spanish, Mexican and American art forms as represented in cattle, horses and horsemen, has created for him a particular niche in the annals of Western art. All his life Don Perceval has been in quest of truth. When he depicts an Assyrian cattle brand or the marking on a horse of the conquistador period, he is combining reality with artistic impact.

His studies have made him probably the most outstanding authority in America on the early horses and cattle brought to this continent in 1519 and also a leading expert on accouterments of the horsemen and the gear of animals.

Don Perceval, born in Woodford, Essex, England, on January 8, 1908, yearned from the time he was a small child amid the mists and greenery of England for some distant arid lands known as "deserts." In later life, when he lived and painted in the deserts, he felt he was fulfilling a childhood longing. His paintings and drawings convey this impression so forcibly that the viewer is convinced of his seeming participation in the events, landscapes and animal scenes that he portrays.

The Perceval family came to Los Angeles from England when Don was a small boy, and it was in the semiarid region of southern California that he grew up, absorbing the lore of the land about which he had dreamed. Perceval roamed the desert southwest, visiting the Hopi and Navaho Indians and the whole wild regions. By the time he was nineteen, Perceval was drawing so well that he did the illustrations for a book by Harry James, *The Treasure of the Hopitu*, his first public venture into art.

While he was still in his early twenties, Don Perceval went to his native England to study art in London at the Heatherly Art School and the Royal College of Art in South Kensington. But the desert called to him again. He went to Spain—that country akin in appearance and spirit to California, whose godmother it was. In Spain Don Perceval began the deep studies and art ventures which eventually led him to his eminence in the field of illustration and painting and historical depiction.

World War II came, and he served four weary years in the Royal Navy amid the fogs of the English coast and as a gunnery instructor on H.M.S. "Excellent."

When he returned to California he became a teacher at Chouinard Art School and then at Pomona College. All this while he was becoming deeply versed in the historic lore of the West, and of Mexico and Spain from which the Latin civilization of western America had sprung.

One ancient custom began to fascinate him.

"Cattle brands are in themselves a definite art form," he suggests. He studied brands and discovered that they went back to the days of the Babylonians and the Egyptians, centuries before the Christian era.

"Cattle brands are not of American or Mexican origin, as many people seem to think," he says. "Both the history of cattle raising and of brands stretch back into the dimness of antiquity. As soon as primitive man became sufficiently domesticated to take pride in ownership, he probably put some sort of mark on his possessions to prevent confusion."

In support of his thesis that brands were in fact art, Don Perceval in 1950 wrote a long illustrated article for the *Brand Book* of the Los Angeles Westerners under the title "Names on Cows," featuring brands ranging from Assyrian bulls to the horses of Cortés, and on into later periods. Out of his absorption with detail came his strong views on the necessity for illustrations to be of as high a quality as the text in so-called history books:

To be of value, illustrations must be historically accurate; otherwise periods tend to merge into a conglomerate mass, thereby defeating the whole purpose of history teaching. Many periods in American history have been allowed to merge together in this way because the historical excellence of the text has not been matched by equal accuracy in the illustrative material used in conjunction with it. Extreme cases can be found wherein the costume shown in the illustration is appropriate for a period two hundred years before the events being described in the text took place. Lesser but equally damaging inaccuracies are so common that a proper sense of period is quite impossible to achieve.

. . . This situation prompted me to do a lot of most rewarding study on the subject of costume, saddlery, and other equipment.

The most astounding, and not uncommon, mistakes occur in the depiction of the Spanish explorers of Mexico and the American Southwest. By way of illustration, I will mention helmets only because what a man wears on his head is, perhaps, the most noticeable thing about him. Spanish Conquistadores are shown wearing either Combed or Peaked Morions regardless of period.

I have seen the bulk of the great collections of armor including the Wallace Collection in London and the Royal Armory in Madrid; I have looked in all the fine books on armor that I can find, and I have yet to see a Morion of either style that was not "late 16th century." During the conquest of Mexico, Cortez and his companions wore helmets with visors, or the lighter late 15th century Sallet (celada, salade or salet). In any case, their armor must have been pre-1518. To show Cortez and company in Combed Morions is an error of some fifty years.

Perceval has pointed out many similar errors in the depiction of the history of the American West, including some by notable painters who made their pictures after the period shown and in the process managed to commit gross errors in regard to saddles and clothing.

"If you're going to teach American history, and this to my mind is essential," Perceval says, "you might as well have the illustrations somewhere near correct because this is essential also."

As his studies progressed and his own painting ability increased, Perceval became

"The Remuda," by Jack Swanson

Jack Swanson branding at Parrott Ranch and riding "Jedediah"

more and more in demand as an illustrator; as a result, he did the drawings for literally dozens of books in the period from 1927 to the present. In addition, he has done hundreds of "free jobs" for friends and historical groups simply out of his interest in the subject matter.

He bought the home of Maynard Dixon in Tucson and lived and painted there for a time before moving to Santa Barbara, where he carries on his art work with artistic excellence and authenticity at his home-studio in the wooded area of Montecito.

An injured horse was Jack Swanson's schoolmate in art classes. This "Case of the Lame Horse" turned out to be the major turning point in the long, rough trail that Swanson was following in his attempt to become a Western painter.

Jack had been born in Duluth, Minnesota, in 1927 but had come to California with his parents when he was still a small child. The family moved around frequently, and he had been in fourteen schools before he graduated from high school.

"I think that I was sort of frustrated as far as formal education was concerned," he comments.

From the age of fourteen he had done a man's work as a horse breaker on ranches, including the Tejon Ranch close to the Ridge Route and the Crofton Cattle Company spreads, also near Tehachapi, California.

"I was already showing signs of my orneriness and to get even with me I was handed all the spoiled horses to work," Jack relates.

During this time it was his good fortune to be on the job with the famous California horseman Frank Martinez, whose reputation extended all over the West. Swanson took many a spill during his horse breaking, and Martinez finally paid him the supreme compliment when he said, "Maybe some day you make vaquero!"

Swanson's first job was at the I. L. Borden Ranch in the Sierra foothills, where standardbred horses were raised. He was sent with seven trotters to the Santa Rosa race meet, "where I cut my eye teeth with standardbred trainers, the fussiest men with a horse there are."

He soon discovered that race-track life did not appeal to him, and from there he started his horse-breaking jobs wherever he could find them. After a Navy hitch of two years during World War II, he and his brother went to Oregon to work on ranches their father had bought, and they supplemented their income by buying wild horses and training them.

"All the time, I would entertain myself drawing," Jack recalls. "Generally it was of anything of interest that happened during the day that I would sketch in the evening. My best admirers and critics were cowboys I worked with, and my sketches were hung in bunkhouses and cook shacks."

He took advantage of the GI Bill and started art school at the College of Arts and Crafts in Oakland, but found that he was impatient with the methods of teaching:

I seemed to be not getting along with modern-type art teachers who didn't think horses were worth painting but pots were.

I brought down a good young quarter stud with me and slept with him back in the mountains above Oakland during the time I was going to art school [he said]. When I decided to leave, I toured the racing circuit with my stud. He was a good one and managed to equal the record for studs at that time on the quarter track.

It was then that the "Case of the Lame Horse" started.

While at a race meet in Stockton, the horse pulled up lame and veterinarians advised Swanson to work him out in salt water for a few months.

Necessity to have some money while I was getting my horse well made me start the GI Bill again in Carmel where a school was located near the ocean [Swanson says]. I'd be working my horse out at daybreak in the waves and then hoof it on up and open up at the school and generally get ten or twelve hours of painting in. Again I was

(Bottom) *"Pickin' Daisies," by Marjorie Reed*
(Top) *Marjorie Reed*

living with my horse, sharing the blanket.

Donald Teague, N.A., asked me one day to pose for a Western illustration. After looking over some of my canvases he took me under his wing, hammering in the basic fundamentals of painting and giving me a boot when I needed it. That last is the most important part of becoming an artist. Another to help me along the way was a tough old Irishman, a great artist, John O'Shea. His work inspired me when I was at my lowest. Meeting my future wife also solidified my desire to make something of my painting.

He and his wife built their own house on a ranch in the Cachagua area of the Carmel Valley close to the California coast, where they breed, raise and train stock horses as a sideline to his studio work.

My feeling towards painting is realism —honesty to detail, thoroughly knowing the subject you're painting and to do the best to record the life of the man who makes his living in the saddle [Swanson remarks]. There's still a big West left but I suspect it'll be gone in my lifetime. I respect the old-timers still left on remote ranches who are hanging on to the traditional ways of horse training. I don't like gimmicks and the fast way of doing things whether in painting or putting a rein on a horse.

Swanson's canvases hang everywhere from the National Cowboy Hall of Fame to collections in Los Angeles, Kansas City and elsewhere.

His most recent adventure is in sculpture, for which his first pieces were cast early in 1968.

So great was the inner urge of Marjorie Reed to paint horses that when she was a girl she walked eighteen miles to sit on a corral fence to watch and sketch them in action. She has since concluded that her painting of horses resulted from frustration because of her great desire to live on a ranch, an ambition which did not materialize.

While Marjorie was yearning for a ranch life, she was busily occupied under the tutelage of her father in learning to draw and paint. Her father, Walter Reed of Springfield, Illinois (where Marjorie was born on February 22, 1915), was a commercial artist, and her mother possessed a fine artistic appreciation. The girl began drawing long before she went to school and then, in her father's studio, designed Christmas cards for major companies and worked for a subsidiary owned by Walt Disney when she was only fourteen.

Her work attracted the attention of Disney, who sought to place her in the animation department of his studios, but, as she says, "I couldn't adjust to the regimentation."

This yearning for a free life in the ranching country could not be satisfied on the outskirts of Los Angeles, where Marjorie Reed grew up after the family moved West. Thus, it was at this period that she would take the eighteen-mile walks to see the horses she wanted to sketch. Later she was able to give full rein to her desire to paint horse and cowboy subjects when she was a visitor at ranches in California, Arizona, Utah, Nevada, Wyoming, Montana and Colorado. She led pack trips into the Tetons to gain material to paint.

She says she was never a good rider, but she took comfort from Charlie Russell's remark that she was "the poorest cowboy of the lot." Of a deeply religious nature, Marjorie Reed feels that through her frustration in being denied a ranching life she was enabled to turn to her art, and to be rewarded by giving pleasure to those who enjoy her work.

"Only by returning the gift of the Creator can we alleviate this frustration," she says about her ability to paint.

In addition to the instruction given her by her father, she studied for a short time at the Chouinard Art School and the Art Center School in Los Angeles. Most of the credit for her formal training she gives to Jack Wilkinson Smith of Alhambra, with whom she studied for two years.

Her extraordinary talent for Western portrayals flowered in a series of twenty paintings showing stagecoaches on the old Butterfield Stage route, the celebrated line which in 1858 began to run from St. Louis, Missouri, to San Francisco across Texas and up through southern California. These paintings attracted national attention and were acquired by James S. Copley, publisher of the *San Diego Union Tribune*. Subsequently, they were used in a book, *Colorful Butterfield*

Walt La Rue

"Movin' On," by Walt La Rue. (Mr. and Mrs. Leroy Johnson, Sun Valley, California.)

Overland Stage.

A Marjorie Reed stagecoach has become synonymous with perfection in this type of art. The animation and fidelity shown in her cowboy and ranch scenes also have won acclaim.

She now lives in the little town of Amado, Arizona, near Tucson, where she conducts an art studio. Few stagecoaches come by, but if they did, Marjorie Reed would be ready to paint them.

"I believe the motion-picture business has helped my schooling as far as my Western painting subjects are concerned," philosophizes Walt La Rue, movie stunt man and cowboy artist. "Where else could a fellow ride on a stagecoach that was just a-flying down the road or be involved in holding up a train? We do it the same way as they used to. The livestock we use gets just as excited. The only thing different is the date—this being the middle 1900's instead of the late 1800's. I have seen stampedes, have been with wagon trains, mountain men, Mexican bandits and horse thieves. I've gotten to see a lot of the old West these days. That's something most contemporary artists don't get a

chance to do. I've been lucky."

La Rue's ability to transform himself into a participant in events that took place eighty or ninety years ago, even in their recreation in the movies today, is typical of the joyous spirit which infuses all his paintings. They have a wide-eyed genuineness that appeals to everyone who loves the real West. His galloping horses, flying lassos, bucking cayuses, and rodeo scenes all bear this individual stamp.

On envelopes and in letters to friends little pencil sketches of the West add the "Walt La Rue" touch to his correspondence—in the fashion of Charlie Russell, whose bubbling spirits led to a similar outlet.

Before I started to paint seriously I made quite a bit of my income drawing cartoons [La Rue says]. For ten years I drew the covers on the official rodeo publication "The Buckboard." These were kind of satire-type cartoons about the real rodeo cowboy, his happiness, his hardships and all the things he encountered.

It's a wonder in a way that Walt La Rue

ever became a chronicler of the West, because he was born in Canada, although of American parents.

> I came to the United States when I was a small boy [La Rue relates], and lived in Montana for a while and then came to California. When school was out every year I took off to the high country where I'd work on pack outfits in the high Sierras. I packed and guided dudes in Yosemite and up above Yosemite. In the winters I broke horses. When I got out of school I went to Montana where I worked for the –X6 near Glacier Park. I wrangled dudes in Glacier. I worked up on Sun River near Augusta and in Choteau, Montana.
>
> When I was rodeoing, I made lots of the little shows and also some of the biggest—Salinas, Madison Square Garden, Los Angeles Coliseum, Great Falls, San Francisco, Portland, Albuquerque, etc.—and won money at most.

La Rue's father was a miner, and Walt had seen the hardships of life when he was a child. Yet these could not stifle some inborn craving he had to express himself. "When I was a small boy I got some pencils and crayons and just went to drawing," he recalls.

For fifteen seasons, later on, he made the rodeo circuit, standing up under the poundings and jostlings while getting into the movies. His formal training consisted of a mere six months at the Otis Art Institute in Los Angeles; it was primarily his inborn talent which carried him forward.

His particular idols have been "Will James" and Charlie Russell. In three words he explains why he does what he does: "I enjoy painting."

> I paint the West because I've been making my living on horseback thirty years and I know that subject better than any other, and I'm also pretty fond of it [he recounts]. Sometimes when I'm painting I really have a tough time getting going. I may get pretty riled up. But when I'm fin-

"The Reluctant Packer," by George Dick. (The artist.)

George Dick

ished and I've done the best I can and the painting looks pretty good, I really get a satisfied feeling and I can't wait to start another.

A naturalist who used to wander around the West with a falcon named Margaret has proceeded from a career with the United States Forest Service and the Fish and Wild-

"The Visitor." Water color by Vic Donahue. (August Neuner, Albuquerque, New Mexico.)

Vic Donahue

life Service to become a painter of cowpunchers. George Dick of Albuquerque blends his two interests and paints flying ducks as well as herds of Herefords.

Dick, born in Manitowoc, Wisconsin, March 12, 1916, graduated in forestry at the University of Michigan and then served in the Army Tank Corps in Europe during World War II. He was in an Army hospital for a while after the war and then tried to get a Ph.D., but he found the weather in Michigan too severe. For his health he went to Jackson Hole, Wyoming, lived in a lean-to and led an outdoor life for two years. At Michigan he had taken a game management course, and this led him to close observations of the animals as he fished all over Wyoming.

He wanted to depict the wildlife around him so he took advantage of the GI Bill and went to the University of New Mexico for four years, where he received a Master's degree in art. His teachers were Kenneth Adams and Randall Davey. From Davey, who painted race horses, Dick gained an interest in horse pictures.

However, he found himself in an artistic trap. He had been influenced by the trend of the times and for two years painted nonobjective subjects. He finally decided that this was not what he wanted to do, and, because of the availability of horse models on ranches all around Albuquerque, he gradually gravitated toward painting them. At the same time, his training in game management continued to give him a great interest in waterfowl and songbirds, so he painted ducks, too. At one time his work with the federal government took him to the Ruby Lake Refuge in Ruby Valley between Elko and Las Vegas, Nevada, near the Humboldt Mountains. In this Pacific flyway area he had opportunity to observe thousands of birds at first hand. Also, in the same region mustangs ran wild.

Alternating between bird and cowboy subjects, he began to achieve widespread notice with both.

Jack Roberts with his painting "The Hunting Party on the Continental Divide, 1854"

"I've only done a few landscapes," Dick says. "I like to have something animated in my pictures, or otherwise I get bored."

He uses the formula of the old masters in mixing his paints, using poppyseed oil and only a small amount of linseed because the latter sets up too fast. He works a great deal with brown because it is one of his favorite colors.

"The mystery of the outdoors and the unknown is what appeals to me, so I am always in search of something new," Dick explains.

Paintings such as "Point of the Run," "Reluctant Packer" and "Border Town" attest to his ability in Western art. He was the first winner of the Purchase Prize of the New Mexico State Fair in 1954.

The nice thing about his kind of work is that when he goes out to paint a cow he may see a duck too!

"An Artist in Search of a Home," might well be the title of the life story of Vic Donahue.

He has been known as a Western painter, illustrator and calendar and magazine artist for many years. But it might not have been imagined by those who saw his Western work that came out of a Vermont studio or a home in Omaha, Nebraska. It took a long while for Donahue to find a permanent resi-

dence that suited him. When he saw it, though, he had no doubts. It is in Tucson, Arizona.

"As soon as I saw Tucson, I knew it was the only place to live and work," Donahue relates.

The long vistas to the desert mountains, the immense saguaros in the desert, the cattle on the ranges, the sunsets, the jaggedness of the peaks—all appealed immediately to Donahue, who was born in Nebraska in 1917. Until he and his wife, Eileen, and their sons, Kelly and Brian, settled in Tucson, he had drawn much upon his imagination for his subjects. While he was working in Vermont and Omaha he had drawn magazine covers of Western subjects that were familiar to many Americans.

During World War II he became one of the first three Marine combat artists in New Guinea and the Russell Islands, and his pictures were placed in the Marine Corps records in Washington.

"Tucson is obviously the place to develop new outlets for both commercial and fine arts," he says. "The entire West Coast region is doing more imaginative work in advertising and the arts than any other part of the nation."

Among his other accomplishments he has illustrated children's books, including *The Mystery of Mound Key* by Robert F. Burgess, published in 1966 by The World Publish-

(Above) M. A. Gomez

(Left) "Pay Day," by M. A. Gomez

ing Company. Donahue's paintings have been featured in galleries in Arizona and New Mexico.

A painter who believes that "beaver trappers had more excitement every morning before breakfast than later-day cowboys had in a lifetime," is turning more and more to historic subjects as a result of his studies. Jack Roberts of Hanging Lake, Glenwood Springs, Colorado, maintains unorthodox views about cowpunchers, although his paintings of them have brought high prices.

"I have concluded that cowboys are a bunch of sissies," he remarks. This does not mean that he has lost interest in the West, however. A particular aspect of the adventurous Western life which appeals to him is that of a hunting expedition in the three-year period between 1854 and 1857 of Sir St. George Gore, the eighth Baronet of Gore Manor, Sligo, Ireland, in the American West.

"The longhorn critter was still free in Mexico and that vast cow country known as the great plains was labeled 'Indian Country' on crude maps of the period," Roberts explains about his plans to illustrate an account of this hunting expedition. He also intends to devote more time to the beaver trappers because of the exciting lives led by these mountain men.

Jack Roberts was born in Oklahoma City on April 1, 1920. His formal art training was at the University of Oklahoma and the American Academy of Art in Chicago, but the greatest inspiration he received was from Harvey Dunn at Grand Central School of Art in New York.

"I regard Harvey Dunn, who died in 1953, as the greatest artist of his generation," Roberts says.

Roberts has done a series for the Equitable Life Assurance Society of New York. Hank Williams, brother of G. Mennen Williams of the shaving cream family, owns about forty of his paintings.

Roberts worked as a cowboy in Burns, Colorado, and from this came his intimate knowledge of range life which he later used in many of his paintings. He became interested in drawing at an early age, and since then has moved steadily toward his goal of "just doing what I want to do."

An Egyptian pyramid, of all things, is the first art subject that Western painter Tony Gomez remembers. His father was painting a pyramid on commission, from a photo.

I can remember Father at the easel while I sat cross-legged on the floor watching him paint [Tony recalls]. I was just a little guy, but I thought Father was crazy—he squared 'em out to look like adobe bricks. Father turned from the easel and pointing to the pyramid said to me, "A hard climb."

It has indeed been, symbolically, a hard climb for Marco Antonio Gomez from that moment in Durango, Mexico (where he was born in 1910), to the high level he has attained in art circles. His father was a portrait painter and had done the features of many prominent Mexicans. When Tony was only eight the family moved to Ashfork, Arizona, in the northern part of that state where the Old West still prevailed in the years prior to World War I.

"I used to ride a lot with Indian kids and when I was galloping along with them the color of the Navaho land and the butte country always fascinated me with its charm and beauty," Tony explains. His chief regret is that he waited so long to take up painting. The necessities of making a living prevented him from devoting much time to the scenes which were constantly beckoning to him.

"I was greatly helped by my father when he was still alive, and since then by my wife and partner, Marge, whose advice and judgment I try to follow because she is so discerning in her taste," Tony says.

His aim has been to try to preserve the best of the past so that the present generation can feel the fascination of a bygone era.

> Russell and Remington didn't do it all, and what they did do is mostly in museums [Tony comments]. "They painted the historic West of their time, and I have tried to learn from these last of the great contemporary masters."

Tony Gomez has constantly improved in recent years in his technical approach, and has won prizes and ribbons in many notable shows. He has been exhibiting in Denver, Taos, New York, Los Angeles, Santa Ana, Palm Springs and cities in Canada. His paintings hang in the homes of buyers from the West Coast to Washington, D.C., and from New York to Paris and West Germany.

He constantly is traveling to the places which appeal to him the most, studying cowboys in action, the Indians, and the landscape.

A father who took his son fishing as soon as the boy could walk can take some of the credit for the later success of the young fisherman as a Western artist.

Conrad Schwiering's first memories go back to the outings he took with his father, Dr. O. C. Schwiering, at one time Dean of Education at the University of Wyoming. The father pointed out the lessons to be learned from wild creatures, from the flowers, the aspen and the pines, and the profound sermons to be listened to by the human heart in the grandeur of mountain peaks such as the Tetons in Wyoming. These early impressions so influenced Conrad Schwiering that when he goes fishing now he doesn't even need to catch a fish. As he puts it, "I see a beautiful reflection or a rich color underneath it in the water and I've had a strike!"

This obsession with art is carried over into almost everything he does. "It's a funny thing to have a profession that is your hobby too," he says. "I really get a great deal of joy out of my work."

Schwiering did not arrive all at once at his goal. He was born in Boulder, Colorado, on August 8, 1916. Between fishing trips with his father when he was old enough to travel and study, he became interested in the art work of Paul Gregg in the *Denver Post*. This interest in art continued during his years at Laramie High School. Later, at the University of Wyoming where he specialized in commerce and legal subjects, he took a minor in art. He studied under Robert A. Grahame and Raphael Lillywhite of Denver. It was advice from Bert Phillips of Taos, New Mexico, however, that directed young Schwiering on the right path in his life work. Phillips,

"Slick Rock Traveler," by Conrad Schwiering. (The artist.)   *Conrad Schwiering on location*

so distinguished in his own painting career, told Schwiering that he should consider all of the contemporary artists and then choose the one he would like most as a teacher. Schwiering made his choice, went to New York City and managed to meet Charles S. Chapman of the National Academy at the Art Students' League. He explained his ambition to have Chapman teach him. Chapman soon decided that the young man had promise, and devoted a great deal of time to his new student.

Since then, with time out for service in the United States Army in World War II when he made infantry film strips and reached the rank of lieutenant colonel, Schwiering has persisted in art of one form or another.

One big break came when, just after the war, Schwiering met Cyrus Boutwell, of Denver, and was asked to show his paintings at the Boutwell Galleries. This started a series of annual exhibitions that in time resulted in Schwiering's being invited to show at Grand Central Art Galleries in New York.

"It is hard not to become emotional amid all this beauty," Schwiering says of the Teton region in Wyoming where he lives, "and I have prayed a lot for the ability to express it."

One Indian with a bowie knife is using it to spread paint instead of skinning buffalo. Echo Hawk, full-blooded Pawnee Indian, born in Pawnee, Oklahoma, actually uses a bowie knife with palette-knife technique in his paintings to obtain special textures and to trap light. Echo Hawk, despite his peaceful use of the bowie knife, knows how to handle weapons, too. He is a twice-wounded veteran of World War II who saw service as a combat infantryman in a regiment in Africa and Italy. His outfit included the famous Bill Mauldin, creator of "Willy and Joe," who were known all over the world.

Echo Hawk is the grandson of another famous Echo Hawk who was a United States cavalry scout under Major Frank North in the Indian Wars. Echo Hawk means "a warrior

Echo Hawk painting on commission from the Aluminum Company of America. He is depicting a part of Tennessee history.

whose deeds are echoed." Echo Hawk has also earned the right to the Pawnee name of "Chaticks-Si-Chaticks," meaning "Man of Men."

"I enjoy my own people, I prefer my own people," Echo Hawk remarks.

In regard to the bowie knife, he explains, "My knife can turn the color better than a brush."

He has painted all sorts of Western scenes from buffalo to Indian powwows, and is considered an authority, both historically and artistically, in his accurate depiction of the American Indian and the West. His great admiration for Winslow Homer, George Catlin, Charlie Russell and Frederic Remington is reflected in his work. One of his notable paintings is "Trail of Tears," showing the Cherokees being driven out of their homelands to the middle of the continent. This painting now hangs in the Gilcrease Institute of History and Art in Tulsa, Oklahoma. He

also was associated with Thomas Hart Benton in the creation of the mural on the wall of the Harry S. Truman Library at Independence, Missouri, showing the opening of the West.

Among his artistic creations have been Christmas cards reflecting the Indian spirit, distributed by Ed Trumbull of Boulder, Colorado. He also does the "Little Chief" comic-strip series for a Sunday supplement.

Echo Hawk believes in an independent approach to art, and despises the technique which "paints in riddles."

He can boast a notable amount of technical training at the Art Institutes in Chicago and Detroit.

For inspiration, he listens to classical music as he paints with his bowie knife.

A college student who was willing to slug it out with his "abstract" art teachers has become one of the West's leading painters of cowboy scenes. Seemingly mild-mannered

Harold Hopkinson was not willing to be thwarted in his desire to paint Western subjects when he was at the University of Wyoming. As a result of his collision with his teachers he was not rated high in the class. Later, though, his apparent obstinacy was justified. He proved that bucking horses could be a better subject than meaningless daubs.

Born in Salt Lake City in 1918, Harold Hopkinson was raised on a ranch in the Bridger Valley of Wyoming during his most impressionable years. Then, when he served in the United States Navy in World War II, he not only received eight battle stars and six ribbons for service aboard battleships in the South Pacific, but also had time to think about his future education. When he came back from the war he went to the University of Wyoming and received B.A. and M.A. degrees in art and administration, but he was unable to enter an art career immediately. He was a ranch hand, then for several years was a locomotive fireman on the Union Pacific Railroad after which he became an art instructor for the University of Wyoming and then Superintendent of Schools in Byron, Wyoming. He served in this later post for ten years, but he was continually torn between education and art. Finally, art won out.

When he made the break, he was able to live in his studio home overlooking the Shoshone River at Byron and to paint every day and often into the night, too. His formal training in art and illustration at the Los Angeles Art Center and in Westport, Connecticut, has given technical excellence to his productions. His material has been so graphic and appealing that it has been used as magazine covers as well as adorning the walls of many homes. He also has specialized in murals, and was one of those helping to create the murals in the Mormon Temple in Los Angeles. In addition, he presented a mural to the Mormon Church in Byron.

When he gets a moment to think back

Harold Hopkinson

on his variegated career, Hopkinson likes to remember the inspiration which started him drawing in the first place. He remembers that he saw examples of the work of Frederic Remington and Charlie Russell on calendars, and these reproductions influenced him to try his own hand at drawing horses and cattle.

A tough old Jersey cow still is the best helper in carrying on an artistic tradition in Mexico, California and Texas. Her hide makes the best *reata* in the world.

This is one of the secrets transmitted from father to son for generations in the art of *reata* braiding. One of the few persons in the West still carrying on this art, which has almost reached the folklore stage because of its rarity, is Ernest Morris of Templeton near San Luis Obispo, California, in a region long noted for its cattlemen and big spreads. Morris, born December 13, 1927 comes by his talent naturally. He is a grandson of Jesse

"Reata Weaver," by Edward Borein from Land of Sunshine, August, 1896

Ernest Morris

Wilkinson, one of the notable cowboys of the old Miller and Lux ranch in California. In his time, Wilkinson could braid an eighty-foot reata ("lariat," as Americanos del Norte say) so strong that it would hold anything with four legs and so smooth that it was a work of art. He it was who taught his grandson Ernest how to do the same thing.

For the most part, modern cowboys cannot handle a reata eighty feet long such as Grandpa Wilkinson used to make, so there is no necessity for it; nearly everybody is content to use a fiber rope. Yet, because he likes to carry on the art, Morris still makes rawhide reatas. Morris is convinced that a dried-up old Jersey produces the best hide for a reata because, "When the fat goes out, the glue comes in, and that's what gives the strength."

It's a wearisome process at best. The hide first is soaked twenty-four hours in water so it will be ready for scraping. Then, after the hair and flesh are off, the hard part starts. The reata braider gets down on his knees with a sharp knife; he cuts the hide round and round in one long piece about the width between the second and third joints on the index finger. The strip is gauged for thickness, and, after

that, it is cornered and beveled so that it will braid smoothly. Four pieces are used for braiding. If, for instance, a sixty-foot reata is wanted, the strips will be cut eighty feet long at the start.

> It's got to have just the right moisture in it for proper braiding [Morris confides]. It's something you can't describe—like kneading bread, you just have to learn. Anyway, after it's braided and dried out you hammer it on an anvil. Then comes the sandpapering, and after that you pull it through the holes in a juniper post—which won't splinter—to put on the finish. The reata then is kept in shape with kidney fat and beef liver for gloss and softness.

Reata braiding is more an avocation than anything else with Morris now, but he still continues it for collectors who besiege him for his beautiful work. At other times he is busy painting Western scenes.

Morris says that he has been drawing and painting as far back as he can remember—

(Left) *Ace Powell at Park Saddle Horse Company Corrals, where he was a top hand for six years*

(Above) *"Company for Supper," by Ace Powell.* (Mrs. Ellen Urich, Ronan, Montana.)

which also is true for riding a horse. He has been a lifelong admirer of the work of Charlie Russell, "Will James" and Ed Borein, because "they have left a true impression of the old West in their art work."

"My love for the open range is such that I want to preserve the memory of the Old West and the California vaquero," Morris says about his painting and the creation of the *reatas*—always, of course, with the help of the old Jersey cows who contribute their hides.

In the language of playing cards, the ace of diamonds always speaks with a loud, clear voice. So it is, too, with Ace Powell, the painter and storyteller whose pictures all bear his distinctive mark, the ace of diamonds. For more than a third of a century this signature of Ace Powell has been on sketches and paintings, all relating to that vast region where the buffalo once roamed in northwest Montana. To many, it is a forbidding and somewhat frightening land, but to Ace Powell the entire region around Glacier Park where he has spent so much of his life is a source of inspira-

tion for painting. He has depicted the cowboy and the Indian in their native haunts and on the horses which made their life possible in the wilderness.

Ace Powell, the son of a cowboy father and a school-teacher mother, has been intimately connected with the cattle business all his life. It is natural that he should have been stimulated by Charlie Russell, who also roamed the Montana countryside, and by Joe De Yong, the pupil and protégé of Russell who likewise was a working cowboy in this region.

"I believe pioneering is America's greatness," says Ace Powell. "It is all I know."

As far back as he can remember he made his living on a horse, until he turned to professional painting in 1938. He was born in Tularosa, New Mexico, on April 3, 1912, and began cowboying when very young. Later, he had one year at Montana State University and some private lessons in painting, but for the most part he has mastered art through observation of the cowboys and the Indians around him.

In a recent booklet, "The Ace of Dia-

monds," written and illustrated by Powell and edited by Van Kirke Nelson, M.D., of Kalispell, Montana, where both live, Powell relates incidents he remembers in the Glacier Park region many years ago. His friends say this publication is another indication that the Ace of Diamonds is destined to carry on successfully in the world of Western art.

A hundred years of cattle-ranching tradition lies behind the man who says he believes that he has "ridden for more cow outfits than any other man today painting and depicting the American cowboy." At his home in the little town of Orogrande in southeastern New Mexico, Clint Worlds likes to remember that he "rode for the last of the big cow outfits and was very fortunate in getting in on the last thirty years of the good, wild, fast-action cowboy life." His mother's people had been cattle ranchers in Kern County, California, since 1870. Worlds can recall that his Uncle Charlie Andreas first put him on a horse in Kern County when he was a tiny boy, and he has been riding ever since.

Worlds was born June 5, 1922, in Kernville on the Kern River in a region long known for its cattle and mining activity. From the time he started drawing when he was eleven, Worlds was influenced by the drawings of "Will James." Later, he became acquainted with Norman Rockwell. Now he credits Bill Bender (who, by coincidence, lives in Oro Grande, California) and Rockwell with having given him more pointers than anyone else about painting. Somewhat in the pattern of "James," Worlds has done his cowboying in many places.

I left home as a very young boy and spent my entire working life drifting from state to state and from ranch to ranch, punching cows, breaking colts, riding rough string, cutting hay, building fences, digging wells, and gathering at roundups. I also guided on the Bright Angel Trail at the Grand Canyon and packed mules into the primitive back country.

Bill Bender relates that, when he was a movie extra in westerns, he rode at Kernville, and in rehearsals galloped back and forth in front of the school where Worlds was a pupil. They later became acquainted, and Worlds recalled how he had wanted to quit his desk

(Far left) *Clint Worlds*

(Left) *"Cow Country Blacksmith," by Clint Worlds. (Joya de Taos Gallery.)*

(Above) *"Portrait of Artist Clarence Ellsworth," by Joseph Stahley. (The artist.)*

(Right) *Joseph Stahley on quarter horse "Jim"*

and join the film riders.

"I do not paint to entertain," Worlds says. "I paint to enlighten, and one must study my work and search out the truth that is there."

In support of his statement of having ridden for more outfits than any other painter, Worlds lists a few of these in different states and in Mexico—including the Nine L, Bar Wagon Wrench, JHL, Hip O, OK, Circle Dot, Steer Head, Quarter Circle, Five and Double S outfits of South Fork Valley, California; the Flying H Moffatt Cattle Company at Gustine, California; the Quarter Circle K's and PAK's at Maricopa, California. He was foreman for the big BAR T Bar outfit at Keene, California, and range foreman for the Seven Cross outfit at Mohave, California, which encompassed nine townships. He rode for the T Lazy S at Battle Mountain, Nevada, and the Box Jigger at Park Station, Nevada, and for Clara Bow and Rex Bell on their Walking Box ranch at Searchlight, Nevada. In Arizona he rode for the famous Chiricahua Cattle Company at Sonoita, the forty-thousand-head Three V outfit at Seligman, and for

the Triangle Cross at Amado. He went through a big roundup in the Sierra Madres in Chihuahua, Mexico, for the Chauvet brothers. His last steady job as a cowboy was for James B. Rogers, the younger son of the late Will Rogers, on his ranch at Randsburg, California. He still rides for a neighbor outfit at Orogrande—the Bar X Quarter Circle. He has his own roping arena at his home and ropes calves in the evenings for relaxation.

Many a cowboy rode his horse into a saloon in the old days, but few are credited with riding a horse hundreds of miles to art school.

Joe Stahley can take credit for this innovation. When he was only fifteen he combined his love of horses and Western art, and rode all the way from his home in Rochester, New York, to Chicago to begin studies at the Chicago Art Institute. He and his horse, Don, underwent "a memorable, broadening experience" on the ride, according to Stahley. This partnership of horse and art has continued on through Stahley's life. His valued companion now is Jim, a husky quarter horse with whom

"Point Rider," by Robert Wagoner. (Saddleback Art Gallery, Santa Ana, California.)

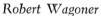

Robert Wagoner

he has shared ranch life, cattle drives, round-ups and brandings. Fortunately for Stahley, he found a wife who also delights in horses and all kinds of Western outdoor life. He has friends among Indians, cowboys, rodeo contestants and ranchers, who are continually supplying him with material for his art subjects. [He learned other facets of art from Dean Cornwell and Nicolai Fechin.]

As with so many painters of this century, he was greatly influenced by "Will James." Both "James" and Stahley were friends of Mr. and Mrs. Earl Snook of Montana, the great collectors of "James" material. It was through this collection that Stahley came in contact with "James."

"Depicting life in the West has been an absorbing interest to me for many years," Stahley says, "my attention being focused upon the cowboy and his horse and their resourcefulness in the big range country."

Besides creating many magazine illustrations for notable publications, he served for four years as art director of Lord and Thomas advertising agency in New York and taught at the Rochester Institute of Technology, specializing in illustration, freehand and still life.

Then he went on to become a set illustrator for Walt Disney and to work at Paramount, Columbia, Metro-Goldwyn-Mayer, and Universal International for sixteen years.

His overwhelming interest, though, has remained in Western painting.

The caliber of his professional standing was shown while he was studying with Harvey Dunn, the National Academician and illustrator, when he was awarded the bronze plaque for the best work of the year.

When Robert Wagoner wrote the nostalgic song "High Country," he undoubtedly was expressing his own lifelong yearning for a ranch of his own. The song, which has enjoyed popularity on television and radio, is an example of only one of his talents. The other, painting, is tied in intimately with his desire for a ranch, and is characterized by his concentration almost entirely upon cowboy and cattle subjects.

Bob Wagoner has had to contend with a paradox for many years. During the daytime he is in the construction business with his father, his duties having ranged from driving heavy machinery to taking charge of the opera-

Paul Salisbury with one of his paintings

tions of the road graders and other large equipment. Then, at night, he has devoted his time to painting. He became interested in art when he was about thirteen—he still is only about forty—but it was not until the decade of 1960's that he began to paint well enough to think about exhibiting. His first major show was at Death Valley, where thousands of persons gather each November for the Death Valley Forty-niner Encampment, of which a major art show, under the direction at various times of John W. Hilton, Bill Bender and Emil (Aim) Morhardt, is one of the notable features.

When Wagoner had been painting in oils only for seven months, he exhibited at this show and, immediately attracting attention, began selling his canvases. His knowledge of cowboys and horses is not secondhand. He has participated in rodeos and been around ranches so much that he knows what goes on. He studied forestry in college and served two years in the Marine Corps, became a flyer and then taught himself to play the guitar and was a professional entertainer for a number of years. All the time, though, he was looking forward to the day when he could have his

own cattle spread. In 1967 he did acquire a ranch as an added inspiration in his painting career.

Bob Wagoner gives credit to Burt Proctor, Frank Tenney Johnson, Olaf Wieghorst and Charlie Dye for providing the kind of example that has encouraged him to carry on. The locales of his exhibitions are constantly becoming more numerous, and he now shows his paintings not only at Death Valley, but at the Saddleback Gallery in Santa Ana, California, and in Phoenix, Arizona, La Galeria, in Sedona, Arizona, and The Gallery of Palm Springs, California.

Born in Marion, Ohio, July 13, 1928, Wagoner has lived for many years in Long Beach, California. His wife Norajean paints china, and his boys seem to have inherited their father's flair for painting and drawing.

One of the paintings of Paul Salisbury is entitled "The Strays," yet the artist has never strayed from his objective of portraying the West as it really is.

Paul Salisbury was born in Richfield, Utah, on November 21, 1904, and he now lives in Provo, not far from his birthplace. In the meantime, though, he has traveled in the wild country of his native state and the surrounding regions, talked with Indians, pioneers and cowboys, and absorbed the meaning of the life they lead. In his studio today he depicts the whole scope of the Western scene from this intimate knowledge gained over many decades.

He began riding horses and trying to draw them when he was only six or seven on his father's ranch near Kanosh Indian Reservation in southern Utah.

He says that he was greatly influenced by the paintings of Frank Tenney Johnson. Salisbury began doing jacket paintings for the *Western Horseman* and the *Desert Magazine* and other publications, and also for banks and libraries and universities. He has held exhibits from Reno, Nevada, to Boston, Massachusetts, and from San Francisco, California, to Atlanta, Georgia. One notable outlet is the Kachina Gallery of Dwight Roberts in Santa Fe. The breadth of his interest is indicated by the titles of some of his paintings: "The Nesters," "Rivers to Cross," "Buffalo Hunters," "Taking a Breather," "Water Hole Conference," "Bringing in the Chuck Wagon," and "The Strays."

If a young artist's imagination has been fired by Michelangelo and Charlie Russell, and on top of this he has become interested in horses, the result may be a fine Western painter. This, at least, has been the case with James E. Boren, who was born and grew up in east Texas, and has striven with persistence and determination toward a painting career. (In addition to Michelangelo and Charlie Russell, he adds that Frederic Remington and Nicolai Fechin—the great Russian artist who spent the latter part of his life in America— also helped to inspire him as he plodded along on the artistic path.) Boren, in recent years, has been the art director of the National Cowboy Hall of Fame, but he did not arrive

James Boren, art director, National Cowboy Hall of Fame

at that position without having worked for it. In addition to his bareback riding on horses beginning when he was nine and his interest in art going back further than that, he has rigorously trained himself to fulfill his artistic aspirations. He has both an A.B. and a M.A. in Fine Arts from the Kansas City Art Institute. His choice of painting subjects has been guided by his surroundings in his native state, and in Oklahoma and Colorado where he also has lived.

"I'm a Westerner—it's what I know and love best," he says.

Despite his duties at the Cowboy Hall of Fame, Boren has continued to paint the cowboy and ranch-life scenes that bear his stamp in color and mood.

The cowboy, the man on the horse, played the starring role in history's most exciting era—that of the American West [he says]. Not only did this environment of men and cattle, outlaws and what-have-you spawn the greatest heroes and include the most exciting situations, but it happened in the most beautiful country anywhere. It happened in Texas, New Mexico, Colorado,

"The Runaway," by James E. Reynolds. (Walter Bimson, Phoenix, Arizona.)

James E. Reynolds

Wyoming and Montana. To me this combination of things, events and surroundings offers an artist the greatest painting material in the world.

Working as he does at the Cowboy Hall of Fame amid great examples of Western art, Boren has the opportunity to meditate upon the motivation and techniques which permitted the artists to reach their eminent position. In no sense a copyist, he still has derived a sense of direction from them. It is this quality that gives to his paintings the fundamental appeal that they possess.

A heritage from the gold country of California animates one artist who has found his love of the Old West nurtured by the majestic surroundings there. James Reynolds of Santa Monica, a third-generation Californian, spent his boyhood summers in the regions around Nevada City and the old town of Washington near the famous Donner Pass road in California. The large herds of cattle driven through Washington (where his grandmother operated a small hotel), and the old wagons, the one-room jail, the Chinese mine and the saloon with its shuttered windows, all entered into the imaginative reservoir of Reynolds, although he did not at once react artistically to its stimulus. After his service for two years in the Navy in World War II, he began to have a yearning to portray the region and the people who had become so familiar to him. This urge to express himself in some art form was so strong that he went to school in Beverly Hills and later to the Allied Arts School in Glendale, where he spent five years studying with such eminent artists as Arthur Beaumont, Charles Payzant and Stan Parkhouse. He was using water colors at this time, and trying to capture in color the ranch life that interested him so much.

He tried ranching and raised everything from white rabbits to cattle, but this was an unsuccessful venture. When he went broke, he decided that he must make a living some other way and carry on his art on the side. As a result, he started to work at Twentieth-Century Fox Films, and since that time has worked there and at MGM, Columbia, Walt

Disney, Warner Brothers and Goldwyn.

Somewhere along the line, remembering a picture by Frederic Remington which had impressed itself upon his mind as a child, he decided he needed a more responsive medium than water colors. He began experimenting with oils, and immediately found what he was seeking.

"There are no fancy statements in my paintings, I just paint the cattleman as honestly as I can," Reynolds says.

James Reynolds was born on November 9, 1926, in Taft, California, near Bakersfield, and now lives in Santa Monica. He finds that, because of intervals between assignments, film-studio work gives him the opportunity to travel throughout the Old West, painting the cattle and horse scenes which intrigue him. He finally has been able to satisfy his yearning to have a small ranch of his own, and his wife and daughter agree that the most beautiful spot they know is the ranch in Oak Creek Canyon in Arizona.

A wife whose faith in her husband's painting ability was so great that it caused her to buy him his first set of paints can take the major credit for having launched "G. Harvey" on his spectacular artistic career in Texas. "G. Harvey" is the signature used by Gerald Harvey Jones of Austin, who can number the President of the United States and other notable figures among his buyers.

"My wife Pat was the first person to notice a talent and to encourage me in this direction," Harvey says gratefully. "After she bought me the paints she managed, when we were always short of funds, to save enough out of her grocery money for art supplies and sketching trips."

A heritage from pioneers of the frontier helped to give Harvey a philosophical and historical tendency which he has been able to utilize to the fullest in his art career. He has become an enthusiastic student of Southwest-

G. *Harvey*

ern lore and has transferred many notable incidents of pioneer days to his canvasses.

"My father was brought up on a ranch and his father, at the age of nineteen, was trail boss of a cattle drive to Kansas from Texas," Harvey relates. "As a child I spent many hours listening to my father talk of the ranch life and frontier days of Texas. I had been painting seven or eight years before I attempted painting Western historical subjects, always collecting material, visiting ranches, reading authentic books, preparing for the day when I would start telling with the brush the story of the days of my grandfather and men like him."

Gerald Harvey Jones was born in San Antonio, Texas in November 1, 1933. Despite his relative youth, he has gained national attention and has had exhibitions in New York and Springfield, Massachusetts, as well as in his native Texas. President Lyndon B. Johnson and Governor John B. Connally of Texas are among those who own his paintings.

One discerning observer of his work, Mrs. James B. Cornette, who operates the Canyon

Painting by G. Harvey

Art Gallery in Canyon, Texas, has said: "Most of Mr. Harvey's inspiration and instruction have come directly from nature and from original research in primary source materials on life in the Southwest during frontier days. Often you can see him in his old straw hat and boots heading with his paint gear to the stockpens or stables, or to the creek beds, rolling countrysides, and the rugged terrain of the Southwest. Here he captures first-hand the rustic beauty of the land and the personality of the animals he loves so well."

Harvey has worked on a series of twelve paintings for the LBJ Ranch near Austin, after having had favorite locations pointed out to him by the President and Mrs. Johnson. At one time he was supervisor of arts and crafts at the Texas Union of the University of Texas. In his sketching jaunts he has encountered many unusual situations ranging, as he says, "from delivering coon hides for a cedar chopper to running after 'wetbacks' along the Mexican border."

A love of freedom that sustained him during dreadful years as a Nazi prisoner in World War II has come to full flowering in America for a Russian-born artist, Constantine Cherkas. He has become a Western painter because the land itself and the people in it combine to stir his artistic emotions.

"Man gains in meaning and depth in such an environment as the American West," Cherkas says. "He becomes an individual, a creator, an independent person. To show this on canvas will be a lifetime task."

Constantine Cherkas was born in Moscow in 1919. He studied art and was admitted to the Moscow Academy of Arts, but his classes were interrupted by the war. He and his wife were seized by the Nazis and placed in forced-labor camps. At the end of the war they waited five years for a visa to the United States.

He is known as a masterful restorer of art works as well as a painter in his own right. He signs his paintings "Constantine" and as a restorer is known as "Cherkas."

After a time in New York and Philadelphia he moved to California, where he has found in that state and the surrounding region the subjects he wants to paint. He has exhibited in many places and won numerous awards. One of his favorite exhibit spots is The

"Where Time Stands Still," by Constantine Cherkas. (The Gallery, Palm Springs, California.)

Gallery of Fred and Paula Penney of Palm Springs.

His work bespeaks the exuberance of the freedom he has so long sought.

Pete Martinez, old-time cowboy, has had a "second career" in Tucson for more than thirty years after having been an artist in New York and Pennsylvania following World War I. In Tucson since 1935 he has operated an art studio and a riding stable, combining his love of horses and painting. He has been a long-time friend of painter Olaf Weighorst with whom he shared a counter at Madison Square Garden in New York when both were struggling young artists selling their horse drawings.

Pete Martinez, born in Porterville, California, in 1894, became a jockey at fourteen, later was cowboy foreman at the Union Land & Cattle Company Ranch in Nevada and studied art in San Francisco and at the Pennsylvania Academy of Fine Arts. He was such a fine horseman that, as he says, "the Army in World War I put me riding horses the other soldiers could not ride." Out of this rough work he got a back injury for which he is paid a U.S. pension. For twenty-three years, despite his injury, he was a horseback riding

Constantine Cherkas

instructor at a boys' camp in the mountains of Pennsylvania.

His paintings, such as "Trail to Home Pastures," deal with his remembered life as a cowboy.

A New Mexico state senator who gave up politics to become a painter because of his inherited interest in horses and cattle is gaining attention in his new profession. Robert M. Lee, born August 13, 1933 in Alamogordo,

Bob Lee with one of his paintings

New Mexico, of the famous Lee ranching family, which included his grandfather O. M. Lee, a frontiersman widely known as a historical character in the West, has had regional exhibits and at the Saddleback Gallery in Santa Ana, California. Both his grandfather and an uncle, V.M. Lee, also were state senators.

"I paint Western art because I was raised with horses, cattle and cowboys," Lee explains. "It is what I know best and I believe people should paint what they know."

The Lee family raises racing quarterhorses. Lee is on the New Mexico State Racing Commission and is a director of the New Mexico Cattle Growers' Association.

The influence of vaqueros, *charros*, and cowboys has gone far beyond the boundaries of the American continent where their role has been so important. It has not been limited to Mexico, to "the American West," or to California on the extreme western mainland. For the vaqueros, in particular, that influence has extended all the way "west of west" to the new state of Hawaii in the Pacific Ocean.

On the island of Hawaii is the only real rival of the famed King Ranch in Texas, which always is referred to, in the round terms of Texas grandiloquence, as "a million acres." The Parker Ranch in Hawaii contains a whopping 262,000 acres and runs 42,000 purebred Herefords, reputedly the largest herd of its kind in the world. It came into being, under a set of strange circumstances, before any of the big ranches in mainland United States

Captain George Vancouver, the explorer, dropped in on King Kamehameha the Great of the Sandwich Islands in 1793 and presented him with some pregnant cows and a sickly bull, the story goes. When the bull died, the King declared the cows to be under a taboo and forbade their being slaughtered. They were allowed to run wild in the mountains and multiplied tremendously. A New England sailor, John Palmer Parker, arrived in the islands about twenty years later and was asked by the King to round up the wild cattle, which had become a menace. Parker had pits dug on the slopes, captured many cattle, killed some, kept others for breeding, and started the ranch that still bears his name. This was early in the nineteenth century, about the time the first artists were painting Indian-and-horse-and-buffalo pictures in the American West.

The Hawaiians naturally were unfamiliar with the handling of cattle, and so they sent to Mexico for vaqueros to come teach them how to cope with the wild and dangerous creatures. Some vaqueros responded and, on arrival, were dubbed "paniolas," a supposed colloquialism for "Española." Hawaiian cowboys to this day are known as "paniolas."

From the start they learned fast. They became so good, in fact, that early in this century they competed in mainland rodeos and won prizes in competition with the best on the continent. At one rodeo in Cheyenne, four paniolas took part, including Eben Pilow, a one-armed roper who was acclaimed world champion in his category. The others, Archie Cleghorn Kaaua, Ikua Purdy and Jack Low, did well too. Purdy won the calf-roping contest.

"Shipping Cattle at Port of Kawaikae," by James K. Parker. (Parker Ranch, Island of Hawaii.)

So strong was the vaquero influence that the philosophy of the Mexicans, derived from centuries on the open range, was communicated in many instances to the paniolas. "Staying on the job" is one element of this philosophy. The paniolas transmit their cattle lore from one generation to another. A veteran of long-time service is Willie Kaniho, foreman of the cowboys on the Parker Ranch, who has been punching cattle there more than fifty-five years.

Artistic possibilities of the paniolas way out there "West of West" have now been recognized. John W. Hilton, the Western painter of 29 Palms, California, maintains a home in Lahaina, Island of Maui, and has been engaged on a series of paintings of the Hawaiian cowboys, their horses, and the cattle. Extraordinary paintings of Parker Ranch life were done by James Parker, uncle of Richard Smart, owner of the ranch. "Uncle Jimmie," as he was known, did not take up painting until he was seventy, and then created pictorial representations of the early days from memory, according to Stella K. Akana,

great-great granddaughter of James Palmer Parker I.

Hawaii has no monopoly on tradition, though. In New Mexico, one vestige of the Old West remains. The State still has a "stock driveway," one of the few left in the United States. Each year it is used by at least one ranch outfit. The driveway is in the San Augustin Plains region near Magdalena.

Five hundred Herefords were driven sixty miles by George Farr and his sons Dave and Ed from their Horse Springs Ranch in the fall of 1967. The Farrs, making the drive in five days, figure that the cattle grazing along the way to the loading pens put on weight, instead of losing it as they do when taken by truck. Also, the drive has become a tradition.

The driveway, from a quarter of a mile to a mile in width, has been in use about fifty years and is kept up by the U.S. Bureau of Land Management. Most other ranchers prefer trucking, but not the Farrs. They have become just about the last steady users of the driveway. Nearly all of New Mexico was talking about their drive because it was written up

(Left) *"Fighting Stallions,"* by James K. Parker. (Parker Ranch, Island of Hawaii.)

(Below) *Roping scene by James K. Parker.* (Parker Ranch, Island of Hawaii.)

James K. Parker (Uncle Jimmie), died February 6, 1963, and was the uncle of the present owner of the Parker Ranch, on the Island of Hawaii. (Richard Smart.)

by veteran reporter Howard Bryan, accompanied by news photos taken by photographer Al Cabral, in the Albuquerque Tribune.

New Mexico and Arizona, as legatees of the Spanish and Mexican periods to which both owe their existence, have not only a particularized interest in cattle and horses and cowboys, but also in the vaquero tradition. It was from the Spanish explorers and vaqueros that the American Indians obtained their first horses, which opened up a new existence for them. In the present age the Indians have produced artists who have dealt powerfully with the horse as an art subject, mostly in water color. Names on these pictures include such artists are Lone Wolf who was taught long ago by Thomas Moran; Beatien Yazz, Harrison Begay, Crumbo, White Bear, Spencer Asah, Gilbert Atencio, Stanley Battese, F. Blackbear Bosin, Pop Chalee, Adee Dodge, Allan Houser, C. Terry Saul, V. Shije, Joseph Tafaga, Quincy Tahoma, James Wayne Yazzie, and Andy Tsinajinie.

CHILDREN CARRY ON COWBOY ART

In the jet age, the horse of history, story and romance can still prance proudly and neigh at the sky because of the children of America.

The popularity of horses is so great among young people that astounding increases in the equine population have been noted in metropolitan areas where riding stables and equestrian trails flourish. From New York to Los Angeles quarter horses, Arabians, Morgans, American saddlebreds and other breeds constantly attract more children who long, amid automobiles and smog, for the outdoors and the thrill of a canter into a mythical land of yesterdays and high adventure.

My own grandchildren have joined in this happy procession, and one of them, Sheila Katherine Herron, daughter of Robert S. Herron, M.D. and Sheila Ainsworth Herron of San Diego, California, is paying her own tribute to horses in art. Her horse drawings have resulted in her enrollment in art-instruction classes, where her work has included a portrait of her own riding mare, Dixie Chips.

I am including this particular drawing in my book as representative of the love of the children of the United States for their horses.

—Grandpa Ed Ainsworth
—Photographs by
Grandma Katherine Ainsworth
and Daddy Robert S. Herron

Sheila Katherine Herron (center) with her quarter horse mare, Dixie Chips; Camilla Herron (right) with her gelding, Knuckles; and (left) Lincoln Herron in front of Dixie Chips.

17

THE VANISHING MUSTANG

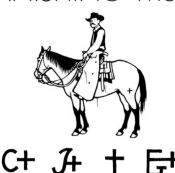

C+ Ɉ+ † Ƌ+

American cowboy, 1930

Far off on the long trail to the horizon, the hoofbeats of the Spanish mustang have sounded fainter and fainter. For a long while, the thunder of their running feet echoed endlessly against the arching skies over two continents, from Canada to Argentina. Then, as their task in the era of the cowboy was accomplished, they began to fade into the distance while this echo diminished from crescendo to a faint obbligato, as if for a muted funeral march.

This gradual exit of the original Spanish horse went almost unnoticed amid the world's preoccupation with births, deaths, the advent of the motor car, social reform, elections, and wars—until one perceptive man who had been brought up in the Texas tradition spoke in a commanding tone of the prospective loss of "the horse that won the West." J. Frank Dobie, who was combination cow hand, his-

torian, folkorist and teacher, decided to share his concern with the reading public. He started a book, *The Mustangs*—which was almost a requiem.

I, as a fellow Texan transplanted to California, was privileged, by the accident of friendship with Dobie, to share in one facet of this literary pursuit of the vanishing mustang. At the time I, too, like most people, was not acquainted with the fact that imminent extinction faced the gallant little horses with their noble ancestry. The reason for their fading away was simple. The need for their special qualities no longer existed in the twentieth century in Texas and California, which had been their special habitats. The more favored breeds such as the quarter horse, the Morgan, the more recently imported Arabian and cross-breds of these had supplanted the true mustang, or diluted his blood by intermixture, to the point where mere remnants of the original Spanish type remained.

Dobie watched all this happening, and, with his profound insight, decided that the moment had come for the chronicle of the mustang to be written before it was too late. As it was, he discovered, he had waited almost too long.

I had become a friend of Dobie on his periodic trips to California because I was a member of a group known as the Westerners, men interested in history, and we entertained him when he came to Los Angeles.

My participation in the mustang saga began unexpectedly in the winter of 1949. Oddly enough, it started not out on the prairies or in the mountains, but in that venerable institution, the California Institute of Technology in Pasadena, which since has become celebrated as the home base of space technology. At that time its Atheneum, a richly decorated building reserved for guests of great importance, was host to Dobie. Dobie was pursuing research for his mustang book in nearby San Marino, in the celebrated Henry E. Huntington Library, repository of every sort of volume, Spanish, Mexican and American, dealing with cow horses, cowboys, and cattle as well as a host of other subjects.

One day he called me and, in a worried tone, asked me to come over to the Atheneum. He knew I had explored the wilds of southwestern Nevada and the contiguous badlands of California and Arizona in search of material for my newspaper column in the *Los Angeles Times*. I was certainly no authority on wild horses, but I had been in their habitat and had witnessed their flights from human beings and seen the companions of their isolation, the wild burros, with primitive line backs, leaping up the walls of the lower Grand Canyon almost like mountain goats.

When I reached the Atheneum, Dobie, with his white hair hanging over his forehead in typical fashion, came to the point at once.

"I'm in a fix," he said. "I'm writing this book about mustangs, but I can't find one anywhere. I've been all over Texas and a lot of other places and haven't located a single one. Can you find me a real mustang?"

I wished later he had asked for an auk or a saber-toothed tiger. It might have been easier. I collided instantly with a fact of which I had been only dimly aware. A real "mustang" is not just any old wild horse. A "mustang" is in as exact a category as a thoroughbred, a Morgan, a quarter horse, or an Arabian, almost as elusive and scarce as the shadow of a dinosaur. Only in isolated California and in parts of Nevada and Arizona did the real Spanish mustang, of the strain landed by Cortés in 1519, precariously survive in tiny bands of undersized, swift, hardy creatures truly as wild as elk, moose, deer or antelope.

My first step was to call on two men who, of all others, were most capable of helping in the search. I asked my old friend Billy Magee, manager for twenty-five years of the 201,000-acre Santa Margarita Rancho along the southern California coast, later turned into Marine Camp Joseph H. Pendleton, and Clyde (Vic) Forsythe, cartoonist and oil painter who had penetrated the wildest regions in the West, to "go out and find a mustang."

Billy got up a wild-horse hunt in the rough mountains of San Diego County between Lake Cuyamaca, Jacumba and the rocky slopes leading down to the Coachella Valley and the Salton Sea. In his fifties he could still ride like a Comanche, but the wild horses—maybe they were mustangs, maybe not—got away anyhow. Disgusted, he put away his lariat for the moment, and went to hunt up some of his old Indian cowboy companions from the Santa Margarita days, for advice. Meantime, Forsythe was over in Arizona appealing to his artist friends who penetrated to rougher places for their pictures than did most cowpunchers. I went over to that frightening country south of Black Can-

(Left) *J. Frank Dobie, the Texan author and folklorist who wrote* The Longhorns *and* The Mustangs.

(Above) (*Left to right*) *Clyde Forsythe, the painter, Bill Magee, California rancher, and J. Frank Dobie inspect a part-mustang while on their way to see a true Spanish mustang.*

yon and Hoover Dam where I had visited a few years before to see the mummy of Queho, the mad killer who murdered prospectors for their shoes, and had himself died wounded and of thirst in a cave in sight of the tantalizing waters of the Colorado River below. Neither Queho's ghost nor all our other allies could produce for us a mustang in the flesh.

Just as we were about to give up, it was Billy Magee, as might have been expected, whose Californiano instincts led him to the goal. He had contacted Alejandro—"Old Alec"—Peters, vaquero supreme whose riding feats among the thirty thousand Herefords on the Santa Margarita had become a legend. Alec had performed some kind of Indian magic with Indian horse hunters over on the Colorado River. They in turn had told him about the one eighteen-months-old mustang colt spared in the general slaughter after a big horse hunt in Nevada, when the colt's mother had been shot while attacking one of the cowboy pursuers. This colt had been traded around until, as a four-year-old, he

finally arrived in Oceanside, California. He belonged to Harol Whitley, son of T. F. Whitley. They had given permission for us to bring Dobie down to see him.

I called up Dobie one day after stalling him off for weeks about the mustang, and said, "Why the hell don't you get your nose out of those books for a day and take a look at some of our old ranches? I've got some swell guys lined up to show you the sights."

We picked him up at the Huntington Library, and headed for the back country. With me were Magee and Forsythe. Dobie made some polite, tentative inquiries about our mustang search, and we shrugged it off as if we had nothing to report. We plunged instead into all kinds of horse talk. Dobie began telling us some of his findings for his book, and how he considered Seabiscut, C. S. Howard's famous winner of the $100,000 Santa Anita Handicap in 1940, as a mustang type despite his listing as a thoroughbred. He also mentioned Will Rogers' favorite cow pony, Soapsuds, as representative of the mustangs.

"Portrait of a Mustang." This grulla, or sand-crane-colored horse, was declared by J. Frank Dobie to be a true descendant of the Spanish horses landed on the American continent in 1519 by Hernando Cortés. The mustang had been captured in the wilds of Nevada and taken to Oceanside, California. (Robert O. Ritchie.)

Forsythe chimed in: "I painted a picture of Will on Soapsuds with Ed Vail of the Santa Rosa Island Rancho on another horse, and I agree on old Soapsuds being the real thing."

Somehow we got on the exactness of the Spanish in everything regarding horses, including the extraordinarily large number of color types they recognized: twenty-three major ones, ranging from "Coyote," a wolf color with a black stripe on the back, to "Rosillo," a clear red, and from "Champurrado," a mixed chocolate, to "Busbayo," a shade between palomino and buckskin.

We gave Dobie the sightseeing works all day in one of the few remaining cattle-and-cow-horse areas of southern California. Amid the giant mistletoe-infested sycamores at the old corrals of Rancho Viejo inland from San Juan Capistrano Mission, Dobie got on the fine quarter horse of ranch manager Arley Leek and went for a canter. He came back, and always something of a poet, exclaimed,

"In town, Time is my master but out here I'm the master of Time."

We went to the magnificent two-story Monterey-type Las Flores ranchhouse of Billy's brother Louis Magee, and then to Santa Margarita where Billy had been the boss so long. The old ranch house, built in 1828, had become the headquarters of the commanding officers of Camp Pendleton. On the long, old porch we sat with Major General Graves B. Erskine, and heard Billy tell of the days when wild horses were so numerous on the Santa Margarita they were eating up the forage of the cattle, and as a result were run over the nearby cliff into the riverbed and killed by the hundreds.

"Out there," said Billy, "we used to dehorn the cattle and the little streams of blood would shoot up and make pools in the cowboys' hat brims."

The sun was beginning to sink when we finally finished the ranch part of the tour.

"By the way," I said to Dobie, "we've got to see one guy in Oceanside for a minute, and then we can be on our way."

We headed for the Whitley *ranchito* on the edge of town where we had arranged for Alec Peters to meet us.

When we arrived, we walked out to an empty corral. Dobie looked around inquiringly, but just then Alec Peters and Mr. Whitley came up and we introduced them. We started chatting about the cattle market as Peters gave a slight signal with his hand.

The sun was low now, reflecting on the water of the Pacific and illuminating the coastal mountains stretching inland towards Mount Palomar. The horizontal beams resembled some giant celestial spotlight focusing on an outdoor stage.

Into this radiance came a boy with a horse.

Dobie's eyes widened unbelievably. He stared fixedly at the horse at the end of the leading rope. The little animal came forward on jump springs. He was a *grulla*, the color of slate-gray feathers, the shade of the sand crane from which his ancestors had derived their name. His one good eye radiated intelligence. The other was a *sarco*, of a frosted-glass-like whitish color that shone in the departing light with a fixed intensity. The boy spoke softly to the horse, and he stood quietly.

"The real thing!" Dobie muttered.

Before us was the Spanish horse personified, the true mustang, the living spirit of a departing breed. His face was flat, with none of the Arabian inward curve; the chest was narrow, the hindquarters flat. Yet we felt as we watched this equine sprite, this buoyant four-footed legend, that any moment there might materialize before us his mighty sires—the prancing war horses bearing Cortés and his conquistadors with the flag of Imperial Spain; the swift coursers carrying Kit Carson and the Pony Express; the tireless mount of Old Cowboy Pecos Bill; the sky-winding son

of chain lightning trying to hurl vaquero Alec Peters to the moon.

Dobie regained his tongue.

"You did it!" he told us. "I guess in my writing I'm like a painter who has to have a living model. Seeing this horse makes everything I've read fall in place for me. Now I can put some guts into my writing."

As Harol spoke soothingly to the *grulla*, Dobie ran his hands over the horse's withers, studied the *sarco* eye, evaluated each line of the lithe, tense body.

It began to grow dark. From somewhere out in the hills there came the long piercing wail of a coyote. Dobie, startled, looked up and asked:

"Dirge or reveille for the mustang?"

When *The Mustangs* came out as a book three years later, in 1952, that question, asked while he was inspecting the *grulla*, was still lacking a reply. Yet the appearance of his tremendously popular book and several seemingly unrelated happenings in the same period were all setting in motion the forces which were to provide the eventual answer.

In Los Angeles, public sentiment aroused by the County Board of Supervisors, led by supervisor Leonard J. Reach, was beginning to manifest itself against the indiscriminate killing of wild horses for pet food. After consultations with Dr. A. G. Feers, county livestock inspector, the Supervisors adopted a resolution condemning the excessive rate of killing of the mustangs and calling for action to stop it. Stuart Hamblen, radio personality, conducted a running campaign against the use of horse meat for pet food.

Many persons felt that beneficial results could be obtained by legislation, because so much of the lands in the states principally involved—Arizona, Nevada, New Mexico and Utah—were owned by the federal government. In these four states, for instance, more than thirty-three million acres were in the

"Will and Eddie," by Clyde Forsythe. The painting portrays Will Rogers on his favorite horse, "Soapsuds," a mustang type, with Ed Vail, rancher, one of Will's pals. "Soapsuds" was painted from life, with Jim Rogers, son of Will, posing in the saddle as his father, about 1940.

National Forests alone.

Out in Nevada, Mrs. Velma B. Johnston of Wadsworth (later of Reno)—known as "Wild Horse Annie"—was revolted by the cruelty of mechanized horse hunts, and began fighting for state and federal controls on the practice on public lands. She made dramatic appearances in Carson City, the state capital, and in Congress in Washington, D.C. After hearing her, Congress adopted regulations prohibiting mechanized roundups of wild horses on the federal domain.

While these efforts were being made to prevent the slaughter of wild horses, a quiet movement was under way in Wyoming to preserve the mustang by continuance of the purity of the blood through breeding. Robert E. Brislawn of the Cayuse Ranch at Oshoto, Wyoming, began with his brother, Ferdinand Brislawn, as early as 1925 to breed mustangs from Indian stock obtained from the Crow, Cheyenne, Shoshone and Ute tribes. These horses included a few Medicine Hats, or "War Bonnets," considered of divine origin by the Sioux, Comanches and other Indians. Finally, Brislawn, his son, Robert E. Brislawn, Jr., and Dr. Lawrence P. Richards of Idaho State College at Pocatello, began to think in terms of establishing a registry for mustangs as had been done with their counterparts, the *criollo* horse of South America, in Chile in 1893, in Argentina in 1923, and in Brazil in 1932.

This dream finally came to realization just five years after the appearance of Dobie's classic, *The Mustangs*. The Spanish Mustang Registry, Inc., was formed as a nonprofit corporation, with Robert E. Brislawn, Sr., as president, on June 14, 1957, at Sundance, Crook County, Wyoming.

The first issue of the *Spanish Mustang News*, a quarterly under the editorship of Susan Field of Colorado Springs, Colorado, began early in 1967 to spread the news of the mustang's fight to exist.

Up in Utah, Tom Holland, just mustered out of the Navy after World War II, had moved to the western part of Iron County in 1946. The big sport around there was mustanging—the chasing of wild horses. Tom took his two boys, Tom, Jr., and Carl, and joined the fun. Before long he became interested in saving the horses as well as chasing them. He also began independently the formation of a group to carry out the idea of rescuing the mustangs before it was too late.

The movement caught on and spread.

"Mustang Annie," Mrs. Velma B. Johnston of Wadsworth and Reno, Nevada, who led successful fight to end airplane and four-wheel-drive truck hunts for mustangs.

"The National Mustang Association," a non-profit corporation, was formed, and on January 13, 1965, through the office of Utah Secretary of State Clyde Miller, received its certificate of incorporation. With the aid of Secretary of State Frank M. Jordan of California and Secretary of State John Koontz of Nevada, permission was obtained to register members in those states, too.

A climax of achievement was reached in 1967. Federal protection was granted to the remaining mustangs in the wilds. The Bureau of Land Management, through its director, Boyd L. Rasmussen, announced that the seventeen thousand mustangs and the eight thousand wild burros that roam the one hundred seventy million acres under the control of the bureau, will be conserved under a sweeping program. This will include co-operation with ranchers where a question of competitive forage is involved, and an attempt to solve the legal problems surrounding unbranded animals. Director Rasmussen also reiterated that in any roundups all motorized vehicles and airplanes will be barred, in line with "Wild Horse Annie's" crusade.

Rasmussen said that the establishment of the 435,000-acre wild horse refuge in Nevada in 1962 and the setting aside of a refuge in Utah in 1965 were preliminary steps in the now-expanded effort to save the mustangs.

"We're sure," he commented, "that many people join us in looking upon these animals as representatives of a colorful and historic chapter in the story of the West."

Intense national attention, of course, had been directed towards the surviving horses by Dobie's *The Mustangs.*

"Their essence was the spirit of freedom," he wrote at the outset. But he was realistic, too.

> Absurd and ridiculous [he emphasized] would be any person who tried to find non-existent similarities between some hammer-headed, ram-nosed, ewe-necked, goat-withered, cat-hammed, sore-backed, hard-mouthed, mean-natured, broom-tailed bronco of the West at the close of the Nineteenth Century and an Arabian of perfection. Just as absurd would it be to regard that bronco as representative of the Andalusian Barbs that Cortez and his handful of men rode to conquer the kingdom of Montezuma. One quality of the original that never withered was hardihood.

When Dobie died on September 18, 1964, true to the last to his own concept of liberty, one of his legacies was his contribution to a fuller realization of "the spirit of freedom" for his few remaining wild friends of the open range. I often feel that, in the corral with Dobie and the *grulla* that evening in Oceanside in 1949, I witnessed the happy turning point in the fate of the vanishing mustang.

THE "SPANISH MUSTANG" CANTERS ONWARD

What is a Spanish mustang?

How can he be defined?

In what way does he differ from other so-called "wild horses"? The name "mustang" is an Anglicized corruption of the Spanish *mestena*, meaning "wild" or "untamed."

The official description of a Spanish mustang as given by the Spanish Mustang Registry established at Sundance, Wyoming, June 14, 1957, with Robert E. Brislawn of Oshoto, Wyoming, as president, is as follows:

The Spanish Mustangs should not be confused with wild horses, as the latter could be of most any breed or mixed breeds.

The purpose of the Spanish Mustang Registry, Inc., is to preserve some of the last remnants of the Spanish Mustangs by registering some of the fine and better authentic animals and from these to perpetuate the Spanish Mustangs for posterity, in the form of a living example of a part of the heritage of the people of the United States.

The Spanish Mustangs, alias the Spanish Barbs, are descendants of the first horses that landed on our Americas.

As to traits and characteristics, the Spanish Mustangs have little in common with the man-made horse of today. They have but five large lumbar vertebrae, 13 to 14 hands in height, and 700 to 900 pounds in weight.

Head characteristics show eyes which are bright and set well out on a flat forehead. A few have bulged foreheads, dished face or roman nose. But all taper to a small muzzle with small crescent-shaped nostrils. Jaws are fairly heavy with a deep throat latch, and teeth are deep set and narrow. The ears are short, slim and lynxlike notched.

Going to the body the horse is equally balanced. There is the same distance from poll to withers as from withers to croup. The legs are strong, clean and round boned. There are no feathers on the legs except for the curly fetlock. The fore arm is long and straight with short round cannon bone. Pasterns are long, springy and let-down for ease of riding. The front legs are straight with very small smooth chestnuts.

The chest is not so wide but V's down nicely and is very deep. The front end should be big and powerful in this respect. The theory here is that if the front end goes the caboose will come along.

The rump is rounded but can be slightly sloping with a fairly low-set tail head. The hind legs set well under the horse and are slightly bended— for strength to hold a cow. Hooves are hard, straight and shiny.

Colors of the Spanish Mustang are wide and varied. They include paints, roans, grullos, buckskins, isabellas, blue corns, appaloosies, albinos and all of the more common solid colors.

The drawing of the bucking mustang was done, from life, in 1907 by Clyde (Vic) Forsythe and belongs to Dr. and Mrs. Robert S. Herron of San Diego, California.

18

VAYA CON DIOS

Man, the perpetual mustanger, aways throws his lasso west. His loop seeks to ensnare new lands, adventure, the spirit of the wilderness, virgin sod, and human happiness. This pursuit of the symbolic wild horses forever fleeing across the far horizon has gone on for millenniums. David the Psalmist must have looked yearningly to the west when he sang of the "green pastures" and the "still waters" in the terminology of the shepherd. Ulysses fixed his gaze upon the Gates of Hercules to the west. The Renaissance moved west to animate an El Greco and a Velázquez. Columbus thought only of one direction on the compass, west. Balboa discovered the Pacific by pressing onward that way. Cortés followed the tradition. Daniel Boone and Kit Carson took only the sunset trail.

Out of this thrust of humanity towards a western goal, no matter how nebulous, came the expansion of the United States across a continent to its ultimate physical limit. Then began the evolution of that phenomenon which we call "the spirit of the West"—an incarnation of venturesomeness, daring, inventiveness, expansion of the soul. From it emerged the robust Westerner, a symbol of masculinity, a free spirit, a cowboy at heart.

From this distillation has come the trend toward a similar robustness in art, an expression of the virility of the westward movement, as if the painter who portrays it were roping all the wild, untamed creativeness of a new age. The cowboy artist has cut out sham and pretense from the herd, and has kept only the best stock for the drive. In his genuineness he captures for himself and for his expanding audience the smell of the crushed sage, the swirl of the dust clouds, the trampling of a thousand hoofs, the bellow of the range

"The Last Round-up," by Clyde Forsythe. (Mr. and Mrs. Bill Bender, Oro Grande, California.)

bulls, the reek of the fighting, untamed horse.

The accomplishments of the painter of the cowboy are specific. He goes beyond mere words, mere art criticism. He is so much a part of a new Renaissance, so swept up in a fever of creation that he has no time for self-appraisal. He has contributed in this age to the thing called Americana. True Americana evolves almost without being noticed. It emerges from the deep wells of national character and consciousness, sometimes instantaneously in moments of great stress, at others by the slow process of growth and evolution.

It always possesses two ingredients: genuineness and sincerity.

"Yankee Doodle" is lasting Americana, born of the patriotic fervor of the human spirit striving for liberty. "The Star-Spangled Banner" endures, despite the handicap of dubious verse structure, because it was born in national crisis and expressed the prayer-cry of a whole people newly baptized in freedom. "O Susanna!" is more than a song; it is the yearning of mortal men for the siren lure of the West. Stephen Foster and "Swanee River" and "Old Folks at Home" embody the plantation era in national annals. New Orleans and "The St. Louis Blues" have given America its jazz, our one indigenous music. Western painters now have broken loose from the European snubbing post.

The Southwestern Cowboy, as a result, has inspired an art form all his own.

Throughout the world, the ideal of American manhood is the lean, rangy Westerner, the heir of the cowboy, recognizable anywhere by his loose-limbed walk and the way he carries his shoulders. If he is not there in person, his prototype in cowboy art is carrying on his presence and his tradition. The speech, the garb, the personality are known everywhere.

Western painters, like all painters, must await the passage of time before history renders its verdict for good or bad on their respective works. Their own generation may like or dislike them, but only posterity has the ultimate word. That concerns the individual. Deeper than this matter of personal fame is the art medium they have jointly created. It already has emerged from the shadows into the lasting sunshine. It already has become Americana.

It passes the test of genuineness and sincerity.

The painters have assured its permanence because of its firm foundations. Its genealogy includes the Moorish saddle, the Spanish rider, the voyages of Columbus, the conquests of Cortés, the feats of the Mexican vaquero and the *charro*, the buffalo boys, the westward trek of the American frontiersmen, the California and Texas cattle and horses, the trail drives, the cowboy. It is compounded of enduring elements.

The rider of the Western range is distant, yet he is near, too. We see him through the mists of time and in his present vigor. He is both body and spirit. He is Will Rogers twirling a lasso and the kid in the back yard roping his dog.

"West" has ceased to be a point of the compass. It has become an immortal mood. The painters have seen to that.

They have thrown their own lasso and captured forever the cowboy in art.

SALUTATIONS AND SUPPLICATIONS

This is my double farewell. It is both an expression of thanks and a voicing of regrets. The thanks go to all those who have helped me so generously in the preparation of *The Cowboy in Art*. The regrets go to those painters of been omitted from this book. I have genuinely cowboy life who, by mistake or chance, have tried to mention the noteworthy artists, both living and dead, who have contributed to "cowboy art." Yet it is inevitable that I have overlooked some. I do not pretend to be an art critic, and my chief aim has been to present biographical material about the painters, both men and women, whose life stories have interested me and who meet the professional test of selling their art work to the public. To those I may have missed in this process of compilation I express my honest apologies. Any apparent slight is unintentional.

My deep and heartfelt appreciation goes to friends both old and new for their gracious and unselfish aid in my research for this book. I was welcomed and helped in many libraries, art galleries and museums. It is impossible to list all these, much as I would like to do so. Yet a few institutions and individuals contributed so greatly

that I must salute them, in the Southwestern tradition, with a hearty "Muchas gracias!"

Among libraries, I received outstanding help from the Monrovia Public Library, the Pasadena Public Library, the Riverside County Library, the San Diego Public Library, the California State Library, the University of California at Los Angeles Library, the Henry E. Huntington Library in San Marino, and the Indio Public Library, all in California; from the Albuquerque Public Library in New Mexico; from the Jalisco State Library and the Benjamin Franklin Library of the United States Information Service, in Guadalajara, Mexico; and from the staff of Artes de Mexico and the staff of the National Anthropological Museum, in Mexico City.

Friends who gave me their unstinted aid include Lorraine Suydam, Carol Densham, Mary Pier, Ruth Banks and Leone Probst of the Monrovia Public Library; Marjorie Donaldson, Chief Librarian, Florence Powers, Reference Librarian, and Josephine M. Pletscher, Art Librarian, of the Pasadena Public Library; Albert Lake, Chief Librarian of the Riverside County Library; and Clara Breed, Chief Librarian of the San Diego Public Library; Ginger Neveau of

Palm Desert and Don Stevning of Coachella, California, co-owners of the Desert Southwest Art Gallery of Palm Desert and the Trailside Galleries of Jackson Hole, Wyoming; Bruce Gelker, owner of the Saddleback Art Galleries of Santa Ana, California, and Phoenix, Arizona; Glenn Faris, Dean Krakel and James Boren of the National Cowboy Hall of Fame and Western Heritage Center, Oklahoma City; Bill Bender of Oro Grande, California; William Riffle of Santa Ana, California; Joe De Yong of Los Angeles; Mrs. Clyde Forsythe of San Marino, California; William Moyers and Fred Harman, Jr., of Albuquerque; Thomas Lewis of the Taos Art Gallery, Taos, New Mexico; Read Mul-

lan of Phoenix; Mary Elizabeth Cornette of the Canyon Art Gallery, Canyon, Texas; Van Kirke Nelson, M.D., of Kalispell, Montana; Ruth Mahood, Chief Curator of History of the Los Angeles County Museum of Natural History, Los Angeles; Don Meadows of Santa Ana, California; Mary Livingston of the Little Gallery, Santa Ana; Maxine Beery, Irving Wills, M.D., and Harold G. Davidson of Santa Barbara, California; Keith Atherton and Sue Jones of San Diego, California; Lori Kielty of Monrovia, California; and many, many more to whom I am just as grateful.

Mecca, California　　　　　ED AINSWORTH
June 7, 1968

COWBOY ART MUSEUMS AND GALLERIES

Western art featuring the American cowboy theme has grown constantly in public favor during the last decade. This trend has resulted in the establishment or expansion of museums and are galleries specializing in cowboy art. These are located all the way from California to New York and from Montana to Florida, including that venerable national shrine, the Smithsonian Institution in Washington, D.C.

Representative of the many museums displaying cowboy paintings and sculpture—although this is by no means a complete list—are the National Cowboy Hall of Fame and Western Heritage Center in Oklahoma City; the Amon Carter Museum in Forth Worth; the Thomas Gilcrease Institute of American History and Art in Tulsa; the Joslyn Art Museum in Omaha; the Montana Historical Society in Helena; the Whitney Gallery of Western Art in Cody, Wyoming; the Charles W. Bowers Memorial Museum in Santa Ana, California; the Remington Art Memorial in Ogdensburg, New York; the Charles M. Russell Gallery in Great Falls, Montana; the Panhandle-Plains Museum in Canyon, Texas; the Merrihill Museum of Fine Arts near Goldendale, Washington; the Museum of New Mexico in Santa Fe;

the California Historical Society in San Francisco and San Marino; the Albert K. Mitchell art collection at the Lovelace Foundation in Albuquerque; and the Read Mullan Gallery of Western Art in Phoenix.

Notable among the galleries displaying enthusiasm for cowboy art are the Desert Southwest Art Gallery of Palm Desert, California, and the Trailside Galleries of Jackson Hole, Wyoming; the Saddleback Art Galleries of Santa Ana, California, and Phoenix, Arizona; the Taos Art Gallery and the Joya de Taos Art Gallery of Taos, New Mexico; the Margaret C. Jamison Galleries and the Kachina Gallery of Santa Fe; the Canyon Art Gallery of Canyon, Texas; the Hammer Galleries, the Grand Central Art Gallery, and the Kennedy Galleries in New York; the Biltmore Art Gallery in Los Angeles; the Old Town Gallery in San Diego; the San Marcos Art Gallery in San Marcos, California; the Fred Maxwell Gallery in San Francisco; the Cyrus Boutwell Gallery in Denver; the Tucker Gallery in Sheridan, Wyoming; the Van Kirke Nelson Trailside Gallery in Kalispell, Montana; O'Brien's Art Emporium in Scottsdale, Arizona; and the John Carter Galleries in Austin, Texas.

INDEX

ACKNOWLEDGMENTS

The author and The World Publishing Company herewith thank the following photographers whose work is reproduced here. All possible care has been taken to identify the photographer of every picture included and to make full acknowledgment for its use. If any errors have accidentally occurred, they will be corrected in subsequent editions, provided notification is sent to the publisher.

Kate Ainsworth: "Cinching Up," p. 83; "White Mustangs," p. 91; Sketchbook exercises, p. 113; "Cowboy," p. 120; p. 124; p. 220. Lee Angle: Painting by Melvin C. Warren, p. 110. Arizona Photographic Associates: "The Race," p. 50; "A Mountain Trail," p. 53; "Indian Scouts," p. 59; "Coming up the Trail," p. 64; "The West of Ross Santee," p. 69; p. 80; "Shepherds Changing Camp," p. 83; "String Team," p. 119; p. 176. Baker Gallery: "Riding Out," p. 184. Ruth Banks: p. 22. Walter Barnes Studio: G. Harvey, p. 214. Milton K. Bell: Drawings by Indians of Tlaxcala Tribe, pp. 12–13; Drawings by an Aztec Artist, pp. 14–15; Charles Schreyvogel, p. 49; "Buffalo Bill on Horseback," p. 60; "The First Borein," p. 63; Edward Borein, p. 63; "Will James" at 16, p. 73; Mustang drawing, p. 165; "Mustangs," p. 167; Midnight and his owner, p. 180; p. 228. Lionel T. Berryhill: Bill Bender and Joie Godshall, p. 79; "The Last Round-up," p. 230. T. A. Burgess: "Spring," p. 127; J. R. Williams, p. 127; "The Land of the Free," p. 128; Trooper rescuing a companion, p. 128; J. R. Williams on "Lizard," p. 168. Camera Arts Studio: "Branding Time," p. 147; "The Strawberry Roan," p. 158. Jane Carter's Camera Center:

"Bucky O'Neill," p. 163. Castelton Modern Art Photo: Paul Salisbury, p. 211. Alfred A. Cohn: "Coming Out," p. 55. Mildred T. Crews: A. Kelly Pruitt, p. 117; "Trail Boss," p. 117. Darol Dickinson: Wayne Hunt, p. 171. Eyewitness Photography: Wash drawing, p. 44. Folsom Photo Lab.: Burt Procter, p. 91. The Gallery: Constantine Cherkas, p. 216. Edward M. Greenwood: Jack Roberts, p. 200. E. A. Grensted: Joseph J. Shebl, p. 174; "Longhorns," p. 174. Denny Hayes: Harold Bugbee, p. 40; Sketch, p. 40. Erwin Helbig: Tom Ryan, p. 157. Zoltan Henczel: "When the Rocks Start to Move," p. 156. Ellen Hert: J. W. Hansen at work on "Liberty," p. 176. Lewis W. Jarett: Echo Hawk painting, p. 204. Dick Kent: "The Strawberry Roan," p. 187; George Dick, p. 198. Tom Knapp: Nick Eggenhofer, p. 118. Dorothea Lange: Maynard Dixon, p. 54. Ralph Morgan: Gerard Curtis Delano, p. 99. National Cowboy Hall of Fame: "The Seventh Cavalry," p. 47; National Cowboy Hall of Fame, p. 137; "Riders of the N-Bar," p. 153; Midnight's grave, p. 180. Karl Obert: "Fremont at Monterey," p. 20; "Reata," p. 21; Sketchbook drawings, p. 24; Rough sketches, p. 24; Sketch made at the Spear Ranch, p. 25; "Welcome for the First Trail Herd," p. 57; Edward Borein, p. 63. Herrington Olson: "Light and Shadow," p. 190. Orren-Ross: Melvin C. Warren, p. 110. Raymond L. Pound: Casey Tibbs, p. 138. Putnam Studios: "Pickin' Daisies," p. 195. R. O. Ritchie: Mustang head drawing, p. 165. Danny Santell: Robert Wagoner, p. 210; "Point Rider," p. 210. Walter F. Scott: Fred Harman, p. 132. Dan Stevning: "Portrait of a Westerner," insert. James Studio: Irvin Shope, p. 155. Peter Von Schmidt: Harold Von Schmidt, p. 95. Les Walsh: Noah Berry, p. 175; Clyde Forsythe, Bill Magee, and J. Frank Dobie, p. 223. Austen West: Ace Powell, p. 207. John Williams: Curtis Wingate, p. 159; "U.S. Cavalryman, 1880," p. 159.